CAREER STORIES

ROMANCE STUDIES

EDITORS

Robert Blue • Kathryn M. Grossman • Thomas A. Hale • Djelal Kadir
Norris J. Lacy • John M. Lipski • Sherry L. Roush • Allan Stoekl

ADVISORY BOARD

Theodore J. Cachey Jr. • Priscilla Ferguson • Hazel Gold • Cathy L. Jrade
William Kennedy • Gwen Kirkpatrick • Rosemary Lloyd • Gerald Prince
Joseph T. Snow • Ronald W. Tobin • Noël Valis

TITLES IN PRINT

Career Stories:
Belle Epoque Novels of Professional Development
JULIETTE M. ROGERS

Reconstructing Women: From Fiction to
Reality in the Nineteenth-Century French Novel
DOROTHY KELLY

Territories of History: Humanism, Rhetoric, and the Historical
Imagination in the Early Chronicles of Spanish America
SARAH H. BECKJORD

CAREER STORIES

Belle Epoque Novels of Professional Development

JULIETTE M. ROGERS

THE PENNSYLVANIA STATE UNIVERSITY PRESS
UNIVERSITY PARK, PENNSYLVANIA

LIBRARY OF CONGRESS
CATALOGING-IN-PUBLICATION DATA

Rogers, Juliette M., 1961–
Career stories : Belle Epoque novels of professional development / Juliette M. Rogers.
    p.   cm. — (Penn State Romance Studies series)
Includes bibliographical references and index.
ISBN 978-0-271-03268-9 (cloth : alk. paper)
ISBN 978-0-271-03269-6 (pbk. : alk. paper)

1. French fiction—Women authors—History and criticism.
2. French fiction—20th century—History and criticism.
3. French fiction—19th century—History and criticism.
4. Women and literature—France—History—20th century.
5. Women and literature—France—History—19th century.
6. Professions in literature.
I. Title.

PQ673.R64 2007
843'.91099287—dc22
2007025869

Copyright © 2007
The Pennsylvania State University
All rights reserved
Printed in the United States of America
Published by The Pennsylvania State University Press,
University Park, PA 16802-1003

The Pennsylvania State University Press
is a member of the
Association of American University Presses.

It is the policy of The Pennsylvania State University Press
to use acid-free paper. Publications on uncoated stock satisfy the
minimum requirements of American National Standard for
Information Sciences—Permanence of Paper for
Printed Library Material, ANSI Z39.48–1992.

This book can be viewed at
http://publications.libraries.psu.edu/eresources/978-0-271-03268-9

For John

CONTENTS

Acknowledgments ix

Introduction 1

1
Innovation and Education:
Historical Contexts from the Belle Epoque 15

2
Literary Contexts:
Bildungsroman, Erziehungsroman, and Berufsroman 43

3
Dreams and Disappointments: Women's Education Novels 79

4
Cervelines: Women Scientists in Novels of
Professional Development 113

5
Indépendantes: Professional Women Writers 149

6
The Composite Novel: Women Lawyers in *Les Dames du Palais* 175

7
After the War 203

Appendixes
Appendix 1: Biographical Sketches 219
Appendix 2: Plot Summaries 223

References 231

Index 239

ACKNOWLEDGMENTS

Over the past ten years, I have benefited from the support of a number of institutions that gave me time off from teaching in order to work on this project. I am grateful for a Camargo Foundation fellowship in Cassis, France, which offered a beautiful setting for writing and reflection. The Center for the Humanities at the University of New Hampshire granted me a semester-long fellowship at the very beginning of the project to read and research the background history of the time period and the women writers, and the Graduate School and the College of Liberal Arts at UNH both granted me summer stipends to work in the Bibliothèque Nationale and the Bibliothèque Marguerite Durand in Paris.

I owe many thanks to the wonderful staff at the UNH library and the librarians at the Bibliothèque Marguerite Durand in Paris who were able to track down hard-to-find books, magazine articles, journals, and other materials from the Belle Epoque. Many people read various parts of the manuscript at different stages, and I am indebted to them for their much needed wisdom and advice: Nadine Bérenguier, Barbara Cooper, Tama Engelking, Diana Holmes, Jennifer Waelti-Walters, and Susan Weiner.

I am grateful to my feline companions Patsy and Eddie, who supervised early drafts from the top of the computer monitor and later ones from the security of my lap; I miss you, Patsy, very much. My daughter Caroline has displayed amazing patience with her preoccupied mom; I am thankful for her ability to lift me out of the mundane with a swirl of her magic wand. John Norman, to whom this book is dedicated, was friend, enabler, and intellectual and moral advisor throughout. For attentions paid while living with me and this book for so many years, he deserves special thanks.

INTRODUCTION

THIS BOOK WILL CONTRIBUTE a new facet to literary histories of the Belle Epoque, one that has not been explored previously: the fascinating subgenre of the *bildungsroman* that flourished briefly during the first decade of the twentieth century in France, and that I have labeled the female *berufsroman*, or novel of women's professional development. I am using terms borrowed from the German, rather than the general French term *roman d'apprentissage* because the German term *bildungsroman* already has several relevant variants that do not exist in French (*erziehungsroman*, or novel of educational development, and *Künstlerroman*, or novel of artistic development). Following that pattern, I derived the term *berufsroman* from the German word for career or avocation, *beruf*.[1]

Such a study will expand our definitions of what "Belle Epoque literature" means beyond the divisive schools of thought that currently exist. In recent years, the breach between studies of the pessimistic and decadent fin-de-siècle era and the optimistic and progressive Belle Epoque has grown wider than ever. For the field of literary history in particular, the production of books examining the fin-de-siècle period has tended to eclipse those that emphasize the Belle Epoque. Such scholars as Gordon Millan, Brian Rigby, and Jill Forbes claim that this divide is based in part on national intellectual trends: "whereas Anglo-American scholars may be happy to think of the period 1870–1914 in France as having been one of fragmentation, repression, and decadence, many French scholars and intellectuals refuse to take up such an unmitigatedly pessimistic and negative position" (Millan, Rigby and Forbes 37–38). French scholars, according to these writers, lean toward a more positive assessment of the turn-of-the-century period and its legacy in contemporary France. Recently, certain Anglo-American scholars have

---

1. Although Marion Heister coined a similar term (*Angestellteroman*) in her 1989 study of German novels, *Winzige Katastrophen*, the emphasis in that expression is on the employee or staff person (*Angestellte* is the German word for employee). The texts studied here, however, do not focus on office workers or employees but instead on professional women and their career aspirations and goals.

crossed the divide and have focused on Belle Epoque optimism, rather than fin-de-siècle decadents. These would include Jennifer Waelti-Walters's influential study, *Feminist Novelists of the Belle Epoque: Love as a Lifestyle* (1990).[2] My own position in this debate lies mainly with the "optimists" as well. This book on early twentieth-century novels of professional development assumes the idealistic and positive interpretation of the time period, with an emphasis on realist fiction and a focus on bourgeois and working-class heroines, rather than the elite echelons portrayed in works by authors of the Decadent (or fin-de-siècle) movement.

Although much can be learned from literary studies of the Decadents and the women authors associated with that group, such as Rachilde, Renée Vivien, and Natalie Barney, these works do not represent a complete picture of women writers from that time period. In fact, by concentrating mainly on the psychoanalytic, sexual, and moral tensions of women writers' works, our understanding of the Belle Epoque and of French feminist literary history is undermined. An investigation of novels written about professional women and the particular dilemmas that they faced during the early twentieth century will provide an original addition to existing literary studies of the time period and will supply a bridge between early twentieth-century women's literature and women's literature in contemporary France.

The Belle Epoque, as its name indicates, has been remembered as a period of happiness and prosperity in French history. After the tragedy and destruction of World War I, the French looked back upon the era 1900 to 1914 as a time of high hopes for the future and for the new century. Optimism for the growth of France and the dynamism of Europe was widespread, and the new age of technological advances inspired everyone with dreams of easier and healthier lives. New modes of transportation (bicycles, automobiles, and airplanes), electric lights, modern plumbing, and other inventions became

---

2. Waelti-Walters's groundbreaking study provides a generally sympathetic survey of many different women writers and has served as a springboard for many new examinations of this period of forgotten literature. Since her book appeared in 1990, four more full-length texts have appeared on one or more of these women writers: Milligan's 1996 *The Forgotten Generation* (on women writers of the interwar period, many of whom began their careers during the Belle Epoque), Goldberg's 1999 *Woman Your Hour Is Sounding* (on women writers during World War I, 1914–19), Collado's 2003 *Colette, Delarue-Mardrus, Tinayre,* and Klijn's 2004 *Une Littérature de circonstance* (on Marcelle Tinayre's early works). Diana Holmes also devoted an entire chapter of her survey of women's writing to three Belle Epoque women writers (*French Women's Writing,* 1996) and she co-edited with Carrie Tarr a collection of essays on women's history, politics, literature, and arts of the Belle Epoque in 2006 (*A Belle Epoque?*).

the symbolic beacons for a society of progress, mobility, and cleanliness.³ In the opening pages of his 1910 sociological study of Parisian women, Uzanne comments on the new era's rapid changes and the benefits provided by new technologies, labeling it a period of *transformisme*: "We cannot help but affirm that our century is interesting to interpret and define with the accentuated movement of its transformism. This world of beings . . . is infinitely more complicated, more difficult, and as a result, more exciting to represent in successive portraits than the world of our peaceful and simplistic ancestors of 1840.⁴ Uzanne's feelings about the complicated and fascinating new era that he was witnessing, with its changes in politics and the sciences, were common among the Belle Epoque population. Although difficulties would inevitably arise, the general sentiment about change and progress was positive.

The popular Exposition Universelle of 1900, held in Paris, attracted more than fifty million visitors who came from all over the world to view the exhibits and to witness the physical proof of a new, modern era. The main attractions included the Palais de l'Electricité, illuminated by five thousand colored lights at night, the electric-powered triple-decker moving sidewalk, and hundreds of displays of new technology. The design of the pavilions and the exhibits all contributed to the general sentiment that "the forces of nature are subdued and tamed; steam and electricity have become our obedient servant. . . . Science serves us ever more diligently and is conquering ignorance and poverty."⁵

In the arts, France attained great recognition during this period as a center for innovative ideas and experimental forms. The movement from representational to nonrepresentational art had begun at the end of the nineteenth century with the Impressionists and Post-Impressionists and continued to grow through the developing philosophy and works of the

3. See Eugen Weber's *France: Fin de Siècle* (1986) for a thorough and entertaining historical account of these modern inventions and the ways in which they changed the everyday life of the French.

4. "On ne saurait affirmer que notre siècle ne soit intéressant à interpréter et à fixer avec le mouvement accentué de son transformisme. Cette société qui disparaît et se renouvelle est transfigurée par de curieux symptômes d'orientation imprévue. Ce monde d'êtres à la veille de subir les métamorphoses que la politique générale, le socialisme, et plus encore la science extraordinairement outillée lui préparent, est infiniment plus compliqué, plus difficile et, par conséquent, plus passionnant à représenter en de successifs portraits que ne fut celui de nos paisibles et simplistes ancêtres de 1840" (Uzanne 5–6).

5. This is an excerpt from the Exposition's inaugural speech by Prime Minister Alexandre Millerand, cited by Paolo Monelli in *La Belle Epoque, 1900–1914: Fifteen Euphoric Years in European History* (1978), pp. 18–19. For an in-depth description of the international pavilions and the science, art, and theater exhibits of the Exposition, see Nigel Gosling's *The Adventurous World of Paris, 1900–1914* (1978), pp. 15–26.

Fauvists and Cubists at the beginning of the twentieth century. Satie, Ravel, and Debussy reached the pinnacle of their successes during the Belle Epoque, as they continued to compose new and controversial musical pieces for an increasing number of admirers and music critics. Writers of all genres experimented with form and content, producing such important and diverse talents as Gide, Proust, Apollinaire, Valéry, and Péguy, to name only a few. These Belle Epoque artists, musicians, and writers found new techniques to present their ideas and provided French culture with a feeling parallel to that of the sciences: progress and hope for the new century.[6]

Accompanying these feelings of optimism and forward-looking thought, certain groups in French society also began to reevaluate the position of women. Historians' accounts of the end of the nineteenth century reveal that support grew rapidly in France for women's pay equity, equal education, and equal job opportunities, among other goals for women's rights during this time. Claire Moses, for instance, claims, "By the [nineteenth] century's end, feminists had a clear sense of direction" (Moses 226).[7] Some of the major legal victories for women's rights included, since 1884, the right to divorce and, in 1907, the right to control their earnings. The French women's suffrage movement also had one of its strongest and most public periods of renewal specifically at the turn of the century. After almost fifteen years of neglect, French suffragist Hubertine Auclert decided to revive her Suffrage des Femmes organization in 1900, due to the increase in men and women receptive to her ideas. Auclert biographer Stephen Hause notes: "The feminist movement that assembled in 1900 was larger and more diverse than the movement of 1885, there were now seven important feminist organizations in France. . . . The combined membership had also doubled. . . . And the growth of the movement was just beginning" (Hause 165).[8] Even though women would have to wait almost forty-five years to receive the right to vote in France, the Belle Epoque period was a turning point in women's suffrage history because of the growing acknowledgment and support of the idea. Feminist organizations of the beginning of the twentieth century thus enjoyed the same optimism and growth found in the economic, technological, and artistic domains of French culture.

---

6. Classic studies of the arts in Paris at the turn of the century include Roger Shattuck's *The Banquet Years* (1955) and Jerrold Seigel's *Bohemian Paris* (1986).

7. For a historical account of working women and labor laws, see also Mary Lynn Stewart, *Women, Work, and the French State: Labour Protection and Social Patriarchy, 1879–1919* (1989).

8. For an in-depth study of the history of the women's suffrage movement, see also Stephen C. Hause with Anne R. Kenney, *Women's Suffrage and Social Politics in the French Third Republic* (1984).

When we shift our attention from the political to the cultural domain in early twentieth-century French studies, however, the most frequently found images of French women are quite different. Popular stereotypes of the French woman usually include visions of decorative "dames," dressed in boa feathers and enormous hats, strolling in the Bois de Boulogne or lounging at the Moulin Rouge. Some critics have commented on these stereotypical images: "Myth has replaced history to such a degree that these words [*la Belle Epoque*] immediately conjure up a music-hall scene: showgirls in black stockings, pink velvet bodices and feathered hats, dancing the cancan" (Jullian 83).[9] It is true that in many canonical literary works of the time, some of the most famous portrayals of female protagonists are those that depict the lives of demimondaines, dancers, maids, or prostitutes.[10] Many writers of the turn-of-the-century era chose to set their novels and their female characters in the decadent atmosphere of bohemian Paris and what is known popularly as "Paris-by-Night."[11] Literary critics of the past two decades have begun to break new paths in the field of fin-de-siècle studies, making excellent additions to the traditional literary analyses of the decadent or perverse qualities of female fictional characters from this era.[12] Recent studies by historians have also contributed greatly to new views of the fin de siècle. Mary Louise Roberts's 2002 *Disruptive Acts: The New Woman in Fin-de-Siècle France,* with its emphasis on major female culture producers, such as the journalists Gyp and Séverine and the magazine editor Marguerite Durand, has demonstrated innovative ways to interpret the subversively feminist activities of women in the arts during the fin-de-siècle period in France.

---

9. By focusing on mondaines, demimondaines, and lesbian couples from the Belle Epoque, Jullian generally serves to reinforce those "mythical" images, rather than providing alternative portraits of women who were not involved in decadent or opulent lifestyles.

10. Examples include Octave Mirbeau's *Le Journal d'une femme de chambre* (1900) or Charles-Louis Philippe's *Bubu de Montparnasse.*

11. The nightlife in Paris cafés, music halls, and nightclubs form the core of this artistic milieu, with venues ranging from the Moulin Rouge and Chat Noir in Montmartre to the Coupole and other Montparnasse cafés on the Left Bank. In his text *The Decadent Imagination, 1880 to 1900,* Jean Pierrot cites Paul Bourget, Maurice Barrès (*Les Taches d'encre,* 1884, or *Les Déracinés,* 1897), Paul Adam and Jean Moréas (*Les Demoiselles Goubert* [Paris: Tresse et Stock, 1886]), Camille Mauclair (*Le Soleil des morts* [Paris: Ollendorff, 1898]), and Bernard Lazare (*Les Portes d'ivoire* [Paris: 1897]) (Pierrot 170–74). See also Jean Paul Crespelle's 1976 text *La Vie quotidienne à Montparnasse à la grande époque, 1905–1930.*

12. The following recent works have been influential in forming my own analysis of the Belle Epoque heroine: Emily Apter's *Feminizing the Fetish: Psychoanalysis and Narrative Obsession in Turn-of-the-Century France* (1991), Elaine Showalter's *Sexual Anarchy: Gender and Culture at the Fin de Siècle* (1990), and Eugen Weber's *France: Fin de Siècle* (1986).

There still exists, however, an unexamined discrepancy between the generalizations made about the perverse or titillating charms of fictional women characters in literature and the activist nature of Belle Epoque feminists engaged in political and social domains. Reasons for this gap are complex, but we can point to two main issues. First, we must acknowledge that women writers have generally held a very weak position in literary histories published in France, both one hundred years ago and today. Nancy Sloan Goldberg, referring to forgotten women writers from the Great War of 1914–18, states that literary historians today have continued "the conventional practice of segregating at the end of their books a short chapter discussing the works of a few disparate women authors, massed together under the rubric *littérature féminine*" (Goldberg xvi). Even when a literary history focuses specifically on women writers, the author sometimes includes a final chapter or epilogue that undermines the innovative qualities of the women studied. In *Histoire de la littérature féminine en France* (1929), Jean Larnac begins with a traditional chronological survey of women writers from the medieval period to the beginning of the twentieth century, then follows with a second section titled "Les Femmes et la littérature" (Women and Literature), including chapters titled "Les Limites du génie féminin" (The Limits of Feminine Creativity), "L'Intelligence féminine" (Feminine Intelligence), and "Le Drame du génie féminin" (The Drama of Feminine Creativity). This second part is devoted to a substantial thesis on the limits of women's creativity and of the female intellect. Larnac thus undermines the most basic purpose of a literary history here: he says that women writers have inferior abilities and can never be great authors. He lapses into banal generalizations about male intellect and female emotion; about women's incapacity to write about anything but themselves; about their inability to write comedy, critical analysis, or history. It is perhaps not surprising that a literary history that concludes in this manner would not inspire many future critics or readers to remember the women authors studied.[13]

---

13. As Collado has shown, a number of male literary historians engaged in this model of literary history when concerned with women writers (Collado 45). I find distinct connections between Larnac's unusual history of women writers and a more recent text, Mona Ozouf's 1995 *Les Mots des femmes*. Ozouf's literary history also concluded with a long essay on "la singularité française" (French singularity), a controversial statement about the limits of French feminism, which, according to certain critics, undermined rather than reinforced the lives and words of the women she had just studied. Such aberrations from the traditional literary history serve as a direct confirmation of Carolyn Heilbrun's claim that writing about a woman's life is often an experimental act. She speaks of women's biography in the following way: "I have read many moving lives of women, but they are painful, the price is high, the anxiety is intense, because there is no script to follow, no story

While in France the tendency is to dismiss or forget women writers, Anglo-American feminist scholars have published more extensively on French women authors, including forgotten or relatively unknown writers. The emphasis of these scholars, however, has been on fin-de-siècle writers whose female protagonists are generally associated with the Decadent movement in French literature, thus once again ignoring or dismissing the works of feminist writers of the Belle Epoque. Mélanie Collado mentions, for example, that for Rachilde, one of the most famous women authors of the Decadent movement, there are more than fifty articles listed in the MLA database in addition to three new books about her work and life that were published in the ten-year period from 1991 to 2001 (Collado 21). Colette has also enjoyed a great deal of critical attention in the past thirty to forty years; Collado claims that more than 250 articles related to Colette appear in the MLA database, and we have seen more than a dozen full-length books on Colette's life and work in a similar time frame (1991–2002). In contrast, when I checked the database for the two other Belle Epoque writers in Collado's study, I found only eight entries total for Marcelle Tinayre and six for Lucie Delarue-Mardrus, including Collado's work on these writers.

To bridge the gap that separates literary and historical portrayals of women from the Belle Epoque in France, I am suggesting here that the novel of women's professional development, or female berufsroman, can provide a "missing link" of sorts, to reconnect the now separate domains of literary, social, and political history for French women during the Belle Epoque.

The novels I have chosen to examine all focus on an aspect of life for French women that no literary study of the Belle Epoque, recent or past, has yet recognized or considered in detail: their professional lives in the public sphere of work. Two surveys of Belle Epoque literature have influenced my choice of texts here: Diana Holmes's contribution to the field in chapter 3 of her 1996 book *French Women's Writing, 1848–1994,* and the full-length book by Jennifer Waelti-Walters cited above, *Feminist Novelists of the Belle Epoque: Love as a Lifestyle* (1990). Holmes in her chapter discusses three novels of women's professional development, and yet the emphasis of her discussion lies not in their careers, but, as indicated by her chapter title, in "Feminism, Romance, and the Popular Novel." In her survey, Waelti-Walters examines the works of thirty different

---

portraying how one is to act, let alone any alternative stories" (Heilbrun 39). When we turn to literary histories about French women authors, we sense that same experimentation: no script, no set story exists for them either.

women authors, discusses more than one hundred books, and covers a wide variety of topics, including family, marriage, love, and education. Only one of her ten chapters addresses the heroines' professional lives or their actions in the public sphere. Similar to Holmes, much of Waelti-Walters's work explores themes related to love and marriage, which, while important to the texts that she has chosen, do not provide the alternative viewpoint that I will bring to Belle Epoque literary studies or French feminist literary history. My goal in this book is to discuss the educational, professional, and social aspirations of working-class and bourgeois female characters in these Belle Epoque novels. Because they parallel activities in the political domain, these novels mark a major departure from stereotypical portraits of women from the beginning of the twentieth century that range from the decadent, hysterical, or perverse sexual being to that of the nurturing and self-sacrificing romantic wife and mother. The French women who wrote these novels of professional development gave their fictional heroines increasingly independent roles, careers, and personalities. From the adventures of a provincial public high school student to the trials of an urban medical professional, the female protagonists portrayed in the novels boldly pursued happiness in the public domain. In the following chapters, I will examine eleven of these novels in detail for their innovative character types and the narrative structures that the authors employed to create such new women protagonists. Four of the works focus on women students and teachers: *Claudine à l'école* (1900, *Claudine at School*) by Colette; *Sévriennes* (1900, *Women of Sèvres*) by Gabrielle Reval; *Institutrice* (1902, *Woman Schoolteacher*) by Esther de Suze; and *L'Un vers l'autre* (1903, *One Toward the Other*) by Louise-Marie Compain. Four texts focus on women in the sciences: *Les Cervelines* (1903, *The Brainy Women*) and *Princesses de Science* (1907, translated as *The Doctor Wife* or *Princesses of Science*) both by Colette Yver; *Pharmacienne* (1907, *Woman Pharmacist*) by Marcelle Babin; and *La Bachelière* (1910, *The Female Graduate*) by Gabrielle Reval. Three focus on women writers: *La Rebelle* (1905, *The Woman Rebel*) by Marcelle Tinayre; *La Vagabonde* (1910, *The Vagabond*) by Colette, and *Les Cervelines* (1903) by Colette Yver. Finally, *Les Dames du Palais* (1909, *Ladies of the Court*), by Colette Yver, focuses on women lawyers.[14]

---

14. All of the authors listed here have short biographical sketches in Appendix 1. All of the novels have short plot summaries in Appendix 2.

This selection of novels is important for several reasons. First, the narrators of these novels all struggle with the same major question: what did happiness in the public sphere actually mean for women during the Belle Epoque? What did it signify for a woman to pursue an education or a career outside the home, and how could she be happy doing so? These were refreshingly new questions for fictional heroines in French literature at the time. In all of these texts, the protagonists are working, thinking women, and although they often struggled with their dual roles in and out of the public sphere, they sought resolutions to them in resourceful ways. While such a category of heroine may appear to be an anomaly in traditional Belle Epoque studies, it reflects both a growing awareness of the position of French women during the turn of the century and the individual efforts being made to change the flat or one-sided portrayals of women that we have inherited from conventional studies of the Belle Epoque. All of these texts have these general traits in common, but each of the novels addresses different aspects of professional growth, career tensions, technical abilities, sexual harassment, and issues for working women in the private domain. Individual authors approach these topics in a variety of ways, and my choice of texts displays the diverse techniques and narrative structures employed.

Finally, I have chosen to study this selection of novels in depth, rather than offer a survey of the many different texts that could and do fall into this category, because the individual literariness of each of these particular texts is also under question here. Dismissed for too long as uninteresting and antifeminist popular literature, these novels in fact often straddle the line between popular fiction and creative literary works in their innovative manipulation of genre. I must disagree with most of my contemporaries who have made great efforts to recuperate these works and to bring them back into the canon, yet who continue to deny their literary qualities. Goldberg, for example, states that "in general, their works duplicated time-honored conventions of the French novel" (xvi). Diana Holmes writes, "The fundamental narrative form employed by all three authors [Yver, Reval, and Tinayre] is the stereotypically feminine form of the romance" (Holmes 1996, 62). Jennifer Milligan concurs with this simplistic view, although she claims that the romance is "re-read" and "revised" after the war. While I certainly agree that the romance narrative does compose a part of some of these writers' novels, it is neither stereotypical nor conventional in form. Many of these novels of professional development twist the requirements of the romance genre to suit their heroines' professional needs or they may even jettison the romance elements completely. Rather than "revising" or "re-reading" the romance, I believe we need to take a new view of these texts and understand them as an innovative contribution to the Belle Epoque, one that would pave the way for new types of heroines and plotlines in later twentieth-century French literature.

To contextualize the actions and thoughts of such original female protagonists and storylines, both historically and socially, in Chapter 1 I describe some of the historical changes in the status of women in France that occurred at the end of the nineteenth and the beginning of the twentieth centuries. These political, social, and cultural improvements for French women opened the doors for the pioneering attitudes of the female characters in these Belle Epoque novels. Professional women heroines appear in great numbers for the first time in French literature during the Belle Epoque, but the novel of professional development and its cousin, the bildungsroman, or coming-of-age novel, had been staples of French literature for years. After surveying in Chapter 1 the historical position of women during the Belle Epoque that provides the setting for these novels, I will, in Chapter 2, examine a number of literary models that existed during the time. The nineteenth century produced very few professional female characters in French literature, and none who attended university or professional schools, as in the Belle Epoque texts that I am studying here. As an example, we do find a number of women who work in Zola's texts, but most are unskilled laborers or those who learn a trade or an assistant's role through an apprenticeship. These women include the laundress Gervaise in *L'Assommoir* (1877), the mineworkers Catherine and Maheude in *Germinal* (1885), the store clerk Denise Baudu in *Au Bonheur des dames* (1883), the artist who replaces her ill husband in "Madame Sourdis" (1874), and the niece Clotilde who acts as secretary for her uncle in *Le Docteur Pascal* (1893). Zola portrays all of these women at work, and in the specific case of *Au Bonheur des dames,* we could even categorize the plot as a berufsroman since it does follow the development of the young heroine and her professional career in the department store. But the main storylines in the other texts do not center on the women's careers and their abilities to adapt to or make changes to their professional domains, therefore they remain outside the definition of a female novel of professional development. I will return to a discussion of professionals, both men and women, in late nineteenth-century French literature in Chapter 2.[15]

---

15. The existence of women professionals historically appears to be key for the creation of literary texts with professional heroines. For example, when we look at the contrast in women's involvement in the medical profession in Europe and the United States, the correlation becomes clear.

Based in part on the bildungsroman, the berufsroman was a unique subgenre during this time period and required a particular style and special features to convey its message. Women authors grounded their female characters in some of the basic molds that male heroes had followed, whether they were teachers and students for the erziehungsroman (novel of educational development), or writers and artists for the Künstlerroman (novel of artistic development). But in order to provide a convincing and appealing fictional account of the *femme nouvelle* (New Woman), the authors invented new narrative structures and new plot devices. They also made significant alterations to the standard character types so that they would conform to the specific plight facing female protagonists. I offer in Chapter 2 an overview of the traditional components of the genre as it appeared at the end of the nineteenth century, with the purpose of outlining the general literary structures and devices that appeared commonly in this type of text. This survey of the texts of male contemporaries will allow us to see clearly the innovative novel-writing strategies women authors developed as they created their own novels of professional development in turn-of-the-century France.

The emphasis on the literariness of these texts is crucial for this book; when we examine the novels in closer detail, we are able to distinguish efforts by individual authors to create narrative structures and fictional protagonists that altered historical and social perceptions of Belle Epoque women professionals. Many of the female characters fall into one of three general categories: communities of women, female pioneers in male fields, and independent women who do not consult with or rely on either women or men for success. The first group is generally present in novels about education: women teachers or students (or both) elaborate a support system among themselves that will strengthen their morale and encourage them to excel in their student and professional lives. In Chapter 3 I focus on the dynamics of different types of women's communities and the effects

---

In the United States, where the first woman doctor—Elizabeth Blackwell—received her degree in 1849, there were numerous women physicians practicing by the end of the century (Elder and Schwarzer 165). Correspondingly, in a three-year period in the early 1880s, we find that three different novels about American women doctors were published in the United States: *Dr. Breen's Practice* (1881) by William Dean Howells, *Dr. Zay* (1882) by Elizabeth Stewart Phelps, and *A Country Doctor* (1884) by Sarah Orne Jewett (Furst 221). In contrast, Germany, which was the last European country to allow women to practice full medicine, in 1899 (Meyer 1997, 146), did not produce novels about women doctors in the nineteenth century. Paulette Meyer has shown that women of Eastern Europe (Russia, Poland, Germany) who wished to pursue a career in medicine had to attend schools in Zurich or Paris since they were refused at their own country's medical school (Meyer 1997, 279).

that they have on the main protagonists in four novels about education and women. These novels contain the strongest links to the traditional erziehungsroman, or novel of educational development. The second type, female pioneers in a male field, usually appears in novels about science and technology. Whether they are scientists, researchers, or interns, the protagonists are usually the only women in their professional schools or work environments. They generally do not have female companions with whom they may confer or in whom they might confide. They therefore must learn their system of values and code of professional behavior predominantly from their fathers, their male classmates, or their male professors or supervisors at work, and they do not have the opportunity to consider a women's community or a women's system of work. In Chapter 4 I examine four novels about women and science and the contradictions that these "pioneers" must work through in order to pursue a career and balance it with their private lives. In these novels, we find an unusual fusion of two very different genres: the bildungsroman and the romance. Each author intertwines the two genres in inventive ways and the results offer a consuming competition for the reader's attention. The third type, independent women, usually develops in novels about writers and artists. Those who work as journalists, novelists, and performers often remain closely connected to critics, colleagues, and admirers. But these particular writers and performers do not seek inspiration or support from any of these groups. They set their own priorities and do not feel the need to collaborate with others to pursue their own professional goals. Chapter 5 includes an analysis of three novels whose subject matter contains the portrayal of a woman writer and the gendered definitions of independence and career goals. Because these women are portrayed as mature and self-sufficient, these novels have limited ties to the traditional novel of development, which usually focuses on a young person who is exploring his or her independence for the first time. Instead, the romance narrative comes to the fore in these texts, but it is deeply influenced by the career decisions that the heroine has made. The public identity of the woman becomes most important for her resolution of her personal decisions; such a switch indicates the transitional nature of the Belle Epoque, a time when stereotypes about women's "instinctive" needs for love and marriage were still firmly planted in bourgeois cultural traditions but loosening their grip on the public's imagination. Finally, in Chapter 6 I examine a novel about Parisian women lawyers. Because very few women practiced law in France at the time, the novel had little or no basis in actual historical trends. The creative choices that the author made when developing a completely new type of professional heroine are thus easily explored. Her decision to elaborate all three groups in this novel, the women's community, the pioneer, and the independent, demonstrates her freedom to produce a variety of fictional models for her readers.

The novels in each of these categories belong to the general division of the berufsroman, or novel of professional development, but because of the varying nature of each work and the narrative compositions of each text, my study of the individual categories will require distinct theoretical approaches for each: sociological theories on professional development, historical theories on the development of science and medicine in Europe, and theories on consumer culture and the production of culture in France, to name a few of the approaches required to study these diverse texts.

A question that naturally arises when we study these women writers and their novels is: what happened to them? Why did they fall into oblivion so completely after World War I? None of the novels studied here has been in print since the 1920s, with the exception of Colette's texts *Claudine à l'école* and *La Vagabonde*. The answers to this question are multiple: canonical exclusion of women writers, decreased interest in the women's rights movements after the war, or changes in the cultural perceptions of working women. In the concluding chapter I address some of the numerous reasons—historical, cultural, and political—for the rapid disappearance of these works, after World War I, from the shelves of libraries and bookstores around France and include a study of some of the texts that replaced them. Not only will we see why the novel of professional and educational development no longer appealed to the readers, but we will understand what traces of the female novel of professional development were carried into the 1920s, by different authors who created different paths in their plot development. Although most of the Belle Epoque novels have remained out of print and unread for the past century, one of the main goals of this book is to demonstrate the role they played and the important place that they hold in French literary history, both as a historical reflection of French women's culture and an innovative phase in feminist literature from France.

1

INNOVATION AND EDUCATION:
HISTORICAL CONTEXTS FROM THE BELLE EPOQUE

THE EVENTS OF THE Third Republic that would have the most significant impact on women's lives, both immediately and on a long-term basis, were the creation of girls' public secondary schools and women's teacher training schools (*les écoles normales*), along with the decision to require primary education for all girls. Before 1870, there had been no official governmental structures that would guarantee a nationalized, public education for girls in France. Although the Falloux law of 1850 had recommended that municipalities of 800 or more inhabitants provide primary education for girls as well as for boys, very few cities and towns were able to provide the necessary funds to support an extra school and extra (female) teachers. Girls' instruction often took place in makeshift buildings with professors "borrowed" from boys' school, or with nuns hired by the town at lower wages. The government supported only a small handful of teacher training schools for women before 1880, making it difficult for women to obtain the degrees necessary to teach in the public schools (the *brevet primaire* and *supérieur* were the minimal diplomas required for teaching). Nuns, on the contrary, needed only a "letter of obedience" from the superiors in their convent to teach in municipal primary schools. After 1867, because the number of inhabitants necessary for the recommendation of a girls' primary school was reduced from 800 to 500, and because the supervision of funding for building construction had become stricter, the number of girls' schools opening increased, reaching an enrollment of 2,316,000 girls in 1880 (Rousselot 370–72). In 1882, a government decree made primary education for all children obligatory.[1]

Secondary education for girls also took several decades to become available to all girls nationwide. The 1867 proposal for secondary education, initiated by Victor Duruy, lasted only three years, until the Commune, and it existed

---

1. For information on primary education in France, see Linda Clark, *Schooling the Daughters of Marianne* (1984), Laura Strumingher, *What Were Little Girls and Boys Made Of? Primary*

only in Paris. It was not until 1880 that the National Assembly passed the Camille Sée Decree, which called for the funding of a national secondary school system for girls (Rousselot 372). In the following year, the National Assembly passed a bill to establish a national women's teaching school, l'Ecole Normale Supérieure de Sèvres, to train women professors for the new secondary schools. Soon after Sèvres, many regional teacher training schools were created to provide qualified, state-educated women schoolteachers for the new girls' primary and secondary schools. This series of national legislative acts meant that girls from all social and economic classes could attend classes, and after 1882, they were required to pass through the primary school level.

According to the new educational system, the schoolteacher became the new source of authority, the new role model during the formative years through adolescence. The new schoolteachers were expected to be models of cleanliness, morality, proper public behavior, and republican civic duty. Mona Ozouf's groundbreaking work on the battles waged between the Catholic Church and the Republic, *L'Ecole, L'Eglise, et la République, 1871–1914* (*School, Church, and Republic*), demonstrates the emphasis on nationalism that education reformers of the Third Republic promoted for both men and women (Ozouf 1982, 103–23). Ozouf observes that one of the major goals for Jules Ferry and other pedagogues of the time had been symbolic as well as practical: they wanted freedom from the church, not only through schools operated independently of the church. *Laicité* (secularism) became a keyword for the campaign for "modern" schooling, and the reformers' primary tool toward achieving that goal was to insist on the notion of national identity rather than on religious or regional affiliations. In its zeal, the republican school supplants God, as Ozouf shows by comparing a geography lesson from a religious school to one from a public school: whereas the text from the religious school includes a celebration of God in its description of the splendors of nature, the text from the republican school includes passages extolling the French citizen in the geographic diversity that makes up France (114)!

To build patriotic pride in the nation, France and Paris were overtly lauded in schools. Education historian Pierre Albertini states categorically, "The education of the schools of the Republic undeniably reinforced the feeling of belonging to the French nation."[2] For Albertini, one of the chief

---

Education in Rural France, 1830–1880 (1983), Jo Burr Margadant's *Madame le Professeur* (1990), esp. the introduction, and the period work by Frederic Ernest Farrington, *The Public Primary School System of France with Special Reference to the Training of Teachers* (1906).

2. "L'enseignement de l'Ecole républicaine a incontestablement renforcé le sentiment d'appartenance à la nation française" (Albertini 75). Albertini labels the entire period from 1870 to

ways for the schools to encourage this growth in nationalist feeling was to add history texts that focused primarily on the nation and on the great figures who had founded France, particularly since the 1789 Revolution. He also cites the development of geography courses on France and the addition of French literature in the primary programs as further examples of the new patriotism that public schools in France were bringing forth under the Jules Ferry reforms.

This new patriotism played a crucial role in transforming Third Republic French society, as Eugen Weber has argued in his classic work *Peasants into Frenchmen: The Modernization of Rural France, 1870–1914* (1976). In particular, schools became a major factor for change in France because they helped students to understand a society that extended beyond their local community. Normally we separate society and school (society educates, school instructs), yet Weber notes that the public schools from the Third Republic provided both instruction and education, describing this particular schooling as: "a major agent of acculturation: shaping individuals to fit into societies and cultures broader than their own, and persuading them that these broader realms are their own" (Weber 1976, 330). This nationalizing force in education influenced both male and female novels of educational development in France at the turn of the century.

In addition to outlining broader social goals, the major reforms for girls' education in the 1880s and 1890s also brought about a very concrete result: by 1900, literacy rates among French women of all classes had increased dramatically. Rather than the bourgeois Madame Bovaries who read sentimental romances to escape from their humdrum lives, women readers now came from all ranks of society, and they demanded a literature that would reflect their own class situations. Between 1900 and 1905, for example, more than a dozen novels were published in France featuring young women studying at the high school and university levels, or teaching girls and women in public schools.[3] Both historians today and analysts from the turn of the century agree that the

---

1960 the "Siècle de Jules Ferry" (the Jules Ferry century) after the man whose reforms changed so notably the way that French children would be educated.

3. Those novels include: *Claudine à l'école* (1900; *Claudine at School*) by Colette-Willy; *Sèvriennes* (1900; *Women of Sèvres*), *Un Lycée de jeunes filles* (1901; *A High School of Young Girls*), and *Lycéennes* (1902; *High School Girls*) by Gabrielle Reval; *L'Institutrice* (1900; *The Woman Schoolteacher*) by R. O'Monroy and R. Vallier; *Institutrice* (1902; *Woman Schoolteacher*) by Esther de Suze; *Le Journal d'une institutrice* (1902; *The Diary of a Woman Schoolteacher*) by Léon Deries; *L'Un vers l'autre* (1903; *One Towards the Other*) by Louise-Marie Compain; *La Maternelle* (1904; *The Nursery School*) and *L'Institutrice de province* (1906; *The Woman Schoolteacher from the Provinces*) by Léon Frapié; and *L'Evadée* (1905; *The Female Fugitive*) by "une

enthusiasm of these new readers was one of the major factors for the sudden popularity of turn-of-the-century women authors whose heroines were independent, educated, and modern—*les femmes nouvelles* (New Women).

One of today's historians of French publishing trends, Anne Sauvy, notes that the increase in literacy was directly linked to one of the highest periods of reading activity among French women: "women achieved literacy in the second half of the XIXth century. From then on, they constitute the most avid readers in the public masses, especially novel readers. The period from 1890 to 1950 is certainly the time when, historically, Frenchwomen read the most."[4] It is significant that these new readers chose novels, and particularly popular novels, as their favorite written materials. These texts were often first published in serial form, in magazines or daily newspapers. Newspapers advertised the serial novel as offering inexpensive installments of fiction that could be read in short time periods, mainly for the benefit of working women who were too busy to pass many consecutive hours at leisure, slowly consuming an entire novel. Historical analyses of the serial novel in France emphasize the practical aspects of its format. Anne-Marie Thiesse, for example, notes that the serial novel worked well with the rhythms of the working-class household because the short installments could be read easily between two domestic tasks and the suspenseful ending of each episode sparked reader interest until the next issue arrived (Thiesse 1984, 21).

This type of *roman-feuilleton,* or serial novel, was most frequently located in the *rez-de-chaussée* (ground floor) section of major daily newspapers.[5] As a part of the daily newspaper, the serial novel turned out to be inexpensive and accessible to women of the working classes for whom the prestige (and cost) of the bound book still held some power of intimidation. Thiesse comments that the school reforms of the Third Republic slowly began to erode that intimidation, "through the early and prolonged contact of all children with textbooks, thanks to the expansion of school libraries and to

---

institutrice de province." These novels all focused specifically on life in *public* schools for girls. Of course, the period also witnessed the publication of countless novels about the plight of the private governess (*institutrice dans une famille*), a traditional role for women found in many novels of the nineteenth century in England and France.

4. "les femmes ont achevé leur alphabétisation dans la seconde moitié du XIX siècle. Elles constituent dès lors la masse de public la plus avide de lectures et surtout de romans. La période qui s'étend de 1890 à 1950 est certainement celle qui a vu historiquement les Françaises lire le plus" (Sauvy 243).

5. This title referred to the physical location of the story on the printed page, since it was usually found on the bottom quarter of the front page (Thiesse 1984, 20).

the wide distribution of book prizes."⁶ The latter, books awarded publicly at the end-of-the-year school prize ceremony, were considered special "aesthetic objects," conserved carefully and proudly displayed in the homes of many generations of French men and women. The serial novel, however, retained its popularity and appeared more and more often in the literary sections of the increasingly popular "women's" magazines that began to flourish during this period.

The rise in the number of periodicals written specifically for women readers may also have links to the creation of a secondary school system for girls, as S. M. Bonvoisin and M. Maignien, historians of the French press, have argued.⁷ The demand for periodicals for women rose so dramatically that between 1892 and 1908 at least twelve different daily, weekly, and monthly newspapers and magazines for a specifically female readership opened their doors in France.⁸ Among the most famous are *La Fronde* (*The Revolt*) founded in 1892 by Marguerite Durand, the only newspaper staffed entirely by women in France, *Femina* (founded 1900), and *La Vie Heureuse* (*The Happy Life*; founded 1902), whose staff members contributed to the creation of the Prix Femina (first called the Prix Vie Heureuse) in 1905, in response to the Prix Goncourt's exclusion of women writers from their prestigious book prize competition.⁹ Although most revues combined articles on current events with advice columns, society news, and literary reviews, some

---

6. "par la mise en contact précoce et prolongée de tous les enfants avec des manuels . . . , grâce aussi à l'expansion des bibliothèques scolaires et aux larges distributions de prix" (Thiesse 1984, 25).

7. "Le succès de cette diversification (de journaux pour femmes) s'inscrit dans l'évolution du statut des femmes au sein de la société française, conséquence de l'obtention d'un certain nombre de droits civils: accès des jeunes filles à l'enseignement secondaire (décret Camille Sée, 1880)" (Bonvoisin and Maignien 17).

8. This phenomenal increase in women's periodicals may have been part of a greater trend during the period 1870–1930, which Anne Marie Thiesse calls "l'âge d'or de la presse française" (the golden age of the French press) (Thiesse 1984, 17–20). Not only did the number of periodicals aimed specifically at a female audience increase, but also the four major daily newspapers augmented their number of women's columns and serial novels that were written mostly by women novelists and intended for female readers.

9. See *La Vie Heureuse* in December 1904, where portraits of the twenty women writers who sat on the first jury appear; the February 1905 issue, where the prize of 5,000 francs is advertised; and the March 1905 issue, where the jury awards Myriam Harry the first Vie Heureuse book prize for her novel *La Conquête de Jerusalem* (*The Conquest of Jerusalem*). Anne Sauvy, in "La Littérature et les femmes" ("Literature and Women"), gives details of the protest raised by women writers against the exclusion of women from the Goncourt Prize and their decision to form a contest of their own (Sauvy 249). Jean Rabaut gives a brief history of the creation of the two differents prizes (Femina and Vie Heureuse) and the decision to combine them into one competition shortly after their creation (Rabaut 151).

of the journals were specifically political (*L'Abeille* [*The Bee*] and *L'Action Féministe* [*Feminist Action*] for example, were newsletters for women's unions), some were specifically literary (*Lectures de la femme* [*Woman's Readings*]), and some were aimed at specific groups of women (*La Femme Nouvelle* [*The New Woman*] was written for high school students and teachers, including job listings). Several of the novelists whom I will study in later chapters contributed articles regularly to women's magazines and newspapers from the turn of the century, in addition to serial fiction. Colette, Marcelle Tinayre, and Colette Yver contributed articles, speeches, and interviews to *La Femme, La Fronde,* and *La Vie Heureuse* during the period 1900–1910, for example.

Camille Pert, a social activist for women, noted in 1910, in her work *Le Travail de la femme* (*Woman's Work*), that very few women had pursued the careers of journalist, dramaturge, or translator, mainly because these jobs did not pay well or provide a source of steady income. She also listed the fact that they were still considered very masculine fields (Pert 298). Not all journalists were of the same opinion. In the November 1905 issue of *La Vie Heureuse,* we find an article written by a male journalist who fears that women were taking over the field of journalism. He claims that 27 percent of all journalists were women, but then adds that his figures were especially true in America and Germany, where women writers were a stronger force than in France.[10] And in Uzanne's 1910 study, *Etudes de sociologie féminine: Parisiennes de ce temps* (*Studies in Feminine Sociology: Parisian Women of Today*), the author claims a large number of women writers: 3,500 women "with blue dyed stocking," including 2,800 who write novels or books for children, 200 who write pedagogical works, and 350 poets (Uzanne 272–73). Although 3,500 feminists (or "blue-stockings") may appear an insignificant number by today's standards, for contemporaries such as Uzanne they appeared to be an overwhelming group that stood ready to invade the literary world.

Pert herself did comment that, with the increase in the number of periodicals and their growing circulations, women might develop more interest in journalism as it became a more feasible means of earning one's living: "The multitude of cheap periodicals [and] newspapers consumes an enormous mass of 'copy'; and if this literature does not bring glory to those who devote themselves to it, it does procure them a modest wage."[11]

---

10. This article was reprinted from the *Figaro* and is located in the column "Evènements et Menus Faits" of *La Vie Heureuse* 27, no. 11, (novembre 1905): 4.

11. "La multitude des publications périodiques à bon marché, des journaux, consomme journellement une énorme masse de 'copie'; et si cette littérature n'apporte point la gloire à ceux qui s'y livrent, elle leur procure un gain modeste" (Pert 298).

Thus Pert considered journalism, whether for a daily newspaper or a women's magazine, primarily as a source of income, rather than as a glorious career for women. It was a practical means for women to earn money, and it was considered only secondarily as a literary endeavor.

Confirming her theory, a well-known journalist from the turn of the century, Séverine, slipped from public memory almost as soon as she died. Her biographer, Evelyne LeGarrec, blames the ephemeral quality of newspaper reporting for her disappearance from the public eye at her death and for her continued invisibility throughout the twentieth century (LeGarrec 306).[12] One of the novels that I will be studying, Marcelle Tinayre's *La Rebelle* (*The Woman Rebel*, 1905), also supports Pert's notion that writing was becoming a practical way for women to live on their own, even though it did not bring fame and glory with it. The story focuses on a heroine who provides for her invalid husband, her son, and herself by writing articles for a women's magazine located in Paris. After her husband's death, she continues to earn a modest living through journalism and thereby remains independent so that she may pursue her own goals and follow her own beliefs.

Other novels about women writers from the Belle Epoque indicate a similar independence of mind and body. In both *La Vagabonde* (*The Vagabond*) by Colette and *Les Cervelines* (*The Brainy Women*) by Colette Yver, the women writers are portrayed as creative individuals who do not need societal approval, the support of a man or husband, or even a network of female friends in order to achieve their goals. Although surrounded by friends, admirers, critics, and suitors, the women writers are portrayed as indifferent to or distant from the conventional restrictions placed on women of their era. Their marginal status within bourgeois society thus confirms some of Pert's concerns that writing was still considered a male field and thus women could not easily pursue such a career at the turn of the century. Yet the number of women writers continued to grow, and their choice of female protagonists who taught and wrote indicates that these types of fictional characters could be considered heroines for women readers of the time.

The secondary school system and the rise in the literacy rate of French women thus caused significant increases in journals, newspapers, and novels written for and by women at the beginning of the twentieth century.

---

12. Other more recent biographies have discussed Séverine's anonymity and have done much to remember this forgotten journalist and newspaper editor. I am thinking, for example, of Christiane Douyère-Demeulenaere's text *Séverine et Vallès: Le cri du peuple* (Paris: Payot, 2003), Paul Couturiau's *Séverine l'insurgée: Biographie* (Paris: Editions du Rocher, 2001), and Jean-Michel Gaillard's *Séverine* (Paris: Plon, 1999), in addition to Roberts's chapters in *Disruptive Acts* (2002).

Jules Bertaut, a literary critic from the turn of the century, goes even further in his claims for the consequences of the new secondary education system for girls. According to Bertaut, not only did the school system produce more young women readers and writers, it also produced more young women protagonists. He explains that obligatory education at the primary level was the main cause for the increase in dynamic young heroines in literary trends: "The great and unique cause to explain this sudden evolution of the young girl (in French literature), can only be education. The young girl owes to required schooling, imposed by the law and accepted by social custom, the personality that she has acquired in the past twenty years."[13] Public education had allowed young girls to become more independent by requiring them to leave their homes on a daily basis to go to school and by encouraging their curiosity and the development of their ideas and opinions. It also promoted a variety of types of young girls, not a single model of submission and devotion to paternal authority. Bertaut believed that these two trends in young women's lives affected the portrayals of them in literature. Finally, they were being described and developed as protagonists with personalities, after centuries of being portrayed as nonentities with no social rank. Bertaut also lists ten different literary types of *jeunes filles* (young girls) found in the novels of his day, including the *revoltée* (the revolted girl), the *intellectuelle* (the intellectual girl), the *fille du peuple* (the daughter of the people), and the *féministe* (the feminist) (Bertaut 165ff.). Another literary critic and popular novelist of the period, Charles-Henri Hirsch, also commented on the "new" *jeune fille moderne* (modern young girl) who had transformed the dull literary model of previous generations: "The differences are very weak between the thousands of young girls of French literature, from Cécile de Volanges to Mademoiselle Renaude Chamot in *Coco de Génie* by Monsieur Louis Dumur. They all seem like fugitives from the same convent. A uniform discipline has bent them to similar ways of acting and thinking."[14] To offer an example of the "new" literary type, Hirsch points to Colette's Claudine character and her refreshing openness and vitality.

---

13. "La grande, l'unique cause pour expliquer cette évolution soudaine de la jeune fille (dans la littérature française), c'est et ce ne peut être que l'instruction. C'est à l'instruction obligatoire, imposée par la loi et acceptée par les moeurs, que la jeune fille doit la personnalité qu'elle s'est acquise depuis une vingtaine d'années seulement" (Bertaut 166).

14. "De très faibles différences existent entre les mille jeunes filles du roman français, de Cécile de Volanges . . . à Mlle Renaude Chamot du *Coco de Génie* de M. Louis Dumur. Toutes semblent évadées du même couvent. Une discipline uniforme les a pliées à des manières analogues d'agir ou de penser" (Hirsch 582).

It must be remembered that not all contemporaries thought as positively about the educational system as did Bertaut or Hirsch. Many felt that the public school system for girls had a negative influence on the female population in France. Some even denounced it as a threat to the Roman Catholic religion in France or to the survival of the French race. Jacques Valdour, under the pseudonym Nic, wrote *Le Lycée corrupteur* (*The Corrupting High School*) in 1909, a general indictment against nonreligious (non–Roman Catholic) public high schools for both boys and girls in France. His pessimistic view of the goals of girls' public high schools becomes evident in his writings, where he claims that the high school is the state's main agent of "intellectual and moral corruption." He also believes that the role of the new girls' high schools is to prevent Christian households from being established (Nic 113). Valdour did not even want to consider the possibility that educated female high school graduates might pursue careers outside the home. From his critique, we can see that he assumed that the women who graduated from public high schools would still be involved with traditionally feminine activities: homemaker, mother, teacher of moral and religious beliefs. They would *fonder un foyer* (start a family). His main fear resided in the fact that these state-educated homemakers might not teach *Roman Catholic* values to their children because of other (i.e., Protestant or republican) values taught in their high schools. But he did not doubt for a moment that women would remain in the home, at the center of the nuclear family.

Furthermore, Valdour believed that the new high school teachers were not only nonreligious, but also antireligious. To prove his point he recounts the story of a girls' schoolteacher who allowed only those high school students who had *not* attended Mass that morning to buy some candy from a passing street vendor. This story had been told and retold several times, and it is difficult to determine what kinds of embellishments or omissions may have been made to the anecdote (Nic 114).[15] Valdour, however, used the tale as a basis for his statements about the "anti-religious Protestantism" at the Ecole Normale Supérieure de Sèvres and the anti-Catholic sentiments that the professors encouraged in the new schoolteachers that Sèvres produced each year for the provincial girls' high schools. Gabrielle Reval, in her novel about the Ecole Normale Supérieure de Sèvres, *Sévriennes* (1900), while giving a generally positive image of the school's mission, also critiques

---

15. According to Valdour, he had read it when it was reproduced in *La Libre parole* following a report given in *Le Messager-matin de l'Allier* based on a story heard in the suburban streets of the city of Moulins.

the austerity and rationality of the Protestant director, Mme Jules Ferron, but for very different reasons than those of Valdour. Literary critics picked up on this criticism and although they gave positive reviews of Reval's texts overall, they continually pointed to the same flaw, the fact that religion never played an important role for any of the heroines of her works. Mme A. Philip de Barjeau's reviews of Reval, for example, in the magazine *La Femme,* give high praise to her literary style and character development,[16] but insist that the lack of religion is the most serious problem in the book, and in "real" high schools, too, because it leaves the students without *une base solide* (a solid base).[17] Paule Branzac, writing for the journal *La Femme Nouvelle* (*The New Woman,* 1 février 1905), mentions similar problems with Reval's texts.[18]

"Nic" was of course not alone in his critique of women's education. Another conservative literary critic and popular novelist from the turn of the century, Léo Clarétie, took a more extreme view of the consequences of women's education and feminism in general for France. In his 1907 study of women's education, *L'Ecole des dames* (*The School for Ladies*), Clarétie wrote that women should have the same rights as men *theoretically,* but that if they actually claimed their rights to equal education and to equal pay, they would have to give up maternity (Clarétie 11). Maternity and feminism were incompatible in Clarétie's eyes, and feminism, if practiced widely, would therefore lead to the extinction of the human race (11).[19] The idea that women had to make a choice between education and maternity, brain and body, was a popular one, backed by medical doctors, priests, and others who maintained older theories on women's anatomy. Many of the novelists analyzed in later chapters in this book also deal with this apparent conflict between motherhood and career, some conceding that it existed, others fighting to prove that both were possible.

---

16. For example: "Quant à la valeur littéraire du livre qui nous occupe, elle est réelle" (As for the literary value of the book that we are concerned with, it is great.), in Mme A. Philip de Barjeau's "Revues littéraires," *La Femme* 23, no. 3, (1 février 1901): 23.

17. For her opinions, see, for example, her later article in 1901: Mme A. Philip de Barjeau, "Revues Littéraires" in *La Femme* 23, no. 15 (1 septembre 1901): 135.

18. Branzac's comparative review of three different novels about women schoolteachers allows her to make such distinctions about Reval's work. See Paule Branzac's article "Livres Nouveaux," which contains a review of *L'Evadée,* by "une institutrice de province" and *Sévriennes* by Gabrielle Reval in *La Femme Nouvelle,* février 1905.

19. Clarétie's concern may seem hysterical today, but in the context of the "depopulation crisis" that occupied the minds of many intellectuals and scientists during the 1890s, the threat of human extinction seemed omnipresent. See Karen Offen's article "Depopulation, Nationalism, and Feminism in Fin-de-Siècle Paris."

A second debate, spawned by the new public schools for girls, centered on whether or not the government should create one unified, coeducational system, cutting the costs of supporting two separate school systems and giving girls and boys the same education. Isabelle Gatti de Gamand, an eloquent girls' school director who had founded the girls' school system in Belgium at the end of the nineteenth century, supported a coeducational system for practical reasons. If the boys' and girls' school systems were melded into one, then girls' education would actually receive more funding, since most French towns had only enough money to support one school and generally gave priority to the boys' school, neglecting girls' instruction. She also believed that a bilateral system channeled girls into a restricted field of possible careers, whereas boys generally had a larger choice of professions, especially those who graduated with the prestigious *baccalauréat* diploma, which was not offered as part of girls' secondary education during the Belle Epoque. In Gatti de Gamand's mind, a single educational system would theoretically give all students equal access to all careers, based on their qualifications and the diplomas held (Gatti de Gamand 21–24).[20]

In the 1930s and later, parallel educations for both sexes would in fact become the norm. But at the beginning of the century, Gatti de Gamand's views did not reflect those of the majority, and most French citizens continued to desire separate schools and curricula for the two sexes. In Colette's text, *Claudine à l'école* (1900), the fictional village of Montigny is in the midst of constructing a brand new school that consists of two separate wings for the boys' and girls' classrooms and dormitories, and two separate teachers' quarters, in spite of the additional cost of providing duplicate facilities. Claudine's curriculum includes obligatory needlepoint, singing lessons, and drawing classes, and her formal schooling terminates with a brevet exam. Her school thus mirrors the decision of the majority of educational leaders, who continued to support different curricula until the 1930s and separate classrooms until the 1960s. Jo Burr Margadant, in her history of women teachers in France, analyzes the advantages of the separate secondary school system for women that existed from 1880 to the 1930s, and specifically the fact that the government trained an entire corps of women teachers to

---

20. Although unusual for the time period, Gatti de Gamand was not alone in her feelings that coeducation would be beneficial for girls: in Nelly Roussel's popular lecture from 1905 titled "L'Eternelle Sacrifiée" ("The Eternal Sacrificed Woman"), she also speaks eloquently for a single education system and notes that the United States, England, and Holland have all converted successfully (Roussel 89).

educate girls. Both cultural and political demands required the government to educate and give authority to the women who would run the new schools, thus producing a new professional class of women in French society (Margadant 249–52).[21]

These political and historical hypotheses for the proliferation of the female erziehungsroman, or novel of educational development, are further supported by the fact that some of the authors of these novels had been public school students or teachers at the end of the nineteenth century. Gabrielle Reval, for example, entered the Ecole Normale Supérieure de Sèvres in 1893, passed the *agrégation* exam, and worked as a schoolteacher before she wrote her trilogy on women's public schools in 1900. Colette attended a provincial public school in her native Burgundian village of Saint-Sauveur-en-Puisaye from 1880 to 1890 before marrying, moving to Paris in 1893, and writing the four novels of the Claudine series from 1899 to 1903.[22] Others wrote historical or political documents and gave public lectures on women's access to higher education and the professions. Louise-Marie Compain, a well-known activist for women's labor law, published *La Femme dans les organisations ouvrières* (*Woman in Workers Organizations*) in 1910, which discusses the role of women in the different unions that existed at the turn of the century. Gabrielle Reval's *L'Avenir de nos filles* (*The Future of Our Daughters*, 1904) lists the pros and cons of different professions that had recently opened up to women. Daniel Lesueur (pseud. for Jeanne Lapauze) also wrote on women and work at the turn of the century: *L'Evolution féminine; ses résultats économiques* (*Feminine Evolution: Economic Results*, 1905).

The new education system for girls thus produced a new mass of readers and writers, but probably most important, it also produced new careerists. Before public schooling, young girls with no family resources who had to find work often went into domestic employment as personal maid, cook, nursemaid, or *la bonne à tout faire* (general housemaid). Generally, they worked long hours for low wages and lived far from their own families, sometimes in deplorable conditions. The *bonne à tout faire* whose responsibilities included cleaning, shopping, cooking, and serving most often worked in petit

---

21. Margadant also explains that the switch to a single curriculum in the 1930s, while benefiting female students who wanted to receive the male baccalauréat degree, would also have some negative results. In particular, the first generations of women schoolteachers and administrators were affected since their training was considered antiquated before they had reached retirement age.

22. The women novelists that I have chosen to study were all of the same generation (six were born between 1869 and 1878), with similar educational backgrounds and middle-class origins. For more biographical information on the nine writers, see Appendix 1.

bourgeois households. Their tasks were grueling, amounting to thirteen or fifteen hours per day, and the young woman's life often remained at the mercy of her employers (Martin-Fugier 19–21). By the turn of the century, a great shortage of domestic help existed in Paris and all over France. Historian Martin-Fugier claims that this lack of employable maids was mainly the result of an increase in demand by petit bourgeois families, who desired a domestic servant for the prestige of being served. She notes that there were numerous petit bourgeois households at the end of the nineteenth century whose incomes were scarcely higher than that of the proletariat, and who thus found it urgent to distinguish themselves from the working classes by hiring a general household maid (36). Martin-Fugier finds that some petit bourgeois would even sacrifice eating nutritionally balanced meals in order to be able to hire a live-in maid and feel as though they belonged to the bourgeoisie (100–101).

With the new century, a new style of domestic help is portrayed in novels, for example, in Octave Mirbeau's *Journal d'une femme de chambre* (*Diary of a Chambermaid*; 1900). The protagonist, Céléstine, recounts her daily life in a bourgeois manor in the provinces, revealing and analyzing the numerous sexual and moral depravities of her employers, neighbors, and village acquaintances. The tone and content of Céléstine's diary rendered Mirbeau's work scandalous in the eyes of his contemporaries. Yet the novel may also be considered subversive because it portrayed a literate maid, one who knew how to read and write well. Although no one may have believed it, the preface stated that Céléstine wrote the entire volume of diary entries, while Mirbeau acted only as the "editor" for the work (Mirbeau 31). Mirbeau presented Céléstine as a heroine who enjoys reading fiction, one who includes comments in her diary about novels she has just finished reading. She also confides to her diary that she finds her "peers"—other maids, servants, and valets from the town—rather dull. To distinguish herself from them, she refers to her urban background and specifically to her education and ability to read: "Upbringing, rubbing shoulders with chic people, the habit of beautiful things, reading Paul Bourget's novels, have saved me from these turpitudes."[23] Even though his tone may be somewhat condescending, Mirbeau created a plausible fictional example of a modern and literate maid for his contemporaries. His protagonist reflects the historical fact that the literacy rate continued in an upward trend among women of the working classes and increased considerably every year during this time period.

23. "L'éducation, le frottement avec les gens chics, l'habitude des belles choses, la lecture des romans de Paul Bourget, m'ont sauvée de ces turpitudes" (Mirbeau 94).

Given Mirbeau's example of the literate maid who feels "above" her peers, we can present an alternative hypothesis for the domestic-help shortage of the Belle Epoque: with a brevet in hand, working-class women were finding more desirable careers opening up for them. Even though they still represented a restricted choice, the new jobs appeared more prestigious, less grueling, and better paying than the standard domestic servant job. Uzanne's "sociological" study of Parisian women from his time is divided into chapters according to profession, with such title chapters as "Ouvrières de Paris" (Women Workers of Paris), "Marchandes et boutiquières" (Women Merchants and Boutique Owners), "Demoiselles et employés de magasin" (Women Shop Employees), and "Dames d'administration" (Ladies of the Administration), which included telephone operators, hospital staff, railroad personnel, typists, and office workers.

Teaching became by far the most popular new profession for women at the turn of the century, probably in part because of the very visible role model that women schoolteachers provided to young girls. This was no surprise, given the government's goals in forming women schoolteachers. More and more histories of the Third Republic's educational goals reveal the wide-ranging socialization strategies that the key governmental reformers and their opponents were struggling to make during this period. The government's efforts included reforms of the guidelines for morals and behavior. School children, of course, were the target for many of the new lessons in ethics and rules of conduct to follow, but equally fascinating is the amount of time devoted in certain pedagogical manuals to setting down rigid guidelines for the behavior and living patterns of the schoolteachers, who appear to be in as much need of reform as the children in some cases.[24]

Because all girls from ages six to thirteen now attended school six days each week, their biological mothers would rather obviously exercise less influence over them. The governmental reformers did not mean to deprive girls of a maternal influence by separating them from their mothers; in fact, it was assumed that all women had innate motherly qualities, and that female schoolteachers could therefore present maternal role models naturally in the classroom to their students (Clark 18). One of these reformers, Jules Rambosson, writing in 1873, even suggests two years of teaching as the best training method for would-be mothers after they had finished

---

24. For more detail on the attention paid to the moral and behavioral guidelines for school teachers, see Linda Clark's *Schooling the Daughters of Marianne* (1984) and Jo Burr Margadant's *Madame le Professeur*.

their own formal schooling, since such a training period would provide hands-on work with children (Rambosson 99).²⁵ The Third Republic's institutionalizing of the definition of mothering would have serious long-term effects on girls and women in the Belle Epoque. An obvious example of this maternal modeling can be found in Gabrielle Reval's heroine Marguerite Triel, in *Sévriennes*. In response to indirect messages from her professors, as Marguerite progresses in her studies to become a teacher, she shifts her emphasis from seeking out maternal professors and role models at her school to developing mothering qualities in herself.

In addition to role models, women schoolteachers were also expected to monitor the conduct of their pupils, as well as their own personal behavior. Historian Linda Clark notes, "Once on the job, woman school teachers should be exemplary in conduct, avoiding local disputes and gossip and keeping a distance from men" (Clark 1984, 16). In Chapter 3, I discuss the difficulties involved for most fictional schoolteachers in attempting to maintain a clean record of behavior, often because of public rumor but also because of personal needs. The private life of the unmarried woman schoolteacher was usually sacrificed to her public duties as teacher and moral guide of her students.

Women's teacher training schools generally recruited from the middle classes, since teaching still offered one of the few respectable employment opportunities for middle-class women during the Third Republic. Primary targets were female students who had finished primary and secondary school requirements with high grades but who were required to earn a living.²⁶ The teaching profession also appealed to young girls of the working and peasant classes, especially because it appeared to be a step up in the world for them. Colette's fictional character Claudine marvels at the fact that so many of her classmates are willing to sacrifice their health and youth by studying long hours indoors in order to become schoolteachers: "In order to not work

---

25. Rambosson also suggests hiring women teachers for other, more practical, considerations: he points out the fact that they would save the state some money, since, according to economic trends of the day, they would have to be paid only one-third the salary of men (Rambosson 98).

26. The post office and department stores also opened their low-level clerical and sales positions to young women during the last part of the nineteenth century and the beginning of the twentieth. These positions, however, perceived as "dens of iniquity," were not desirable jobs for women of the bourgeoisie, even though many women who worked there came from the lower ranks of the middle class. See, for example, Michael B. Miller's discussion of "les demoiselles de magasin" in *The Bon Marché: Bourgeois Culture and the Department Store, 1869–1920* (Princeton: Princeton University Press, 1981), pp. 192–97.

in the fields or at the loom, they had preferred to make their skins yellow and their chests hollow and deform their right shoulders" (Colette 2001a, 124).[27] This statement from *Claudine à l'école* reflects the reality in France: the number of young women applying for teaching positions at the turn of the century outnumbered the positions available by astounding percentages. Lesueur mentions that a call for applicants in 1899 to fill 193 posts for female primary schoolteachers in the Seine department received 7,000 applications. As a result, some critics began to recommend that schoolteachers discourage young high school students from trying to enter the teaching field, since such a high demand existed for the few positions available (Lesueur 234–38). Yet due to the reigning pedagogical practices, where learning from role models prevailed, professors continued to encourage tacitly their students to become teachers.

In spite of the prestige and promise of an easier life, the teaching profession in reality was a difficult one, filled with long hours, low pay, poor living conditions, spiteful town citizens, and unsympathetic school administrators. Feminists, socialists, and even the president of the Republic spoke out on the inequity of the woman schoolteacher's career. The newspaper *L'Action féministe* (*Feminist Action*) reports that on October 30, 1909, President Fallières spoke at the inauguration of the Hôtel de la Ligue de l'Enseignement (Hotel for the League of Education) on the necessity of women's equality in French society: "I am among those who believe that women should be equal to men in social life. If the laws have not yet consecrated this equality, I wish that the difference in salaries that exists between women and men in society disappeared."[28] Not only were women schoolteachers paid less than their male counterparts, their teaching assignments and actual working hours were often longer. And the educator's career was an isolating one for single women, sometimes leading to a life of solitude and depression. Emilie Carles, in her autobiographical account of her teaching career in the French Alps, *Une Soupe aux herbes sauvages* (translated as *A Life of Her Own*), discusses her loneliness during her initial years as a teacher in several tiny alpine villages, before her marriage and permanent assignment to a school in her home town (Carles 89–91, 125–26). These facts were translated in the

---

27. "pour ne pas travailler dans la terre ou dans la toile, elles ont préféré jaunir leur peau, creuser leur poitrine et déformer leur épaule droite" (Colette 133). For English translations of Colette's *Claudine* series, I have used the White translation.

28. "Je suis de ceux qui pensent que les femmes doivent être à l'égalité avec les hommes dans la vie sociale. Si les lois n'ont pas encore consacré cette égalité, je fais des voeux pour que la différence des traitements qui existe entre les femmes et les hommes dans la société disparaisse" (Fallières 24–25).

fictional accounts of women schoolteachers as well: in every single women's education novel that I examine in Chapter 3, the teachers all note problems with adjusting to their assigned school and town. In Louise-Marie Compain's 1903 novel, *L'Un vers l'autre* (*One Toward the Other*), both the experienced school director and the heroine Laure Deborda, a novice in her first year as a schoolteacher, are the subject of menacing gossip by townspeople who are suspicious of the new "godless" professors. Marie-Thérèse Romane, the main protagonist of Esther de Suze's 1902 novel, *Institutrice* (*Schoolteacher*), enjoys her new teaching job but must leave the school and the town after vicious rumors were spread that she has been involved in an affair with the mayor. This pattern in the novels, based on personal accounts of the teaching profession and cultural and social biases against unmarried women teachers, contributes to the production of a renunciation plot structure, essential for a deeper understanding of the novels as a genre.

In addition to the incentives to read, write, and teach, the opening of secondary schools for women sent out the message that women should be well educated and should have access to higher learning. With the new interest in university-level educations for women, other more prestigious professions, such as law and medicine, previously controlled by men, also became legally open to women during the turn-of-the-century period. Although some of these professional schools were now accessible officially, it must be noted that some remained closed to women, even to those who had earned the baccalaureat diploma, until after the Belle Epoque. Those schools that had "officially" opened their doors to women still held up many barriers to female applicants: it was common practice for the men in charge to discourage women from pursuing advanced degrees and from practicing the profession. To understand some of the reasons for the difficulties that women encountered when trying to enter these careers, it is helpful to first examine the numerous changes that these professions themselves underwent during the nineteenth century in France.

In many sociological and historical theories of professionalization, women's entrance into the "free" professions is noticeably absent. By "free" professions, I mean the category known in French as *les professions libres*: law, engineering, and medicine, for examples. Women's absence from sociological accounts of professionalization theory probably stems from the fact that women have been allowed into these professions only in the past century, and in significant numbers only in the past forty years. All professionalization theories, however, include some of the same general structures, processes, and ideals involved in the creation and perpetuation of the professions. These basic structures will provide us with a clearer picture of the restrictive and regulated environment under which the supposedly "autonomous" professionals worked, an environment that is applicable to both men and women.

During the nineteenth century, certain high-status social groups felt they were losing their traditional stability and prestige. Beginning with Napoléon's decree for the baccalauréat, new exams were created to control entrance to professional schools and thus to the liberal professions. They often reflected the classical and elite training found in some expensive preparatory schools, but particularly in Napoléon's national system of lycées. Created in 1808 under the guise of a republican rhetoric of public education open to all (male) citizens, the baccalauréat almost immediately became "one of the most powerful stratifying devices in French society" (Weiss 20).[29] The content of the baccalauréat focused on a classical curriculum and required, for example, that the philosophy questions be delivered in Latin (22), thus excluding candidates who had not engaged in traditional studies promoted by the lycées. It also reinforced the notion that a literary and classical education was essential for the formation of a "well-rounded" professional, even those involved in the sciences and law. There were obvious political reasons for requiring the classical education found in the state-run high schools, such as Napoléon's wish to create order and hierarchy in his empire. But it also included an underlying prejudice for members of the upper classes, who had traditionally held positions in these professions. John H. Weiss notes that the baccalauréat not only provided barriers for the working classes, but created unity among different strata of the bourgeoisie as well (23). The baccalauréat thus required elitism and an implied disregard for practical or technical education. These qualities would affect the social status of students admitted to schools of law and medicine throughout the nineteenth and even into the twentieth centuries. For those students who did not have an upper-class background, there would often be socialization in school to identify with the bourgeoisie whose members considered themselves superior to the members of the commercial, agricultural, and industrial professions (23). Philip Elliott in his text *Sociology of the Professions* discusses the equal importance of status socialization when compared to role socialization in professional schools: "Role socialisation consists of training in the skills

---

29. See also Christophe Charle's 1987 text *Les Elites de la République, 1880–1900*.

of a future role; status socialisation involves acquiring a more general social identity and patterns of behaviour acceptable to people in the future status position" (Elliott 77). Gaston Valran, a Belle Epoque author, confirms this emphasis on status socialization, and in particular the focus on professional work as a form of service rather than as a means for economic gain. In 1908 he wrote about the importance of a professional's contributions to society: "We generally consider that one chooses to exercise a liberal profession, not for professional profit, but out of concern for social welfare."[30]

The combined importance of one's status and behavior, in addition to one's technical role, emerges from the historical view that professions and professional associations were formed and grew out of two opposing forces. First, there are the socially elite groups that had always claimed membership to professional classes, due to ideals of service to the crown, rather than to technical ability. Second, with the rise of industrial and commercial societies in the nineteenth century and their technical advances, a strong notion of professional knowledge and competence developed, especially in the latter half of the nineteenth century, according to Elliott. The results of these two forces were a combination of the two philosophies, which remain firmly in place today, so that the defining characteristics of professions, even now, contain, for example, the idea that doctors or professors or others involved in "the liberal professions" should dislike competition, advertising, and profit, and that they should believe in the principle of payment in order to work rather than working for pay (Elliott 52–53). Thus, although members of the liberal professions required some technical training, which placed them in the same category as members of commercial or industrial professions, they were socialized to identify with members of an elite class who focused on service.

Magali Larson's work *The Rise of Professionalism,* in which she focuses on the developing relationship of new professions to the market, adds to this historical view of professionalization. She analyzes the act of creating a demand for new professional services and examines the control of this demand by professional organizations, with the help of the state. She explains that, unlike the early capitalist industries, the new professions "were not exploiting already existing markets but were instead working to create them" (Larson 10). In order to develop a credible reputation and eliminate nonprofessional competitors, the professions were required to standardize

---

30. "On estime généralement que l'on choisit d'exercer une profession libérale non pour en retirer un profit professionnel mais par souci de l'intérêt social" (cited in Vagogne 7).

their practices and to regulate the education of their members. In order to achieve these goals, they relied on state protection and state-enforced penalties against unlicensed practitioners, as well as on state-mandated "monopolies of competence" for universities and professional schools, which would be the only institutions allowed to confer diplomas on new members of the professions (15).

Although the previous comments apply specifically to men in professions, some of the same underlying characteristics are true for the women professionals portrayed in Belle Epoque novels. In literary works, the conflicts and the successes of women trying to enter traditionally male domains—law, medicine, engineering—quickly became the subjects of novels about women's professional development. One of the first parallels with the general observations we have just made about the liberal professions is the fact that most of the female protagonists are either members of the bourgeoisie or aspire to that class. They usually hold such traditional bourgeois values as duty, responsibility, and service to one's family and country. Although some protagonists must work in order to earn a living (especially those who are widowed or orphaned), most of the professional women claim a love for knowledge and service above all other goals. This second parallel, the general denial of any desire for wealth, fame, and competition is indeed part of the practice of status and role socialization that takes place during the years of professional training for both men and women. But such desires certainly do exist, and they are apparent to the husbands, parents, and colleagues who are close to the women professionals. Their situation is thus open to a different kind of attack than the one directed against schoolteachers, because they do not work for selfless reasons. Whereas schoolteachers are rarely portrayed as ladder-climbing competitors (the highest rank they could strive for was usually the directorship of a school), women lawyers, scientists, and researchers who have tasted even a small amount of success are often described as ravenous for renown in their field. Ambition may have been acceptable for men in the professions, as it implied an eagerness to serve both state and self, but in women, any desire for advancement was usually translated as aggressive and egotistical and as such was severely critiqued by supervisors and outsiders.

A third parallel to general practices in professionalism lies in the need for technical training. All of the protagonists studied in this book are deeply involved in clinical studies, lab experiments, and other practical applications of their professions. In Chapter 4, where the focus is on the "feminization" of the scientific and medical professions in France, each of the professional development novels discussed is liberally sprinkled with technical jargon or scientific terms. All four novels narrate, in various degrees of detail, the educational process for the scientific professions. Finally, many of the women who are portrayed as successful professionals have found a particular niche for themselves, as women, in the field of scientific study. The ability to find a new "market" for their skills and to maintain that they are particularly well trained for that market enables them to gain a certain authority in their field, as Magali Larson claims. For example, a prominent woman doctor in Yver's *Princesses de sciences* (*Princesses of Science*) specializes in gynecology and women patients, or a young woman lawyer in Yver's *Dames du Palais* (*Ladies of the Court*) earns a considerable reputation by gaining expertise in divorce law and child-custody cases. Thus, many of the general principles of the history and theory of professional development in Western Europe apply directly to the women protagonists in these novels.

In spite of some traits shared with general professional development theory in France, there remain several distinct differences in women's professional experiences. In the battle to allow women to practice law in France, for example, it was not just role and status socialization that were essential for access into the legal profession, as a brief look at the historical case of Jeanne Chauvin demonstrates. Jeanne Chauvin, the first woman to defend a dissertation thesis in law in 1892, was refused admission to the bar and the right to try cases in 1897. Eugen Weber explains that after these refusals, Chauvin "went to court, and lost on the ground that the legal profession should be reserved for men, who alone exercised civic rights" (Weber 1986, 96). Such a court decision confirms Magali Larson's theory that the professions must call on the state to aid in controlling the entrance of new members. The court in this case, however, was not eliminating a "nonprofessional" or "unlicensed" competitor; Mme Chauvin held the required degrees to practice and had undergone the necessary role and status socialization mandated by the legal world. Instead of pointing to unprofessional behavior or inadequate technical training, her lack of civic rights, based on her sex alone, was the reason for dismissing this potential lawyer. Later, in November 1900, following a shift in arguments, the National Assembly passed a bill allowing women to practice law, as Edmond Milland of *Le Figaro* noted. Milland's report of the Senate debate that preceded the bill's passage indicates that the shift made by the opponents eventually led to a weaker argument for them. While in 1897 one of the key components of the opposition's line of reasoning had been Mme Chauvin's lack of civic rights, based on her sex, the debate in 1900 centered on the character and nature of women, which may be considered a socialized skill. M. Gourju, senator from the Rhône and opponent to women lawyers, stated, "women govern humanity with their beauty, their heart, their grace, and they must not envy the legal power of man."[31] Their new position was easily attacked: M. Tillayre, the author of the bill, claimed that if women had stronger hearts than men, they would make better lawyers. He further noted that his appeal was not only for feminist reasons but also for "legitimate claims—the freedom of the professions."[32] Although the latter statement may appear to indicate his rather dubious belief that feminist reasons were *not* legitimate claims, the importance of upholding the "liberty" of the free professions stands out clearly. The vote following Tillayre's speech passed the bill overwhelmingly: 172 to 34.

To demonstrate the enthusiasm for the new law, the front page of *Le Petit Journal* (no. 527, 23 décembre 1900) contained a full-page illustration of the first woman lawyer in France, Mme Petit, standing in the Appellate Court of Paris. It was reported that she went through the *prestation de serment* (oath taking) only twenty-four hours after the official decree was passed, so that she could join the bar and begin to practice law immediately (*Le Figaro*, 6 décembre 1900). Within the first several years, the number of women attorneys in France increased, but not considerably. An article titled "The Beginnings of Women Lawyers" ("Débuts des femmes avocats") in the September 1905 issue of *La Vie Heureuse* reports that only four women had chosen to exercise their right to practice law in France. And in 1910, Camille Pert's study found that after the first years of the century, the numbers had leveled off, probably due to the continuing resistance from male lawyers and law students, and to social and cultural definitions of women's nature that would prohibit them from pursuing a career in law. Yet the right to practice law was considered a remarkable victory for the women's rights movement of the early twentieth century (Weber 1986, 96).

That feeling is evident in the voice of the book reviewer for *La Vie Heureuse* who criticized Gustave Hue's novel, *L'Avocate* (*The Woman Lawyer*, 1903). The reviewer is angered because the protagonist, Jeanne Hardy, was never shown trying cases in the courthouse. The heroine's decision to abandon her law career also disappointed the reviewer, who felt that the opportunity

---

31. "les femmes gouvernent l'humanité avec leur beauté, leur coeur, leur grâce, et elles ne doivent pas envier le pouvoir légal de l'homme" (*Figaro*, 14 novembre 1900). Milland's report is given in full in *L'Histoire de France à travers les journaux du temps passé: La Belle Epoque, 1898–1914* (Paris: L'Arbre Verdoyant, 1984)), p. 94.

32. "revendications légitimes—la liberté des professions." Ibid.

for women to practice law was an important right that needed to be promoted rather than critiqued in literature. She chastised Hue for neglecting to underline this message in his book "because the career of the woman lawyer is one that is accessible to women and because today women have more and more need to earn a living . . . he [Hue] proves nothing against the practice of the austere legal profession by the women of tomorrow."[33] This excerpt indicates the book reviewer's wish to inform her reading public that the field of law was indeed open to women, and to encourage those readers who might be interested in pursuing a career in law. One further critique of Hue's novel was that Jeanne Hardy was not realistically portrayed as a lawyer, since Hue had described his heroine as young and beautiful. Most lawyers, in the reviewer's opinion, were neither (ix). A few years later the novelist Colette Yver published *Les Dames du Palais* (*Ladies of the Court*, 1909), in which she counteracts those stereotypical images: Yver develops portraits of a variety of women lawyers who are old and young, pretty and ugly, married and single. Thus in contrast to Pert's statistics that showed a static number of women lawyers in France, Yver's fictional account implies a blossoming of new women attorneys that allowed for many different types of women to practice law.

The medical profession also underwent turmoil and debate over the decision to allow women to practice. One might expect less resistance from traditionalists, since mainstream social and cultural mores promoted the values of care and nurturance in women. These skills were required for the practice of medicine and part of both the role and the status socialization in medical school. In theory, the medical profession should have been considered an appropriate field for women, and the precedents set by the Empress Eugénie in the 1860s, when she authorized women's admittance to the Ecole de Médicine de Paris by an imperial decree, would lead one to believe that by 1900 many women would be practicing medicine. Yet a relatively small number of women actually attended medical school or received a medical degree in the nineteenth century.[34] Weber notes that between 1882 and 1903 the number of women doctors in France showed only a small increase, from seven to ninety-five (Weber 1986, 95).

---

33. "parce que la carrière d'avocate est une de celles accessibles aux femmes et parce que, aujourd'hui, les femmes ont de plus en plus besoin de gagner leur vie . . . il [Hue] ne prouve rien contre l'exercice de l'austère profession d'avocate par les femmes de demain" (ix) (*La Vie Heureuse*, *Supplément avec guide du lecteur* 2, no. 1 [janvier 1903]: viii–ix). See also *La Femme* 25, no. 6, (15 mars 1903): 48.

34. Benefiting from the Empress Eugénie's support, Madeleine Gibelin Brès was the first woman in France to receive a medical degree in 1870. One reason for the relatively small number of women

The new prestige and power of the medical doctor in French society, as demonstrated by Foucault and others, also brought out resistance and hostility from both male students and male doctors to the idea of women studying and practicing medicine.[35] The sexual harassment of those women who did enter the medical profession was therefore well known and well documented at the turn of the century. Weber recounts an incident of a woman who had tried to enter medical school being burned in effigy by her classmates.[36]

Several authors from the Belle Epoque period wrote about women in the medical field: Colette Yver and Gabrielle Reval wrote on women studying or practicing as doctors, and Marcelle Babin wrote about a woman who studied to become a doctor, but ended up in the field of pharmacy. These authors address specifically the issues of harassment from male colleagues in school and on the job and about mistrust and hostility from clients. The main protagonist of *Pharmacienne* (1907), Danielle Dormeuil, openly discusses the disruptive behavior of the medical students at her school, which was intended to discourage her from attending classes and continuing her studies. She also unknowingly became the object of an unusual experiment devised by one of her own professors, an event that led to a long illness and her forced decision to switch to the field of pharmacy. The career of the pharmacist, because of its sedentary, storekeeper aspects, was considered a profession more suitable for women. In Colette Yver's novel *Les Cervelines* (*The Brainy Women,* 1903), one of the heroine's male classmates pays a waiter at a formal dinner to "accidentally" pour gravy all over her silk blouse. When she goes to the kitchen to clean up, the ringleader of the prank follows her there and steals a velvet collar from her in order to spread harmful lies about her, insinuating promiscuous behavior. The narrator comments that these pranks are signs of a deeper jealousy and hatred: "They [the male

---

in medical school is probably the fact that a baccalauréat was required to enter the universities. Public schools for girls did not award this diploma until 1924 (Moses 175).

35. I am referring, of course to Michel Foucault's 1962 *La Naissance de la clinique*. Mainstream views of the country doctor, who emphasized reduced suffering and pain, were not prestigious, barely a cut above a tradesman: Charles Bovary, in *Madame Bovary,* is a good example of the lack of prestige and status for the country doctor. It was only with the rise of the clinics and professional schools that the power relations between patient and doctor changed dramatically in the nineteenth century. For further discussion, see Chapter 4 on women scientists and doctors.

36. For an historical account of discouragement of women in the medical profession, see Weber's *France: Fin-de-siècle*, pp. 95–96.

students] were envious of her, of her intelligence, her science, her work.... They were—these lazy little ladies' men, keen on their careers—so many enemies from whom she always had to protect herself."[37]

In January 1901, in an effort to combat the negative and injurious behavior against women in medical schools, a women's school director named Mme Alphen opened a private hospital staffed entirely by female medical interns from her school. The journal *La Femme* reported that an all-female staff of medical interns would greatly reduce the tensions for women doctors in the abusive work environment of a mixed-sex hospital. Furthermore, the article noted that it would encourage women to develop their "special aptitudes" in medicine, perhaps implying the female traits of caring, healing, and nurturance, but could also have pointed to specialized "women's" fields (gynecology, obstetrics, or pediatrics) (*La Femme* janvier 1901, 10).

One topic that has rarely been addressed in sociological theories of professional development until recently is the tension between domestic and professional work. This lack is perhaps due to the fact that male professionals, about whom most theories of professional development have been written, assumed that others (wife, parents, domestic help) would attend to the domestic affairs of their private lives and thus did not address this issue directly. For example, in an analysis of the centrality of work to the private lives of professionals, Elliott does indicate the correspondence between work and leisure time activities in the professions.[38] In his study, however, he makes no mention of domestic or familial responsibilities or everyday activities in the private domain.

Turning to women's professional development novels from the Belle Epoque, it becomes apparent that these traditional definitions of the professional were already out-of-date one hundred years ago. The preponderance

---

37. "ils (les étudiants) étaient envieux d'elle, de son intelligence, de sa science, de son travail. ... C'étaient—ces petits hommes paresseux, galants, âpres à leur métier—autant d'ennemis dont elle avait à se garder toujours" (Yver 1903, 146). A 1990 French novel, *Catherine Courage* by Jacques Duquesne, narrates the trials and triumphs of a turn-of-the-century woman doctor, demonstrating the continued fascination in France with women in the medical field of the Belle Epoque. Jacques Duquesne also wrote the screenplay for the four-and-a-half-hour televised version of the novel in 1993.

38. Based on a study of university professors, advertising executives, and dentists, Elliott claims that if the intellectual content of the profession and the amount of contact with professional colleagues are both high, the similarity between work and leisure activities will also be high. Thus, university professors will pursue hobbies during their leisure time that overlap with or are related to activities of their profession, as opposed to advertising executives and dentists, who usually choose hobbies that are very different from their professional activities (Elliott 138).

of concern with the home and of direct involvement in domestic decisions indicates that a dramatically different experience has existed for women professionals for more than a century. The fictional characters created during the Belle Epoque often longed to find ways to combine the traditional duties of housewife and mother with the new responsibilities of their chosen professional career. When seeking a solution that would permit such a delicate balance of domestic and public work, the protagonists often modified their home environments. These novels include women researchers whose most important room of the house is their study and women doctors who built examination rooms and even laboratories in their homes. These professional women spend at least part of each day in the public domain, whether the lecture hall, the pharmacy, the hospital, or the clinic. Yet their rearrangement of their own homes permits them to stay in closer contact with domestic concerns and to oversee the daily management of private affairs. This arrangement not only reflected historical practices of the time but also indicates the novelists' attempts to develop professional female protagonists who could be understood as nurturing or maternal characters. The goals and the challenges found in nonteaching professions, namely, the need to balance public and private duties, thus yield new types of professional heroines and conflicts in Belle Epoque literature.

From this brief survey of the professional development of women in France, we can understand how the activities of heroines in certain Belle Epoque novels reflected the changes that were occurring in French society. Not only did the heroines engage in new fields of study and work, they also discussed the challenges their careers presented to them and the discrimination they confronted. The novels' popularity and proliferation may have been a result of how closely they paralleled the changes in the political and social realms of French culture: they thus act as a bridge in Belle Epoque studies between fictional women characters in the domain of literature and active women students and professionals in the domain of social history.

Before considering the relation of these novels to the culture that produced them, it is crucial to first look at their status as literary objects. For clues to what made these topics and these women writers so popular during the Belle Epoque—and then so forgettable in literary histories of the era—it is necessary to study the key narrative and generic elements of this particular subgenre of the bildungsroman, or coming-of-age novel.

Although the women writers have been forgotten, several major male authors from the end of the nineteenth century who wrote novels in the form of the berufsroman are still studied and read today. The women novelists who followed them created new plots and different character types, thus a brief survey of the typical literary devices and protagonist profiles found in the bildungsroman will help to illuminate the reasons why women's novels appealed to the Belle Epoque readers of France and offer an explanation for their absence from most twentieth-century literary histories of the Belle Epoque.

2

LITERARY CONTEXTS:
BILDUNGSROMAN, ERZIEHUNGSROMAN,
AND BERUFSROMAN

WOMEN WRITERS OF THE Belle Epoque who developed plots about the education and professional careers of modern women brought surprising innovations to a genre that had existed for some time in Europe. Although novels of professional or educational development may appear to readers today to be odd little subgenres of the bildungsroman (coming-of-age novel), in fact they enjoyed a strong level of popularity as a novel type throughout the nineteenth century. Examples as diverse as Stendhal's *Le Rouge et le noir*, Flaubert's *Education sentimentale*, or even Zola's *Docteur Pascal* witness the professional development of a protagonist: one who undergoes both professional and personal trials and who experiences moments of success and frustration along the way.

One of the typical elements of the French novel of development found in these classic nineteenth-century works is the Paris-province opposition: the hero leaves behind his family and friends in the country to seek his fortune and learn about himself in the nation's capital. Victor Brombert, in his 1961 study of intellectual heroes in French fiction, comments on this fascination with Paris for the youth of France by noting, "ever increasing numbers of moneyless young men of humble birth launched into literary and artistic careers," and he attributes it to the Romantic movement, the cult of success, and to the "democratization" of literature (Brombert 37).[1] Brombert claims that, in addition to the Paris-province migration and the formation of circles or *cénacles* of young intellectuals, the nineteenth century witnessed the rise of the male intellectual in French literature as a result of the emergence of a university bureaucracy. Men from many different social classes

---

1. Although Brombert did not focus on the bildungsroman or its subgenres in his study, his examination of the figure of the intellectual in French literature reveals the structure of the novel of development in many French works from the 1880s to the middle of the twentieth century in France.

were clamoring for a diploma with the hope of gaining a stable, if somewhat modest, career: "Not only Barrès, according to whom all Frenchmen dream of becoming bureaucrats, but men such as Gabriel Monod repeatedly call attention to the dangerous plethora of university graduates and to the 'bureaucratic plague' which, they feel, sap the energies of the country" (39). Thus, many nineteenth-century French authors concentrated on the development of a bourgeois character, whether he be the son of peasants or of high-level professionals, and they dealt specifically with the young man's interactions within the institutions in which he works and the society into which he was born.

Contemporaries of Belle Epoque women novelists include such writers as Maurice Barrès, Paul Bourget, or André Gide.[2] These men wrote novels about educational or professional development either a few years before or contemporaneously with these women. In their narratives, the male authors include heroes who were high school students or teachers, law and medical students, archeologists, historians, and politicians. Although these writers were often diametrically opposed to Belle Epoque women writers in their political leanings and their views on education, they also chose to employ the form of the novel of development, and specifically the novel of professional or educational development, to comment on the major upheavals that were taking place in French society during the first decades of the Third Republic.

I am limiting my comments in this chapter to novels of development that focus on male characters because very few fictional female characters in the late nineteenth century were involved in narratives of educational or professional development. That is, very few pursue advanced education at the high school or university level; the number of female characters pursuing careers in the liberal or scientific professions was also very small. This is not meant to imply that female characters were not involved in various quest plots in novels of the nineteenth century, especially in texts written by women. Alison Finch's 2000 study *Women's Writing in Nineteenth-Century France* provides a thoroughly comprehensive overview of all kinds of women's writing: poetry, prose, memoirs, journalism, children's fiction, and political texts. In her discussion of novels, Finch includes many

---

2. These are just a few names; other men who wrote novels about professional or educational development include Anatole France: *Les Opinions de Jérôme Coignard* (1893) and *L'Histoire contemporaine*, (1896–1901), both with professors as the main protagonist; Roger Martin du Gard: *Devenir!* (1909, about a failed writer) and *Jean Barois* (1913, about a professor who becomes a scholar-activist).

of the fictional women who populated works by such well-known authors as Germaine de Staël and George Sand, as well as those created by forgotten writers like Sophie Ulliac-Trémadeure and Thérèse Bentzon. These last two did create female characters who worked or planned to work: in Ulliac-Trémadeure's 1838 *Emilie ou la jeune fille auteur,* for example, the protagonist is obsessed with writing and, to a certain extent, with fame (Finch 106). In Bentzon's 1880 *Yette* the protagonist prepares for a career in teaching, but she decides to marry before she can take the job that she is offered (177). These two nineteenth-century women writers created stories that could fall into the general category of the novel of professional development, but they were not contemporaries of the women writers I am focusing on here and thus would not have had the same kind of influence on them that the male authors of the Belle Epoque did.

The term *bildungsroman* has its historical base in early nineteenth-century German literary history, originating with the lectures of Professor Karl von Morgenstern, who is attributed with the first use of the word. Wilhelm Dilthey popularized the term in 1870, and the form of literature it has come to represent spread during the second half of the nineteenth-century into France and England, creating its own traditions in each of those national literary cultures (Hardin xiii). The main focus of the term corresponds to the German word *Bildung* which translates as "formation," "education," or "cultivation." Later uses of the term have removed it from its historical origins and give it the more general definition that critics still attach to it today. For example, German critics Jacobs and Krause define the bildungsroman as "the intellectual and social development of a central figure who, after going out into the world and experiencing both defeats and triumphs, comes to a better understanding of self and to a generally affirmative view of the world" (Jacobs and Krause 20, quoted in Hardin xiii). Their more general definition eliminates much of the historic specificity of the original bildungsroman, but even the last condition in the definition, that there be a "generally affirmative view of the world," is too specific when we are discussing late nineteenth-century and twentieth-century forms of this genre. Jeffrey Sammons, for example, claims that we cannot expect the bildungsroman to contain an individual's reconciliation with society: "It does not matter whether the process of *Bildung* succeeds or fails, whether the protagonist achieves an accommodation with life and society or not.... There must be a sense of evolutionary change within the self, a teleology of individuality, even if the novel, as many do, comes to doubt or deny the possibility of achieving a gratifying result" (Sammons 41). In both the male and female versions of the turn-of-the-century texts to be studied here, the authors rarely give a positive conclusion and often leave the novel with an ambiguous final word about French society and the protagonist's place in it.

Authors also strayed from the traditional ideological limits of the bildungsroman by moving beyond the bourgeois hero, to include working-class protagonists who did not fit the original type. In France, such writers as Vallès, Zola, and Barrès dealt more directly with class conflict and focused on the emergence of working-class protagonists, thus casting in doubt the notion that the bildungsroman must have a bourgeois hero at its center. Most French working-class characters, however, try to overcome their impoverished backgrounds in order to pursue dreams connected with a life of ease and wealth (Vallès's *Le Bachelier,* for example), searching to attain certain bourgeois ideals. Almost all of the protagonists in this volume foster aspirations that fall into the ideological category of "bourgeois," even when that protagonist's economic status or family background places him or her in the working class.[3]

In another study that departs from the bourgeois humanism of the original German literary definition, M. M. Bakhtin draws a major distinction between the novel of emergence, in which society is a static backdrop for the actions of the hero, and those novels in which the world emerges at the same time that the hero does (Bakhtin 19, 23). This later category is of special interest to Bakhtin; it is one in which the hero "emerges along with the world and he reflects the historical emergence of the world itself. He is no longer within an epoch, but on the border between two epochs, at the transition point from one to the other" (Bakhtin 23). During the Belle Epoque, we find both types of texts, though the second type, those "historical-cultural" novels of emergence that explore the transitions in French society at the same time that they explore transitions in their protagonists' lives, are of particular interest in this book.

The process of emergence is a complicated matter in the novel of development because the protagonist frequently must find his or her own path, making detours and falling into traps along the way. Walter Sokel, in his discussion of the existentialist version of the bildungsroman as it applies to specific Russian and French texts from the mid-nineteenth to mid-twentieth

---

3. Sammons states, "the concept of *Bildung* is intensely bourgeois; it carries with it many assumptions about the autonomy and relative integrity of the self, its potential self-creative energies, its relative range of options within material, social, even psychological determinants" (Sammons 42).

centuries, brings out this key element. He states that the young hero must learn by "false starts": "For long stretches he is lost in what will later turn out to be illusion, error, pursuit of false goals. Thorough exposure to these is the chief vehicle by which formation of character or *Bildung* is attained" (Sokel 333). All the novels under study here follow this general description as they depict protagonists who take misleading paths and often err from their original goals. One of Sokel's contributions to the definition of the novel of development is his distinction between the traditional forces of development and those found in the narratives of "existential education" that he is studying, and his distinction is key for our study of Belle Epoque novels of development. Sokel claims that the traditional hero of a novel of development experiences change through his social interactions with other people and physical changes (seeing new places, experiencing new cultures). In contrast, development for existentialist characters occurs mainly on an interior level (333). All of the protagonists I study here, both male and female, achieve their goals through a combination of exteriorized and interiorized experiences. The texts diverge significantly in style and ideology from the "existential education" novels that Sokel chose to explore, yet they all share this modern feature of interiorized self-discovery.

Denis Pernot's outline of the *erziehungsroman* and *Künstlerroman* provided the basis for sketching the new category that I have called the "berufsroman," based on the German word *beruf*, which means "profession," "career," or "avocation." For the novel of education, Pernot explains that the German term *Erziehen* is clearly pedagogical in nature, and that the root of *Künstlerroman* (*Kunst* or *Kunstler*) focuses specifically on art and artist (Pernot 109–10). Following the patterns stated above, the term I have selected to discuss novels where professional apprenticeship or development occurs is the *berufsroman*, since *beruf* is the German term for "avocation" or "career." In the following pages I will draw distinctions between all three of these subgenres of the bildungsroman.

Two Belle Epoque examples of the novel of educational development, or *erziehungsroman*, are Paul Bourget's *Le Disciple* (*The Disciple*, 1889) and Maurice Barrès's *Les Déracinés* (*The Uprooted*, 1897).[4] These writers not only specialized in the education novel model, they offered striking critical

---

4. Both of these works are featured in Denis Pernot's important study *Le Roman de socialisation, 1889–1914* (1998). In the same category, Bourget also wrote *L'Etape* (1902), about a brother and sister studying to become high school teachers in Paris. Barrès's *Les Déracinés* is part 1 of his trilogy, *Le Roman de l'energie nationale*.

exposés of the school system and the intellectualization of the working classes in their texts. The main characters of the Barrès novel were specifically subject to the forces described in Chapter 1, that is, those pedagogical models that sought to "nationalize" the French peasant and turn him into a "Frenchman," as Eugen Weber asserts. Barrès transforms his protagonists into "national" citizens with national ambitions to match; as he creates his youthful misfits, he focuses his critique on the education system's transition from regional instructors to national educators. The students are at first exhilarated by the high school teacher's rhetoric of nationalism and then disappointed in their local surroundings.

A great variety of novels of professional development exist from the time period: here I will concentrate on two about archeologist-historians, professionals who were commonly called "Orientalists" during the Belle Epoque: André Gide's *L'Immoraliste* (*The Immoralist, 1902*) and Myriam Harry's *La Conquête de Jérusalem* (*The Conquest of Jerusalem,* 1904). Relatively unknown today, Harry's novel created a stir when it was published: nominated for the Prix Goncourt in 1904, it won the very first Prix Vie Heureuse ever awarded. I include her novel here in this overview of male influences because her work focuses on a male protagonist, and it circulated mainly among male readers and critics when it first appeared. Although many women's magazines also reviewed and admired her work and protested heatedly her exclusion from the Prix Goncourt competition in 1904, Harry's male protagonist for *La Conquete de Jérusalem,* Hélie, affords more insightful comparisons with novels containing men in the leading role (and specifically with Michel in Gide's *L'Immoraliste*), rather than with novels featuring the female archeologist-historians studied later (see Chapter 4).

These two examples will provide us with a general overview of the major traits associated with the berufsroman genre as well as an understanding of the strong critique of professional institutions that would become a hallmark of Belle Epoque novels on women's professional development. Analyzing turn-of-the-century versions of the novel of development or emergence and their main cultural critiques of French society will allow us to understand more completely the literary climate that existed when Belle Epoque women novelists began to create their own tales about students and professionals.

Men and women held very different positions in French society at the time of the Belle Epoque. Nevertheless, these male-centered novels contain many of the same features as novels with female characters and women's stories.

For example, although they may not apply in exactly the same situations, the protagonist categories found in novels by women writers—the community, the pioneer, and the independent (see Introduction)—appear frequently in these earlier androcentric novels. For example, the strong community of male students in *Les Déracinés* is similar to those found in novels about educational development in women. In Bourget's *Le Disciple,* the protagonist Greslou is a student and a tutor, but his way of life corresponds more to the type of the independent, a character usually found in novels about women writers, artists, or performers. At the beginning of Bourget's later novel, *L'Etape* (1902), the protagonist, who is studying to become a philosophy teacher, has two friends, but he strays from their philosophy and becomes a loner. The main character is not an independent, however, because he wishes to work inside the institutional codes of both the university and the church. He would most likely fit the category of the pioneer, which occurs mainly in novels about women scientists and doctors.

Just as aspects of these protagonist categories can be found in the male-authored works, certain narrative structures apply to both women's and men's stories about professional and educational development. One of the primary features of the education novel's narrative is the socialization and conduct codes learned by new members of a given profession and social class. The narrator often describes the details of this socialization process at length, along with the development and testing of the prescribed set of technical skills needed to perform daily tasks in the profession. If the apprentice is an insider, usually with a father and other male family members already practicing and well respected in the professional community, the transition period for the novice is often experienced as a "natural" series of learning events, with little or no difficulty in adapting to the social expectations of the institution. Such is the case for Gide's character Michel in *L'Immoraliste;* his father's reputation and specialized knowledge affords Michel easy access into the profession at the young age of twenty-one. But if the apprentice is an outsider, with no family ties to the professional institution that she or he has chosen, there are usually some conflicts and difficulties in the adaptation period. Some of the characters in *Les Déracinés* fall into this category, as does Bourget's main character, Greslou, in *Le Disciple.*

Finally, if the apprentice is an outsider not only professionally but also socially and economically, there are many conflicts with language, attitude, demeanor, and cultural inferences. Adaptation is difficult or impossible for the student or novice who is both poor and maladjusted. Like Zola and Vallès, Belle Epoque writers created heroes who struggled with class differences, often without success and without honor, and often alongside colleagues who were comfortably born and raised in the bourgeois elite but who did little to help the poor. In Barrès's *Les Déracinés,* economic difficulties become a major impediment for some of the characters and frustrate their pursuit of advanced professional degrees in law or medicine. Male protagonists in particular often find that the major obstacles that they face arise from the *economic* class that they are supposed to belong to in a particular profession.[5]

In spite of these similarities between men and women's professional development narratives, there are many contrasts between the two during the Belle Epoque. An enumeration of these differences elucidates the innovative manner in which women writers chose to rework the genre when they turned the focus to female protagonists. First, the mentor-disciple relationship is an overwhelmingly central theme for novels on men's education. In Bourget, Barrès, and parts of Gide's work, we find a very strong dependence on this association between the experienced professor or colleague and the beginning student or young apprentice. For these authors, the mentor is essential to the protagonist's development at school, and the relationship usually proceeds according to prescribed codes of conduct or, occasionally, outside of the boundaries considered "acceptable" in the institution. Thus the mentor-disciple relationship may take the plotline of these novels down unusual and sometimes destructive paths. The title of Bourget's text *Le Disciple* indicates to the reader from the outset that the central plot will revolve around this crucial relationship. Although some novels about women students and their desires for a strong relationship with their professors or supervisors are discussed in Chapter 3, more often than not, Belle Epoque women's novels lack a powerful mentor figure. The reasons for this lack are varied: in certain fields, such as the sciences, there were few women in positions of authority who could mentor the younger female colleagues. The men in power often abuse their position and don't take their female students seriously. In other domains, such as education, where the staff was entirely female, the mentor figures are distant and cold or their behavior provides inappropriate examples for their students. In contrast to novels with male protagonists, female protagonists must often fend for themselves or learn by negative example from those in authority.

---

5. In contrast, women characters often must undergo socialization to conform to specific *gender* norms associated with a profession.

A second element frequently found in novels written by male authors is the criminal act: theft, embezzlement, assassination, rape, or murder occurs at least once in all the novels studied here. Men commit most of the crimes in these texts, and they come from any social class, although most often the criminals are members of the working classes or poverty-stricken bourgeois. Often as a result of real or perceived disenfranchisement, the young student or professional strikes out, usually in desperation. He attacks those who represent the professional institution (or the society at large) that refuses to accept his individual efforts and his deviations from the norm. Common to novels written by men or focusing on male protagonists, these types of unlawful activities are noticeably absent from most women writers' novels of educational or professional development, even when the heroine comes from a working-class background or finds herself in dire financial or social situations.

The presence of crime in novels with male protagonists and, correspondingly, the lack of such criminal activity in novels with female characters are probably due in part to the fact that being realist novelists, the authors may have wished to reflect the current trends in criminality, which included very few women criminals. Belle Epoque judge and criminologist Louis Proal in his 1890 text *La Criminalité féminine* (*Feminine Criminality*) states that the female-to-male ratio of accused criminals was one to seven.[6] He does not include in his ratio the crimes that he considered impossible for women (crimes from a profession: forgery, misappropriation of funds, misuse of corporate funds, or that required physical force: armed robbery, murder, assault and battery). And he also places in a special category those crimes that he labels "women only"—abortion, infanticide, and adultery—for which women were held to a different, much more severe set of laws.[7] In the general categories, women are in the minority except for poisoning, where they rival men.

---

6. Proal states, "To compare women's and men's criminality we must take crimes that are equally accessible to either sex, such as arson, poisoning, assassination, theft, breach of trust, breach of contract, adultery." (Pour comparer la criminalité de la femme à celle de l'homme, il faut prendre des crimes, qui sont également à la portée de l'un et de l'autre sexe, tels que l'incendie, l'empoisonnement, l'assassinat, le vol, l'abus de confiance, les délits de parole et l'adultère) (Proal 1890, 8)).

7. The fact that Proal considers abortion a "women only" crime demonstrates the prejudice inherent not only in this particular sociologist's views, but also in his society's values, since his work was respected during the time period. We can assume from his categories that, even though men probably performed at least some of the abortions, it was only the women who were prosecuted for the crime. Similarly, with infanticide, it was possible (and even probable) that both men and women were equally involved in the criminal act, but only women were brought to court for this particular crime.

Another possible reason for the scarcity of crimes in women writers' novels may have been the anticipated audience for the books. There was still much concern about the negative effects of reading novels for women and young girls. Then as now there were many worries about youth exposure to violent images and ideas. In his 1900 work *Crime et suicide passionnels* (*Suicide and Crimes of Passion*), Proal describes the popularity of novels about legal proceedings and famous crimes, explaining that they are available everywhere: "Advertised on great colored posters, they show a murder or a scene of debauchery.... On all the walls of Paris, we see assassinated men, abused children, and women attending orgies. All these images are engraved in the brains of passersby (Proal 1900, 411).[8] Although Proal claims that any passerby would see these images, many women writers, knowing that their works would be reviewed in women's magazines and would find popularity with a mainly female audience, may have tried to steer clear of these shocking or scandalous images.

A third key element that differs in men's and women's novels of professional development lies in the incorporation of a romance plot into the narrative. Although almost all novels of educational and professional development that focus on female protagonists include a romance plot to varying degrees, the romance element is often secondary or even nonexistent in such novels with male protagonists. The most obvious explanation for the difference in these conventions is that traditional expectations for women's novels stipulated a romance component, whereas novels written for a male audience did not.[9] Romance narratives do exist, however, particularly in men's novels of educational development, although not as consistently as in women's novels. For example, while the romance element is crucial for understanding the development of the protagonist in Bourget's *Le Disciple*, in Barrès's *Les Déracinés* the romance narrative is of secondary importance.

A final contrast between male and female novels of educational or professional development is the portrayal of technical and professional skills. The social codes described above, and which we find in both male and female

---

8. "Les romans judiciaires qui reproduisent le récit de crimes célèbrent sont très populaires; ils sont publiés en feuilleton par les petits journaux à cinq centimes et pénètrent partout. Annoncés par de grandes affiches coloriées, qui représentent une scène de meurtre ou de débauche.... Sur tous les murs de Paris, on voit des hommes assassinés, des enfants martyrisés, des femmes assistant à des scènes d'orgie. Toutes ces images se gravent dans le cerveau des passants." (Proal 1900, 411)

9. Although this is the most apparent explanation, it does not account for the many variations we see in women's novels of educational and professional development during the Belle Epoque. In Chapters 3 and 4, I will demonstrate how romance plot conventions were often modified and sometimes turned upside down so that the newer narrative twists of the professionalization plot could co-exist with the romance plot simultaneously.

novels, are usually accompanied by a set of required technical or aptitudinal codes, generally considered the basic tools of a profession: the actual facts, processes, and procedures that the student must acquire in order to be able to practice the law, perform surgery, teach students, conduct research, or do whatever the particular career track requires. The novel of educational development contains the most detailed descriptions of coursework, exams, lab experiments, and other situations where the protagonist learns the basic tools of the trade. The novel of professional development also frequently gives detailed accounts of both the everyday work of a particular profession and the exceptional moments in the protagonist's budding career, whether it is an important court case, a major scientific breakthrough, the reviews of his or her latest publication, or the first day of a new term in a new school. Because these particulars are the defining factors of what constitutes a career, the basic tools and practices of the trade, it would seem to be a necessary part of any novel on professional development. Yet most Belle Epoque novels of professional development that contain *male* protagonists do not provide detailed descriptions, and some offer only sketchy accounts of the actual work of the young professional. Most of the novels discussed in this chapter contain relatively few details on the work-related activities of the protagonist, and often they are included only as a backdrop to the main action of the story.

In contrast, the description of workplace activity is consistently one of the defining characteristics of the women's novel of professional development and is present throughout the texts studied in Chapters 3 through 6. A possible reason for this divergence is that readers (and authors) found the actual descriptions of women in the workplace either fascinating or titillating, and therefore the writers spent more time elaborating their descriptions of their female protagonists' activities at work. They could also have been concerned with offering detailed and realistic portrayals of women, since skeptics and critics of the *femme nouvelle* existed in large numbers during the period.

Such technical information gives the reader an insight into the expectations and practices of the profession and into the necessary social and material obligations that each institution required of its members. Most authors of the berufsroman counter these required codes with the questions and disruptions of his or her protagonist. Almost all protagonists go through periods of doubt about their profession, about its methods and goals, and about their colleagues or those in supervisory positions. Even if the hero blindly follows all professional codes, she or he often finds that there is a high personal price to pay for adherence to an institution's requirements. Many protagonists seek alternate paths that will allow them to expand the profession's limitations or at least give them more freedom in their work and their lives. At times, these new paths lead to reintegration within the traditional norms of the profession. For a great majority of these novels, however, both with male and female characters, the protagonist must decide either to conform to the rules or to quit.

Thus, a major trait that both men's and women's novels share is the type of conclusion. In almost all the novels discussed in this chapter, as well as almost all women's novels discussed in the following chapters, the main protagonist questions the institutional codes during the development of the plot. By the final pages of the narrative, the main character usually chooses to leave or is required to leave his or her original profession. This defining feature of the genre, which I have labeled the "renunciation" plot structure, exists for both men and women, even though the reasons for the departures vary widely and could be understood as a major point of contrast between the two sexes.

The nature of the plot structure results in a major dilemma for this particular subgenre of the bildungsroman; that is, no conclusion is available that will cast a positive light on professional activity. On one hand, if the protagonists find success in their chosen profession, it means that they have learned to repress their curiosity and inventiveness in order to conform to the dictates of the profession. On the other hand, if they decide to quit the profession to pursue other paths, their choice implies defeat or, at the least, a lack of ability. In either scenario, the conclusion in these novels tends toward a negative view of the professions and ends in renunciation. Critics and readers, however, have interpreted the decision to leave in different ways: for men it is considered a heroic mark of independence, demonstrating that the individual will is stronger than the suffocating demands of French bourgeois society. But when women leave behind their professional careers in these novels, it has been considered an antifeminist sign that they are capitulating to the demands of a sexist society. The dual nature of these interpretations and their repercussions has, not surprisingly, affected the reception of these texts over time.

Missing Socialization: Bourget and *Le Disciple*

Paul Bourget's 1889 novel *Le Disciple* offers an intriguing example of a Belle Epoque novel about the education and professional development of a young man. This text closely followed the infamous trial of Bourget's own "disciple" from Algeria, and it put the discussion of training and professional apprenticeship in the limelight of public debate. Paul Bourget, having been educated in the public schools of the Third Republic, became a devout disciple of the determinist philosopher Taine. He renounced Catholicism at fifteen and embraced the Naturalist school of thought. But around the age of thirty-five, Bourget began to stray from the rigid prescriptions of Taine's positivism and back toward the safer ideas of moralistic responsibility and conservatism espoused by the Catholic Church. Thus Bourget's first "pure" experience as an intellectual disciple was jettisoned, although with many relapses, for a return to his childhood faith in institutionalized religion.

Although being a devoted disciple was not easy for Bourget, he found that being a strong mentor was even more problematic. One of his own disciples, Henri Chambige, misconstrued Bourget's early agnostic and positivist philosophies, with devastating effects. As a young Algerian law student, Chambige met Bourget in Paris in 1887 and was "converted" in particular by reading Bourget's novel *André Cornélis* (1887), the story of a young man who suspects that his stepfather killed his father. When he returned to Algeria, Chambige became the lover of a married woman and convinced her to commit a double suicide with him, but then failed to follow through with his half of the suicide pact. Chambige and his crime became an international scandal on a scale with England's Jack the Ripper, from the same year, 1888.[10] When Chambige was tried for murder and condemned to forced labor by the Algerian courts, the attorney general's arguments included the statement that Chambige had fallen under the unhealthy and negative influence of certain famous Parisian writers, thereby attacking indirectly Bourget and his novel of decadent irresponsibility (Angenot 53).

The very next year, Bourget published his first major success, *Le Disciple*, a narrative that related closely to the Chambige trial and to Bourget's excruciating experience with a disciple gone awry. Bourget devotes the major part of the novel to the narrative written by the disciple figure, Robert Greslou, a private tutor and admirer of the philosopher Sixte. Greslou is charged with the murder of his employer's daughter, Mlle Charlotte de Jussat-Randon. Although he did not, in fact, kill her (in the sense of pulling the trigger), he did fail to go through with his half of a double-suicide pact that he had

---

10. For an in-depth analysis of Bourget's relation to the infamous Chambige affair of 1888, see Marc Angenot's "On est toujours le disciple de quelqu'un, ou le mystère du pousse-au-crime" (One is always the disciple of someone, or the mystery of the invitation to crime), particularly pp. 52–55.

devised for Charlotte and himself. In the novel, Greslou describes how the published works on love and the passions by his mentor Sixte had inspired his relationship with Charlotte. Bourget's fictional plot is very similar to the outline of the Chambige affair, with the dramatic variation that the woman who is seduced and dies is a young unmarried innocent, rather than the middle-aged adulterer whom Chambige had manipulated.

To begin, Bourget offers a biography of the life and career of Sixte, followed by a brief section in the voice of Sixte himself, so that the novel opens with a direct understanding of the principles that he has constructed. This section of the novel is a major departure from the classic bildungsroman, which usually narrates the life of the young disciple, not that of the elder mentor. Even when the narrator's voice is omniscient, the traditional bildungsroman emphasizes the perspective of the young novice, who is considered the central character of the work. Bourget overturns the conventions of the genre by beginning the text with the mentor's life story, thus establishing his story as the dominant narrative. He does so for obvious reasons, relating to his involvement as possible mentor in the Affaire Chambige, but the results of such rearrangements are important for the development of this literary genre. Adrien Sixte could be understood both as Bourget himself and as a transformed model of Bourget's own guide, Taine. Sixte is portrayed positively, as a man of complete moral rectitude, but also a human being completely incapable of teaching moral responsibility to his disciples.

After the section on Sixte, Bourget switches the narrative voice over to Greslou. The pupil's distorted interpretations of the mentor's philosophy are thus juxtaposed with the original version that appears just a few pages earlier. In his statements, Greslou returns again and again to specific quotations from Sixte's work *La Théorie des passions* (*Theory of the Passions*) to demonstrate that he had merely been following the words of his teacher in his experiment with love and death.[11] As we follow the developing theories of this deluded individual, we understand the ways in which Greslou has easily, but mistakenly, twisted the thoughts and ideals of his mentor as he tried to apply them to practical situations.

---

11. It is interesting to note that Greslou is not simply portrayed as a reader-disciple. Contemporaries noticed that he took his power as an advisor very seriously, suggesting readings that would persuade his young love interest to submit to his will. In his work on suicide and crimes of passion, Proal uses a hunter's metaphor for the fictional character Greslou: "Les écrivains, qui dans leurs romans ont décrit les procédés de la séduction, n'ont pas manqué d'observer que les séducteurs se servent de lectures pour arriver à leur but. Dans *Le Disciple* de Paul Bourget, Robert Greslou, voulant se faire aimer de Charlotte, a soin de lui faire des lectures sentimentales. Le jour où la jeune

One of the key items that concerns Bourget is the relationship of the student with his teacher and the problems that arise when the student misconstrues the teachings or when the teachings lack substantial moral content. Bourget's text places a large part of the blame on the student character, Greslou, and especially on his weaker powers of thought and analysis. This negative attitude toward the Greslou character lies in direct contrast to the classic bildungsroman, where the plot often revolves around a series of mistakes or "false starts," as Walter Sokel labels them, by the main character. The main character usually learns from these errors and is able to grow from them. In *Le Disciple,* the Greslou character never recovers from his flawed interpretations of Sixte, and his defective reasoning leads to tragic results.

The narrator does reproach the mentor character Sixte as well, for his amoral position and the deficit of traditional societal values in his teachings, even though these are not the main targets of blame. The Sixte character's philosophical ideology is critiqued in particular for its lack of adaptability to the "real" world, from which Adrien Sixte has basically removed himself. When his pupil tries to apply Sixte's esoteric theories about the passions to the provincial world of a bourgeois French family that has employed him, those theories are quickly deformed into unthinkable tenets.

Underlying this more obvious critique about teachers whose heads are in the clouds and their weaker pupils who dangerously misinterpret their mentor's teachings, Bourget's commentary extends to a larger social issue that was much discussed during the period. One of his great concerns was the problem of citizens from the French countryside or from provincial cities who, through free public education, had abandoned the traditional trades of their forefathers, left behind their native lands and customs, and gone to live in the nation's capital.[12] Both Sixte and Greslou are men of the "people," both are from the French provinces, and both are outsiders to Parisian culture, intellectually and socially. Adrien Sixte, for example, is

---

fille vient lui demander des conseils pour ses lectures, il comprend qu'il la tient, comme un chasseur tient son gibier quand il l'a au bout du fusil" (Proal 1900, 415–16). (Writers who in their novels have described the procedures for seduction have not failed to observe that seducers employ readings to attain their goals. In *The Disciple* by Paul Bourget, Robert Greslou, wanting to make Charlotte fall in love with him, takes care to read sentimental texts to her. The day when the young girl comes to him asking for reading suggestions, he understands that he's got her, as a hunter has got his prey when it's at the end of his rifle.)

12. For an excellent analysis of Bourget's thesis, and the larger debate in France during the period, see Marie-Christine Leps's 1992 text *Apprehending the Criminal: The Production of Deviance in Nineteenth-Century Discourse,* esp. pp. 181–91.

the son of a humble clockmaker from Nancy who, following the advice of Adrien's professors, wishes that Adrien go to a teacher training school and become a *fonctionnaire* (civil servant). Adrien wants to become a clockmaker like his father. As a compromise, he remains at home but instead of studying clocks, he studies metaphysics. He eventually leaves his hometown of Nancy, but he remains completely removed from the social, political, and intellectual circles of the new city that he inhabits, Paris.

Further, the coping mechanisms that this provincial intellectual uses to adapt to life in the capital are skewed and thus doomed to failure. The narrator states that in fifteen years in Paris, Sixte has never accepted a dinner invitation, never gone to the theater, never read a newspaper. He never greets the local shopkeepers or the neighbors in his apartment building, even though one neighbor is a professor at the Collège de France and a potential colleague. Sixte's understanding of social and cultural matters is null, and he disdains or rejects all social customs, including church attendance.

From a sociological viewpoint, this lack is a result of Sixte's refusal to attend the teacher training school or any other institution of professional learning where status socialization would have been a normal part of the education process. He focused only on the technical aspects of his career: the ideas and the problems surrounding various philosophical issues. Because he missed the professional socialization process, the mentor had no understanding of his pupil's misdoings and was thus deemed either a fool or a fraud by the judge who summoned him for questioning. As mentioned earlier, in the male novel of educational or professional development, the emphasis is usually on the socialization process that takes place in school rather than on the technical skills required of a student. Here, Bourget focuses on the deficient socialization process that Sixte underwent and the detrimental effects that this had on his career and on his pupils' lives.

Sixte's lack of social awareness, a result of his reclusive life, explains why he at first does not see his pupil's murder charge as a failure of his own teachings. During a long monologue that includes the thought processes of this philosopher, the reader discovers that Sixte does not consider himself responsible and in fact does not feel any remorse for his student's actions. He does not even question the judge's accusations or wonder if Greslou may perhaps be innocent. Instead he begins to analyze the situation as he would a philosophical knot, hoping to find different reasons for Greslou's crime (Bourget 1889, 74). Both the narrator who describes him and the judge who questions him in the opening chapters of the novel return to the idea that Sixte is simultaneously an extremely simple and naïve man concerning daily life and a highly sophisticated intellectual in abstract theories concerning ideas (49).

Bourget takes a different approach in explaining the aberrations of the disciple figure, Greslou. The diary of the disciple explains that he is also a boy from the provinces, and his family is a mix of peasant and civil servant. The paternal figure is completely analytical, idealistic, and interested in theory, while the maternal figure is entirely consigned to the realm of the physical, material world. Greslou, from an early age, feels the pull of these two different forces in his life and takes on a split identity. His dual personality compels Greslou to find strength in Sixte's philosophical treatise because it appeared that Sixte had been able to systematize passion and theorize scientifically about love. Thus his theories seemed to unite the two separate spheres that had drawn Greslou apart and placed them into one coherent philosophy.

Greslou's family background also contributes to his idea that he is an individual who deserves a lifestyle superior to the hand he has been dealt. This unrealistic ideal comes from his mother's preferential treatment of his father. For example, she told Greslou that, as an intellectual, his father deserved a preferred status and therefore was exempt from certain mundane tasks required of everyone else: "This idea was not formulated at the time in my child's brain with clarity, but it deposited the seed of what would be later one of my youthful convictions, that is, that the same rules do not govern very intelligent men and others" (Bourget 1889, 102).[13] It becomes obvious to the reader of Greslou's diary that he considers himself in this same "superior" category as his father. The seed planted in his head during his childhood has blossomed into an array of excuses and rationalizations for his erratic and immoral behavior.

In addition to distancing countrymen and peasants from their native provinces, Bourget believes that the new Third Republic education system promotes equality among all students. But equality is faulty because while it is possible in the protected site of the classroom, once the students have left the school, they are confronted with economic and social differences in French society. Greslou is either incapable of adapting to these new codes or merely unwilling to do so. What matters is that the socialization

---

13. "Cette idée ne se formulait pas dès lors dans mon cerveau d'enfant avec cette netteté, mais elle y déposait le germe de ce qui allait être plus tard une des convictions de ma jeunesse, à savoir que les mêmes règles ne gouvernent pas les hommes très intelligents et les autres" (Bourget 1889, 102).

process that he underwent in the educational system has blinded him to the fact that his new employer, M. de Jussat-Randon, will never allow him to marry his only daughter and become a member of their upper-class family. As a poor student employed to tutor the son of M. de Jussat-Randon, Greslou is not in the same social or economic class as the de Jussat-Randon family and will never be permitted into their society on an equal footing.[14] In his diary, Greslou gives a direct example of this fact: he is allowed to eat with the family in the dining room on nights when they are alone; when guests visit, Greslou is relegated to the kitchen with the rest of the domestic staff. In spite of these rather obvious reminders of his social rank, Greslou never firmly grasps the nature of his status with regard to the de Jussat-Randon family.

The narrator's underlying critique of Greslou is thus twofold. First, the mixed (and conflicting) cultural backgrounds of his parents have caused Greslou's confused morality. This cultural "mixing" is a result of the newer mobility of the working classes and the lack of regional ties that the public education system has promoted. It is implied that Greslou would have been better off had he remained in his father's profession, the more concrete world of civil engineering. Second, the school system awakened intellectual appetites and aspirations that he could not manage. Instead of a teaching career in Clermont-Ferrand, he chose to go to Paris to try to pursue a university degree in philosophy. When he failed the entrance exams, he was left to a life of abstract theorizing that his intellect could not master. These are the main reasons for his deranged ideas about love and death that end so tragically, according to Bourget.

In this novel of education, the ending remains negative. That is, the disciple is not reintegrated with society, as is generally the case in the classic eighteenth-century bildungsroman, nor is there hope for marriage or for a continuation of the disciple's development. Bourget's overall vision for his novel of emergence is a pessimistic one. His cynicism and his critique of the

---

14. A brief comparison between Paul Bourget and women writers who developed mentor-disciple models in their berufsroman reveals that they both contain critiques of social classes, but with the directions reversed. While Bourget blames the delusional Greslou for his wild idea that he might marry the upper-class woman he loves, Charlotte Jussat-Randon, he never for a moment critiques the rigid class system that governs the provincial family for whom Greslou works. In contrast, when we look at Gabrielle Reval's novels, for example, on the education of young women (*Sévriennes*) and on young women's first teaching experiences in the provinces (*Un Lycée de jeunes filles*), we will find the opposite concern. She does not focus blame on those female students who, leaving the Ecole Normale Supérieure de Sèvres for a teaching post in the countryside, run into conflicts with their new students' parents, administrators, and other town citizens. Instead, the focus is on the inflexibility and lack of modernity in the provinces that create deep mistrust of the

radical shift from rural to urban lifestyles that was taking place in the nineteenth century were also major focal points for one of his more successful disciples, Maurice Barrès, and his novel *Les Déracinés* (*The Uprooted*).

The State-Run Mentor: Barrès's *Les Déracinés*

In the mid-1880s, Maurice Barrès chose Bourget as his mentor, to help him write, edit, and negotiate with publishing houses. Surprisingly, Bourget was happy to comply with this request, even after the disastrous events of the Chambige affair. As part of this apprenticeship, Bourget dictated entire passages to Barrès, who for the most part copied them directly into his texts with few alterations (Bompaire-Evesque 224–25). He found publishers who would agree to read and publish Barrès's texts, and he even convinced Barrès to make major changes in his novels, such as the final passage in the final volume of Barrès's trilogy *Le Roman de l'énergie nationale* (*The Novel of National Energy*) (Frandon 230–40).[15] Reflecting their relationship, the first novel of Barrès's trilogy, the 1897 novel *Les Déracinés,* is also a story about professional apprenticeship and training.

These two authors, although they diverged in literary forms, with Bourget preferring high society romance novels and Barrès preferring political thesis novels, and in political opinions, with Barrès taking the far right xenophobic view at the beginning of the twentieth century, nonetheless agreed wholeheartedly on one thing: their views that the mentor-disciple relationship represented an extremely volatile but fundamental rapport in the building of moral, social, and intellectual values for young men.

In Bourget's *Le Disciple*, the main target for blame in the death of Mlle de Jussat-Randon was the disciple. Although the mentor Sixte had a negative influence, the author makes it clear that the crime that Greslou

---

newcomers from Sèvres. While Bourget critiqued those students who left behind their parents' trades and ventured forth to Paris for advanced degrees, Reval critiques those who stayed behind in the provinces, with their closed minds and ancient prejudices against unmarried women. Reval's critique of the education system is strong, yet it is not nearly as deeply rooted in antirepublicanism as Bourget's critique is. See Chapter 3 for a discussion of Reval and other women writers' novels about teachers and students.

15. Both Bourget and Barrès were from Nancy, which may account for the strong mentor-disciple bond between the two.

committed is not Sixte's fault, since he never held any official role in Greslou's life. Aside from two meetings in Sixte's office and several letters exchanged, Greslou and Sixte did not have a close personal relationship. He was never the teacher, editor, or employer of Greslou, but merely an author who had a strong impact on Greslou's intellectual development. Therefore when Greslou was tried for murder, it was shown that Sixte never willfully imposed his philosophical ideals on Greslou, but rather that the disciple Greslou misinterpreted those principles and used them to rationalize his murderous actions.

In contrast, in *Les Déracinés*, Barrès shifts the blame for failure and murder away from the seven main "disciple" characters, who are portrayed almost as victims and for whom we feel pity and concern. The narrative instead focuses much of the blame on the mentors, and in particular on Bouteiller, a direct representative of the state, whose official capacity as advisor and educator has permanently and purposefully redirected the students' goals and ambitions away from their homeland (Lorraine) to Paris, in order to benefit the centralized Third Republic government located there.[16] After the students graduate, they spend several years in the military or at home, but all eventually flock to Paris to pursue the dreams and fortunes that their teacher Bouteiller has led them to desire there.

Following the pattern of the more traditional bildungsroman, Barrès does not give us as much information about the mentor Bouteiller, in contrast to Bourget's unusually open description of Sixte. But Barrès's narrator does provide some key information about the mentor's background and his ambitions. In the opening chapters of the text, Bouteiller is a young professor of philosophy who has recently transferred to the public high school of Nancy, where he meets the main characters of the novel, all high school students in his class. Bouteiller, like some of his students, is the son of a working-class family. According to his patron, the baron Jacques de Reinach, at the age of nine Bouteiller worked in Lille as a mason's assistant during the day while studying at night, finally winning a grant at age twelve to go through high school and the university system (Barrès 306–7).[17]

---

16. The tone of the *roman à thèse* (thesis novel) is much stronger in Barrès's text than in Bourget's; a number of chapters discuss the pitfalls of teaching students to identify themselves with the nation and its capital rather than with their own region and home cities.

17. It is interesting to note that Bouteiller, like Sixte in *Le Disciple,* is described as learning in isolation, independent of a system of mentors or protectors. His sponsor Reinach explains how Bouteiller was an autodidact until he reached the age of twelve: "Malgré ce surmenage, Bouteiller prenait sur ses nuits de gamin pour étudier, et à douze ans, *sans jamais avoir eu de maître,* il obtenait

Bouteiller is almost a caricature of the ideal Third Republic high school teacher: completely devoted to the goals of the state, he promotes its mission over all others, whether they are familial, religious, regional, or any other. French historians Mona Ozouf and Pierre Albertini indicate that patriotism was essential to republican education reformers because it was considered the one link that could unify the different subjects at school and, eventually, the different generations in France. Third Republic schoolteachers for boys were quite aware of this goal, as one professor from 1884 demonstrated when he claimed that it was the professors' duty to inspire respect and admiration for the nation in each student: "To make sincere patriots, that is still our goal in teaching French history; to make good citizens, that is our ideal in giving civic lessons" (Ozouf 1982, 114).[18] The speeches and lectures that Bouteiller spouts remind us of the discourses professed by Third Republic schoolteachers: he promotes national pride, good citizenship, and honest patriots in his classroom. As Bouteiller's political career begins to take root, he lectures to a group of congressmen and Parisian businessmen about the duties and obligations of the public school teacher toward the children of France and in particular for the need to teach philosophy to high school students: "The teacher is the representative of the state; his mission is to give the reality of being French to the children born in France. What is France? A collection of individuals? A territory? No, it is a grouping of ideas."[19] Although this speech is given to members of Parliament, whom he hopes will support his political aspirations, he gives very similar lectures to his seventeen-year-old students in their philosophy course.[20] He is an enthusiastic teacher who

---

au concours une bourse" (Barrès 307, emphasis added). (Despite the overwork, Bouteiller spent his nights as a child studying, and at the age of twelve, *without ever having had a teacher,* he obtained a competitive grant.) It is only when he has entered the teaching profession that Bouteiller becomes a "protégé" of Gambetta and Reinach and profits from the mentor-disciple system himself.

18. "Faire des patriotes sincères, tel est encore notre but en enseignant l'histoire de France; faire de bons citoyens, tel est notre idéal en donnant l'enseignement civique" (Ozouf 1982, 114).

19. "L'Instituteur est le représentant de l'Etat; il a mission de donner la réalité de Français aux enfants nés sur le sol de France. Qu'est-ce, en effet, que la France? Une collection d'individus? Un territoire? Non pas, mais un ensemble d'idées. La France, c'est l'ensemble des notions que tous les penseurs républicains ont élaborées et qui composent la tradition de notre parti. On est français autant qu'on les possède dans l'âme.... Sans philosophie d'Etat, pas d'unité nationale réelle" (Barrès 305).

20. In this, Barrès's high school teacher contrasts strongly with many women's high school teachers. In Compain's novel *L'Un vers l'autre* (1903), for example, the main protagonist, Laure Deborda, complains that she has to cram the heads of her literature students with too many facts for the onerous exam system created by the government, and therefore she never has enough time to discuss "les idées" with them. Of course, had there existed a philosophy course for girls' high schools during this period there might have been more opportunity for the discussion of ideas. I discuss Compain's novel in depth in Chapter 3.

inspires his students and obviously understands that his duty as a role model for the future leaders of France is a serious undertaking. Yet his allegiance to the ideals and goals of the republican regime are sometimes too academic for the politicians he tries to woo and, at the same time, too politically biased for his work as a teacher of ethics and philosophy.

Although there is some truth in Barrès's powerful portrait of the zealous Third Republic schoolteacher, it should be noted that a growing debate has revealed that schools in the provinces in fact honored and promoted regionalism and provincial customs much more than was previously suspected. Anne-Marie Thiesse in her 1997 work *Ils apprenaient la France* (*They Taught France*) contends that regional customs and traditions were often taught in schools as part of the patriotic discourse. In fact, Thiesse remarks that local and national identities were often presented to students as "perfectly in union" (parfaitement solidaires), and that the local identity was proposed as the "irrefutable foundation" (la fondation irréfutable) for the national (Thiesse 1). Very often, the local identity or *petite patrie* was assigned a maternal role while the larger national identity was considered more abstract. Therefore educating students to have pride in their nation often began with pride in local customs. Although Thiesse's position may appear to contradict the previous notions discussed, namely, that Third Republic pedagogues were trying to standardize and nationalize the French population, her hypothesis accomplishes much in explaining why Barrès was so thoroughly obsessed with the traditions and culture of his local region, Lorraine. The stunning defeat to the Germans in 1870 had, of course, been the primary reason for his ultrapatriotism. But the early emphasis on the *petite patrie* in the public schools may also have influenced Barrès as a student, since he firmly believed that the local and regional traditions were the foundation and the starting point for all feelings of national and patriotic identity. Thiesse also notes that the Education Ministry and public school teachers were promoting rural vocations and a provincial lifestyle for their students through their constant deploring of the rural exodus and transformations caused by industrialization (9). According to this strategy, teachers claimed that rather than erasing the artisanal traditions of the countryside, modernization would perfect them.

Contrary to the exhortations of professors and government officials to remain local, the press and the public held strongly to the notion that the mythic rural France, the *real* France, was being destroyed by the mass exodus to the cities that was spurred on by industrialization. Following that general trend, Bourget and Barrès created fictional high school students who dreamt of nothing but Paris and high school teachers who preached Paris, Republic, and modernity above all else to their students.

As a mentor, Barrès's public school teacher is a rigid and duty-bound individual who does not allow personal affection to enter his relationships with his students.[21] When the government calls him to take a position in a Parisian high school only a few months after arriving in Nancy, he gives the students a stirring lecture on the importance of following the demands of the state, even when personal choice might draw one to a different path. He claims that he must take the job even though he has grown fond of his pupils in Nancy. Barrès implies that Bouteiller's ambitious professional goals and his reverence for the Republicans in power in the nation's capital were the two main factors that had a real influence on his decision to leave Nancy for Paris. Yet Bouteiller goes through the motions of testing his students and asks them to vote on whether or not he should abandon them for Paris. Having learned their republican lessons well, they unanimously vote for him to leave them, with the exception of the more conservative Saint-Phlin character (Barrès 89–91).

We can easily understand the importance of the mentor's influence in *Les Déracinés* when, four years after Bouteiller's departure, his disciples arrive eagerly in Paris, full of the dreams and aspirations he had pumped into them. Even though he had spent only a short time with them in Nancy, the power of his words remains in their hearts. In classic bildungsroman tradition, shortly after they arrive the young men are faced with the harsh realities of succeeding or merely surviving in the metropolis. As they stumble with these "false starts," they naturally turn to their mentor to find help and reassurance.[22] These encounters with Bouteiller are among the most openly critical and cruel passages of the novel. Although he still holds the attitudes he maintained while in Nancy, his new career in politics and his devout adherence to republican principles leave the students stunned, humiliated, and disappointed (Barrès 330–35). The poorest students of the group, Racadot and Mouchefrin, go to him to find tutoring jobs so they can afford to stay in Paris and continue their studies in law and medicine. Bouteiller is indifferent to their story and does no more than offer them some stale words of encouragement before sending them on their way empty-handed. The two understand that "they were nothing in his eyes" (ils étaient à ses yeux du néant) and retreat in humiliation from his study (183).

---

21. In this, Bouteiller resembles some of the women school directors whom we find in Belle Epoque novels, such as Mme Jules Ferron in Gabrielle Reval's *Les Sévriennes* (1900).

22. I use the term *naturally*, although this reaction occurs only in male students in these novels. While women also show disappointment with their mentors for not having prepared them sufficiently for the "real world" outside of school (in novels by Reval, Colette, Yver, and Tinayre), they

When the two wealthy students in the group, Sturel and Roemerspacher, go to Bouteiller to announce their new journal, *La Vraie République*, funded by Racadot's unexpected inheritance and edited by Sturel, they are greeted with scarcely concealed "derision," (raillerie) "joking" (gouaillerie) and "a mocking look" (un regard moqueur) (Barrès 331). These initial reactions by Bouteiller are in part due to jealousy, since Bouteiller had always dreamed of running a newspaper himself. But he also objects to the intentions of Sturel and the group, who want the newspaper to represent the new ideals and political viewpoints of their own generation rather than that of the established Gambettistes or Republicans in power. Bouteiller gives them a stern lecture on the importance of obedience, discipline, and abnegation and sends them away disappointed. Sturel and Roemerspacher had hoped that he would join them and write for the newspaper, but Bouteiller has become part of the entrenched political group that they were hoping to challenge.[23]

Disappointment in the mentor is a typical reaction among young students and budding professionals in the novel of education or professional development. In that respect, Bourget's disciple Greslou was unusual because he clung tenaciously to every word of his mentor, twisting Sixte's words to fit his schemes. Among Barrès's disciples, Racadot and Mouchefrin are the most similar to Greslou; they also commit a heinous murder in order to follow their dream and to be accepted by their bourgeois peers. And like Greslou, Racadot and Mouchefrin constantly refer to their mentor's goals when expressing their own. They do not, however, assume that their crime is simply a natural extension of Bouteiller's philosophy, and Bouteiller is never accused openly of corrupting the two young men's lives. The blame falls solely on them. The others, in contrast, grow disenchanted or disappointed with Bouteiller.

The students of *Les Déracinés* are more representative of the disciple type than Greslou, yet even as they move beyond the initial reverence and imitation to the later phases of disillusionment and rejection, they still return to Bouteiller's principles as they begin to shape their own thoughts. At the end of *Les Déracinés*, Bouteiller's most devoted disciple, Suret-Lefort, gives an inspired speech of gratitude at the victory party celebrating Bouteiller's election as representative for Nancy in the Chambre

---

rarely return to their mentor's doorstep looking for help, whether in the form of advice, political or moral support, or money. Male protagonists, on the other hand, often seek out their former teachers or mentors for all of these reasons in order to pursue their objectives or to redefine their goals.

23. Other possible role models, such as the journalist Portalis or the philosopher Taine, are also discarded along the way in *Les Déracinés* as corrupt, self-interested, or destructive.

des Députés (House of Representatives). Sturel and Roemerspacher are disappointed that he refused to join their newspaper but admit that, in spite of their differences with him, they should have returned to one of Bouteiller's original principles with regard to Racadot's and Mouchefrin's trial and should have testified against their old friends for the good of the Republic. On several occasions, Barrès underlines the fact that even if their mentor has fallen short of the students' initial worship, his ideals and principles remain firmly planted in their psyches. Only Saint-Phlin, who never believed in Bouteiller wholeheartedly, leaves behind Paris and all his high school friends to reestablish himself in his hometown in Lorraine with his family. For the other young disciples, the mentor's influence generally continues to affect their goals and principles.

These two novels offer varying examples of the male mentor-disciple relationship in the late nineteenth-century novel of educational development. Although both authors follow some of the traditional patterns of the classic bildungsroman, Bourget reconfigures many of the standard traits and Barrès offers a variety of mentor-disciple relationships. Thus both authors create innovative deviations from the standard and at the same time integrate a number of pedagogical critiques and political debates from the late nineteenth century on education and politics into their plotlines. As such, both texts contain the qualities that Bakhtin requires of a novel of "emergence," where the protagonist and his surroundings appear to emerge and transform themselves simultaneously.

These works also illustrate how the issues of proper status and role socialization (or the lack thereof, in the case of Greslou, Racadot, and Mouchefrin) seriously affected the student wishing to become a member of a particular profession. Shifting the focus from educational to professional development will provide a different perspective on the genre, but the same issues—mentor-disciple relationships, criminal acts, and socialization problems—crop up in the male berufsroman from this time period.

Vagabond Orientalists: Gide's *L'Immoraliste* and Harry's *La Conquête de Jérusalem*

Gide's classic text *L'Immoraliste* (1902) is not usually read in the framework of the novel of professional development, yet it follows many of the standard patterns of that genre, with some deviations from the norm. The portrait that Gide offers of Michel is that of a young man in his midtwenties at the beginning of his career as an archeologist-historian, or, using the title defined by Edward Saïd, an "Orientalist."[24] Following the mold for a typical professional protagonist, Michel is devoted entirely to his research, having been raised to be an archeologist like his father. Michel's entire world is scholarly, specifically related to textual studies of the Orient, and at age twenty he published under his father's name the highly successful *Essai sur les cultes phrygiens* (*Essay on Phrygian Cults*), launching his career and gaining renown for himself among well-established researchers in the field. Michel describes himself at this early stage as inexperienced in life and the world around him, even though he is an expert in Orientalist studies. As such, Michel could be understood as a typical nineteenth-century Orientalist.[25] Gradually, as he comes into contact with the actual people and places he had been studying in texts, he finds that his previous conceptions about his subject matter were too bookish and that his scholarly studies would never again be as attractive as they had been with his father in Paris. When he must battle a life-threatening illness during his honeymoon trip to Tunisia, his priorities for work and living change considerably. In classic bildungsroman fashion, Michel's research plans and his projected career undergo major "detours" or "false starts," and during the course of the novel, both Michel and his career are transformed.

Michel's first mentor, his father, has a considerable influence on him while he is a young man: he is responsible for his career path, his marriage to Marceline, and his travels to northern Africa. Following his recovery and return to France, Michel is attracted to a very different type of mentor, his colleague Ménalque, but not for his professional standards or as a professional role model. In fact, he states that he had avoided Ménalque at the very beginning of his career because his reputation was that of an eccentric peer who did not follow traditional academic methods. After Michel's transformative experience in Tunisia, he finds that he enjoys Ménalque's company specifically because of his marginal tastes and his interests in all things

---

24. In his text *Orientalism*, Saïd gives the broad definition of "Orientalist studies" as "everything from the editing and translation of texts to numismatic, anthropological, archeological, sociological, economic, historical, literary, and cultural studies in every known Asiatic and North African civilization, ancient and modern" (Saïd 52).

25. Gide's character follows the pattern of many Orientalists. Saïd states, "Even the rapport between an Orientalist and the Orient was textual" (52). According to Saïd, certain early nineteenth-century German Orientalists were "cured" of their taste for the subject after their first direct contact with the culture. Michel's first trip to Tunisia was also transformative; the experience did cure him of his desire to pursue abstract, purely textual research on the Orient. At the same time, however, his taste for the physical pleasures and beauty of the Orient increased dramatically.

decadent and exotic. Because his research and values have changed, he can now appreciate the principles, or, rather, "antiprinciples" of a colleague such as Ménalque. During their conversations, they discuss the constraints of the profession, including their bourgeois associates, and the confinement of academic discourse.

There is, of course, an incongruity in their mentor-disciple relationship, based on one of Ménalque's main diatribes against their academic colleagues and against Parisian bourgeois society in general: "Each one proposes a patron for himself, then imitates him; he does not even choose the patron that he imitates; he accepts a patron already chosen" (Gide 115).[26] Although Michel appears to view Ménalque as a sort of mentor (patron), to do so would be to fall into the trap of imitation that Ménalque specifically warns against. Ménalque must be viewed therefore as more of an antimentor, one whom Michel can see as a fellow "immoralist" or outsider, but not one to imitate and follow, as he did his father.

As Michel's days focus less and less on research and more and more on living, the time spent on writing, reading, and teaching diminishes. Michel's "immoral" nature distracts him from his wife, but in our discussion it is important to recognize that it also leads him away from his work and his professional goals. Although he does return to Paris to take up a prestigious teaching position at the Collège de France, there is little in the novel about his courses, students, or research. During the summer before he begins the new position, Michel spends the late afternoons and evenings at his summer farm in Normandy carefully preparing his lectures. But the morning horseback rides he takes with Charles, the farmer's son, are his first priority.

Thus, typical of the male berufsroman, very few scenes in Gide's text depict Michel at work. In one of the only detailed descriptions of a public lecture, the narrator relates the misunderstandings and negative reception of Michel's new research by both colleagues and students. Following this defeating experience, Michel becomes less interested in the course he teaches at the university and the specific references to his professional activities wane considerably throughout the rest of his narrative. This easy renunciation may be understood as a sign of Michel's lack of socialization during his school years. His private education under the tutelage of his father did not include the necessary status socialization that would be helpful to him after his father's death. For example, during the first year of married life

---

26. "Chacun se propose un patron, puis l'imite; même il ne choisit pas le patron qu'il imite; il accepte un patron tout choisi" (Gide 115).

with Marceline, Michel is noticeably uncomfortable during parties and social gatherings at his home. Rather than seeing these events as an opportunity to mix with colleagues and members of his social class, he finds them exhausting or boring trials of his patience. He is much happier to spend time with the working-class men on the farm in Normandy and with the Arab boys that he meets during his convalescence in North Africa.

During the second summer at La Morinière, his farm in Normandy, he spends no time at all on teaching preparation or on research. He instead becomes involved with petty crimes, such as poaching on his own lands, because it allows him to associate with Alcide, the second son of his farm manager Bocage, in an intimate setting. This poaching is the only actual "crime" in *L'Immoraliste,* making it fall slightly outside the typical category for men's novels on educational or professional development where we usually find more serious crimes, such as attempted murder or assault. There are instances of extramarital sex, which Michel indulges in and which hurt Marceline. Although not a crime for men during the Belle Epoque, adultery was certainly a violation of the marriage pact. And there is of course the larger issue of homosexuality that Michel explores throughout the text, and which was, again, not considered a crime but was a marginalizing experience for most gay men during the Belle Epoque.[27] Finally, Marceline's prolonged illness and death at the end of the narrative may be interpreted as a "crime," since they resulted from Michel's incessant demands to travel and his ignorance of her declining health. During the last stages of her illness, Michel sought pleasure for himself instead of tending to her needs, thus bringing on her death indirectly through negligence. Although perhaps a moral crime, it is not on the same level as the assassination, embezzlement, or robberies that we find in other male novels of educational and professional development from the same time period.

By the end of the novel, Michel's resolve to continue his work has been completely disrupted; his wife's death during their second trip to North Africa was the final blow that caused him to completely abandon Western ways. Yet he appeals to his European colleagues to help lift himself out of the paralyzing depression into which he has fallen. In fact, the entire novel is framed by this request to his French peers: the story is preceded by a plea,

---

27. Critics have in fact suggested that Ménalque, Michel's new friend and colleague, is based on Oscar Wilde, whose trial and imprisonment for homosexuality in England a few years earlier had been an important homophobic declaration. It was in Paris that Wilde found refuge when released from prison in 1898.

or a letter of recommendation of sorts, written to the *président du conseil* (prime minister of France), the brother of one of Michel's friends who has answered Michel's call for help. And as the novel concludes, we find a small glimmer of hope that he might be reintegrated into the professional circles he had abandoned in France after his first trip to Tunisia.

Gide's novel differs from the other male novels of development studied so far because he allows his character the freedom to *choose* to leave his profession: neither financial difficulty nor intellectual deficiency nor lack of insider connections to the profession force Michel to make this decision. Michel has the money, intelligence, and personal connections to excel in his field, and nevertheless he decides to quit. It is because he has all these assets but is still unable to challenge his colleagues' old-fashioned opinions and their tight hold on institutional codes that he feels prevented from opening up new paths of research. Michel's reasons for renouncing his chosen profession therefore are different from those of Mouchefrin, Surel, or Greslou and are more like those of many female professional protagonists, because the women often quit based on a conscious decision that it would be the best thing for them. The conclusions for novels about women, however, rarely end with the contemplation of a possible return to the profession with the help of friends in high places.

My studies of male-authored works writing about professional and educational development are not meant to imply that there are certain intrinsically "male" habits in fin-de-siècle novel writing. Rather, these similarities may be interpreted as typical of male protagonists of the Belle Epoque. To demonstrate this, one need only look at another novel of professional development, *La Conquête de Jérusalem* (*The Conquest of Jerusalem*), written by a woman, Myriam Harry. Her novel about the archeologist Hélie Jamain and his research in the Middle East, though written by a woman, involves some of the same issues concerning a male protagonist's development.

Published in 1904, less than two years after *L'Immoraliste*, Myriam Harry's text begins with a similar protagonist in a similar setting. At age twenty-six, Hélie Jamain has lost both his parents, has inherited a sizable fortune, and has a great affection for the study of ancient and "oriental" languages and cultures. In the opening chapter, he has just arrived in Jerusalem, where he describes himself in a direct fashion to the people he meets: "I am an Orientalist and I plan to undertake archeological studies" (Harry 13).[28] Much like Michel's first trip in *L'Immoraliste*, Hélie's first

---

28. "Je suis orientaliste et je me propose d'entreprendre des travaux d'archéologie" (Harry 13).

encounter with the land he has been studying theoretically is a shock for the young bookworm, one that both disappoints and surprises him and plants him in a hospital bed as well. And like Michel, Hélie's research is transformed radically as a result of his direct contact with the culture that he had been previously studying solely through texts.[29] Originally focused on research in early Christian sites, Hélie is seduced by the "Orient" and switches to a study of premessianic rites and ruins.

This crucial shift is foreshadowed on page 1, when Hélie flees from a mobbed Christian church with its masses of pilgrims celebrating Palm Sunday and escapes to the solitude of a nearby minaret tower where he watches his first dramatic sunrise over Jerusalem (Harry 1904, 7–9). His interest in the early Christian era fades quickly as his research in that field appears arid, yielding nothing, both in the parchments he examines and the archeological digs he engages in (24). This example of a false start, typical of the bildungsroman, yields better results than Michel's in Gide's *L'Immoraliste* because Hélie's switch to a new topic provides him with excellent resources, and eventually he produces an innovative research project that is received enthusiastically by scholars back in France.

Hélie, however, shares some features with Gide's protagonist as it is during his honeymoon trip that Hélie's switch becomes definitive. He and his new wife had planned on traveling through the ancient holy lands of Christianity to visit Galilee, Nazareth, and other Christian cities. When Cécile's devout attitudes in these regions frustrate Hélie's desire to consummate their marriage, they move on to Syria and the ruins at Baalbek. Here Cécile relaxes her moral standards, and at the same time Hélie discovers that his true passion lies in the more "exotic" ancient cultures of the non-Christian Orient.

In contrast to other novels of professional development about young men, the narrative in Harry's text gives many details of Hélie's research: his digs, his discoveries, his frustrations, and the news of his first publications and their reception in France are all well documented in the novel, in contrast to Gide's limited reports on Michel's research. But in the domain of the mentor-disciple relationship, the two novels are quite similar in tone.

---

29. In Chapter 4, I will study two female "orientalists" (Marceline Rhonans in Yver's *Les Cervelines* and Gaude Malvos in Reval's *La Bachelière*), both of whom have not yet taken their first voyage to the Orient, and who therefore are still working and publishing in the excited "bookish" stage of their careers. At the conclusion of *Les Cervelines,* Marceline is headed to Lebanon for her first visit

Hélie does not have any success in locating a person who could help him in Jerusalem, and it is suggested indirectly that his feelings of bewilderment and his frustration in his research are in part due to his lack of guidance. The Lazarist priests, who had originally encouraged him to go to Jerusalem after his promising work first appeared in France, reject Hélie completely when he marries Cécile because she is a Protestant missionary, a competitor to their Catholic cause. When Hélie runs into one of them by chance in Nazareth, the betrayed priest angrily cries, "Maledictus sis apostata!" (Harry 1904, 44). Hélie is crushed when he learns that he has been excommunicated from the Catholic Church, burned in effigy, and labeled a "renegade" by these scholar-priests because of his Protestant marriage (92). Another possible mentor, the Protestant minister Zorn, whom Cécile admires and follows in all of her own missionary work, is rejected by Hélie. He believes Zorn is a stuffy prude who does not understand impartial intellectual research. Zorn therefore cannot provide Hélie with a good research mentor either. In truth, Zorn is a rival to Hélie, since Cécile finds more in common with Zorn than with her own husband.

Hélie eventually finds a figure in whom he can confide, Count Béhémond, but like Ménalque in *L'Immoraliste,* this man is more of an antimentor than an authority figure. He is certainly not a recognized leader in his field, since most inhabitants of the city consider him an eccentric. Wearing the costume of a medieval Crusader (including hair shirt, coat of mail, cape, and sword), he rides around the city of Jerusalem looking for new recruits to reconquer the city for the glory of France. His main sidekick is a comical image of a decadent doctor who smokes hashish all day, occasionally rousing himself to mumble, "Vanity, all is vanity and smoke" (Harry 1904, 118).[30] Although the count might not appear to be a likely mentor, Hélie enjoys his detachment from the political and religious quarrels that divide Jerusalem. The count speaks in somewhat romantic terms, but his advice is helpful to Hélie, particularly concerning Cécile, but also on more general topics about living and pursuing one's dreams.

Hélie's lack of a research advisor in his field becomes treacherous, and without support and direction, he falls into unscrupulous hands. He depends completely on his dragoman Slamine, who first showed him the precious

---

to archaeological sites (and perhaps, eventually, a disappointment with her career). Despite their "novice" stage, these two protagonists undergo considerable shock and dramatic changes in their careers, all while remaining in France.

30. "Vanité, tout est vanité et fumée" (Harry 1904, 118).

Moabite artifacts whose unusual inscriptions and carvings would make Hélie famous in the Parisian world of archeology and confirm his reputation as a scholar. When their relationship falls apart, Slamine is in a perfect position to jeopardize Hélie's reputation, which he does by claiming that the artifacts were false, produced recently by locals in a hidden location in the desert.[31] Alarmed by these charges, several members of the Académie conduct investigations and several museums return their collections to Hélie. His work as an "orientalist" is scrutinized and reconsidered as potentially unreliable. Hélie then loses interest in his research and finds it disheartening to continue with his work. Like Gide in *L'Immoraliste,* Myriam Harry develops her male protagonist's difficulties with institutional codes in this novel of professional development. The decision that Hélie made to change his research project leads to his renunciation of his primary career plans.

In *La Conquête de Jérusalem,* however, some of the major conflicts arise at home, between the opposing ideologies of Catholic (or pagan) husband and Protestant wife, rather than between the researcher and his peers. As Hélie watches his career crumble before his eyes, his wife Cécile enjoys a successful career as a Lutheran missionary, writing for the newsletter, organizing charity balls, and distributing Bibles, clothes, and medical supplies. Her mentor, Pastor Zorn, is a powerful figure who helps her to move up the ladder in the Protestant community of Jerusalem. Not only is she more successful than Hélie, she decides to attack her husband as a rival when he publishes the first part of his major study *La Resurrection du paganisme* (*The Resurrection of Paganism*).

By publishing that work, Hélie made it clear he was no longer working for the promotion of the Protestant mission, and Cécile and her mentor Zorn thus begin to wage war against him. They steal a chapter of his manuscript from his desk, ransack his study, publish Slamine's false accusations, and generally encourage the downfall of Hélie's "idolatrous" work. Hélie's battle with the institution's codes begins with the religious intolerance of his own wife and friend but then extends to include the academy's ready willingness to believe the charges made against his research. Hélie is frustrated but helpless to change their single-minded views of his work.

---

31. Harry's portrait of the cunning and devious Arab Slamine is an obvious example of colonialist attitudes in Orientalist writings of the Third Republic, similar to Gide's portraits of the Arab boys who play with and steal from Michel in *L'Immoraliste*. But Michel does not depend on the Tunisian children for his career and reputation, while Hélie is shown to be completely dependent not only on the raw materials Slamine provides for his successes in Parisian academic circles, but also on Slamine's word that the artifacts are indeed authentic. Without those artifacts, Hélie is just

The conflict between husband and wife is one of the major differences between Myriam Harry's work and that of Gide or any of the other writers studied in this chapter. There are female characters in the other texts; for example, Marceline is certainly an important figure in Michel's life in *L'Immoraliste,* but she does not have any influence over his decisions about work or his choice of research field. In Bourget and Barrès, the women are either romantic interests or sources of money, but they have no direct influence over the men's education or careers. None of the other women characters appears to have a competing career, whereas Cécile sees her work in the Lutheran missionary community as a key component in her life. Hélie finds her work potentially threatening and stops to ask himself the following, "This deaconess, my wife, could she be ambitious/careerist?" (Harry 1904, 152),³² not realizing the extent to which her career is important to her. When he later discovers Cécile's aggressive efforts to tear down his work, he is disappointed and discouraged by her actions. This aspect of Harry's novel aligns it more closely to the married couples in women writers' novels featuring a female professional protagonist, where the battles waged are frequently in the home as well as in the public sphere.³³

Although Harry and Gide make very different use of the female characters in their novels, their works are comparable because neither writer includes crimes against others. In contrast to Barrès and Bourget, the protagonist in Harry's text does not commit a murder, attack, or rape. Hélie is a victim of an assault by religious zealots at the beginning of the novel, and he commits adultery. There are several tragic events, such as Cécile's accidental poisoning death by her godfather and Hélie's suicide at the conclusion of the text, but again, these are not crimes against others committed by the protagonist. By not including crime, Myriam Harry follows the general pattern of most women writers of educational or professional development novels of the era . Harry was able to achieve the intended aesthetic goals in her text without resorting to the more serious offenses that male authors deployed in their texts.

In all four of the novels studied here, the authors refuse to follow some of the defining patterns and archetypes for the classic eighteenth-century male bildungsroman. For example, there is no happy reintegration with family

---

an ordinary scholar, or, even worse, when Slamine claims they are false, he is viewed as a promoter of counterfeit objects.

32. "Cette diaconesse, ma femme, serait-elle ambitieuse?" (Harry 1904, 152).
33. I will return to the issue of husband-wife rivalries in more detail in Chapters 4 and 6.

and society at the conclusion of these texts. Although there is a vague hint of some sort of reconciliation at the end of *L'Immoraliste,* it does not reverse the general concluding mood, which is one of exile and alienation. In Bourget's text, the focus begins on the mentor figure, thus emphasizing his role over that of the disciple. And in Barrès's text, the multiple protagonists take a variety of approaches to fulfill their desires and thus offer the reader a number of different quest plotlines to absorb. These authors played with narrative conventions and rewrote the genre to suit their own political or stylistic objectives. Women writers, as we will see in the following chapters, were even more aggressive in their alterations to the traditional novel of development.

One final element that the authors either distort or eliminate is the interplay of quest and romance. The traditional bildungsroman often contains a strong element of quest, with the young protagonist leaving his home to seek his fortune, undergo adventures, and return home with a new, more elevated status. In all of these novels, the young man does leave home, whether for Paris or "the Orient," in order to further his career or education. The trials that each protagonist undergoes do teach him important lessons about himself, although sometimes these lessons are misunderstood (*Le Disciple*), disappointing (*Les Déracinés*), or ostracizing (*La Conquête de Jérusalem* and *L'Immoraliste*). Although two of the protagonists in these novels marry, only a very small portion of the narratives is devoted to a romance plot. This contrasts greatly from novels about women's educational or professional development. In those texts, quest and romance are normally both present, usually intertwined, and frequently act as conflicting plot elements.

Several studies of the twentieth-century female novel of development indicate that many of the traditional definitions of the bildungsroman effectively exclude women from the role of protagonist for the simple reason that women were excluded from the public sphere and were allowed to pursue a quest only insofar as it related to their subsequent marriage and motherhood.[34] Any sense of self or individual growth was subsumed to the roles of mothering and service to the husband and family. While male heroes of the classic bildungsroman often do marry after returning from their adventures and reintegrating with their society, their marriage is viewed as a form of reward

---

34. Two excellent examples of such studies include Esther Kleinbord Labovitz's *The Myth of the Heroine: The Female Bildungsroman in the Twentieth Century* and Annis Pratt's *Archetypal Patterns in Women's Fiction,* especially Chapter 2 on the novel of development, by Barbara White and Annis Pratt.

for the deeds accomplished on their adventures. For the female heroines of most nineteenth-century novels, however, marriage is not a by-product but rather the main goal of the protagonist's quest. This pattern would change in the beginning of the twentieth century with the arrival of the female novel of educational or professional development.

Women authors of the Belle Epoque, analogous to their male colleagues, chose their own innovations to the genre. In doing so, they redesigned the novels of education and professional development in order to invent the outlines for a new women's novel for the new century. They did so clearly to fulfill a different reading population's expectations and to describe a woman's challenges in the worlds of advanced education and professional careers. Their changes also created a new literary style for the French reading public. These novels about women students and professionals contained some of the same elements found in male novels of educational and professional development from the Belle Epoque, and the authors and the works we have studied here were among the most significant in laying the foundations for the blossoming of new types of women protagonists that appeared at the beginning of the twentieth century and the new narratives that would match these women's goals.

3

DREAMS AND DISAPPOINTMENTS: WOMEN'S EDUCATION NOVELS

LESS THAN TWENTY YEARS after the French Republic passed a law requiring primary education for both boys and girls, the surprising *Claudine à l'école* (*Claudine at School*) took Paris by storm. The charming schoolgirl heroine created a fad for Claudine hats, cigarettes, soap, perfume, and other items. The public demanded a theatrical version of the story and, of course, more Claudine novels. How could an education novel, and specifically a girls' education novel, produce such a monstrous popular response? To answer this question, I will examine the development of the image of the girls' school, both in *Claudine à l'école* and in other more sober female education novels from the early years of the twentieth century. Historically, the images of girls' schools put forth in these novels offered readers an insider's view of this relatively new social structure within French culture. But the novels also demonstrated the women authors' mixed narrative techniques: while these writers used certain familiar bildungsroman structures, they also introduced new aspects to the novel of educational development, such as the "official" women's community, utopian subcultures for women, and most important, the emergence of girls and women alongside (although not necessarily in parallel with) the emergence of general French society.

In these works, two social spheres are set in contrast with the heroine's development: the general French society of the turn of the century, and the specific women's community found inside the school. In this chapter I will focus on four different women's education novels, each offering a different example of these dual societies. The first, Colette's *Claudine à l'école* (1900)[1] takes place in a generally unchanging provincial village and could therefore be understood to belong to the first category of bildungsroman, or novel of development, that Bakhtin describes, where the protagonist emerges in a private way against the backdrop of a static society (Bakhtin 19). But the public school that the protagonist is attending throughout the novel

---

1. For a brief plot summary of this novel, see Appendix 2.

actually begins the process of emergence along with the main character, thus classifying the novel in the second category of Bakhtinian novel of development, those in which protagonist and social structure emerge simultaneously (23). Likewise, in Gabrielle Reval's *Sévriennes* (*Women of Sèvres,* 1900),[2] the city of Paris is a backdrop so distant from the women's world of the Ecole Normale Supérieure de Sèvres that it goes almost unnoticed, rarely mentioned in the narrative. In contrast, the school's pedagogical philosophy makes rapid changes, but not always in step with or as a result of the personal emergence of Marguerite, the main heroine. *Sévriennes* thus provides an interesting divergence from Bakhtin's second category of the novel of development. Louise-Marie Compain's *L'Un vers l'autre* (*The One Toward the Other,* 1903)[3] takes place in a relatively volatile world, both because of the feminist thoughts and actions of the heroine, Laure, and because of conservative political forces beyond her control in the city where she is teaching. Yet her own school appears to be a relatively stable force in her life, a tranquil oasis for her during a period of radical changes and emergence. Finally, Esther de Suze's *Institutrice* (*Woman Schoolteacher,* 1902)[4] transpires in an isolated Alpine village that does not accept change. The heroine, Marie-Thérèse, finds herself in a quiet and sleepy girls elementary school that is similarly immutable, and her own coming of age proceeds against these two very static backdrops. As we shall see, the heroines' character development and their force in both the "real" and the "academic" worlds change considerably, depending on the type of environments in which each author has chosen to set her particular heroine.

These different environments also produce changes to the traditional bildungsroman traits discussed in Chapter 2. Many of the main protagonists have difficulty finding mentors who are strong or nurturing role models. Further, the classic move from the provinces to Paris is usually absent, although in *Sévriennes* we find heroines who move to Sèvres, in the suburbs of Paris, in order to pursue their teacher training degrees. And finally, the lessons learned along the way are not the same as those that men learn: the false starts and other detours that the traditional bildungsroman hero makes while pursuing his goals are usually delayed until the ending of the female novel of education, with a renunciation of school or teaching or both. The idea of a successful reintegration with the heroine's family and society at

---

2. For a brief plot summary of this novel, see Appendix 2.
3. For a brief plot summary of this novel, see Appendix 2.
4. For a brief plot summary of this novel, see Appendix 2.

the conclusion of the texts is also quite rare, although one novel, *L'Un vers l'autre,* does reunite the heroine Laure with her estranged husband at the end of the story. Thus some of the basic structures of the archetypal bildungsroman are modified or eliminated to accommodate the new female student or teacher character, depending on the social environment of the school and the community where she lives.

The authors of the novel of women's educational development also included several innovative narrative structures in their texts, such as the development of a utopian subculture and the enactment of rites of passage. On one hand, the description of a rite of passage follows closely the patterns of the traditional bildungsroman but it also permits the writer to disclose accurate depictions to readers of the pedagogical practices and innovations for French girls and women during the time period. On the other hand, the creation of a utopian women's space in the novels allows for a range of critiques of the national education system for girls, from wildly sarcastic, as in *Claudine à l'école,* to mildly disapproving, as in *Sévriennes*. While these first two novels direct their attentions to the problems that arise within the school system itself, those in the second group, *L'Un vers l'autre* and *Institutrice,* focus on pressures issuing from sources outside the schools that affect the ways in which the women protagonists are able to learn and teach. Each novelist also divulges a more idealized vision of what the national education system could and should provide for girls and for women teachers. These visions include cooperative superintendents, enthusiastic teachers, and supportive townspeople. At the very least, the heroine offers some suggested improvements for her own school.

Whether or not the world surrounding the heroine is stable or changing, for the individual protagonist who is beginning a new stage in life, there is usually some required ceremonial ritual, a marker of change, or what turn-of-the-century cultural anthropologist van Gennep labeled "les rites de passage" (rites of passage) in his work of the same name.[5] It is useful to employ the three stages that form van Gennep's definition of the rite of passage—the preliminal, liminal, and postliminal stages—and the accompanying "territorial passage" to the site of the actual event, especially when discussing these key moments of change in the women's education novels.

The education system in France (and in many Western societies) has traditionally been based on a series of hierarchical exams; the passage of each one gives the student access to a new level of learning and a new status in the

---

5. Arnold van Gennep's original *Les Rites de passage* (1909) describes the rites of passage of "timeless" non-Western cultures that he had studied during the early part of the twentieth century.

educational and social community. The exams for the *brevet,* the *baccalauréat,* the *licence,* the *capès,* and the *agrégation* still exist today in French education. One of the major rites of passage for French students therefore was (and still is) the final exam. Although all students may now take the baccalauréat exam at the end of the high school years, at the turn of the century, girls' schools offered the brevet exams at the primary and superior levels. For small village schools, the series of written and oral exams were given at the chief town of the department by a group of professors chosen from regional schools. All eligible students from the surrounding area assembled for two or three days to undergo the exams together. This relatively new social and cultural event for girls continued to arouse curiosity in the general public, and we find a correspondingly detailed view of this particular rite of passage and its various stages in Colette's description of Claudine's brevet exams in *Claudine à l'école.*

There is first the "territorial passage," ushering the students away from the village of Montigny to the site of the exam, an unnamed central city for the Fresnois region. All the eligible students and the headmistress, Mlle Sergent, take the coach to a nearby train station and embark on the three-hour train trip together (Colette 1984a, 123–24). During the preliminary stages, Claudine notes her separation from her cat Fanchette (123) and the joking or risqué comments from the drunken coach driver and three traveling salesmen that their group receives during their departure from Montigny (123–24). Once they have arrived at the hotel where they will be staying, she notes their incorporation into the new setting through a communal meal at the hotel (125). The liminal stage for this rite of passage includes the students' huddled counsel with the headmistress before and after each exam (136, 139, 149, 155–56, 162), the description of the exams themselves, including specific questions and various attempts at cheating, and then the group's walk over to the posted lists of students who have passed (*les reçues*) after the exams are over.

Within each individual ceremony, there are several stages that are repeated and ritualized, such as the walk to see the grades posted on the school door. Immediately after the last written exam, "They put us out,

---

He eventually began to apply these theories to French society in his later works. I find the categories especially helpful in defining the newly established patterns and exercises for girls' education. Furthermore, I find that when discussing the fictional portrayals of the new schools for girls, van Gennep's interest in and focus on the sacred versus secular debates are of particular relevance, since they were hotly contested topics during the turn of the century in France.

feverish and noisy at the thought that, this very evening, we should read, on a big list nailed to the door the names of the candidates who had qualified for the Orals the next day" (Colette 2001a, 135).[6] After dinner, the students have their eyes glued on their teacher, Mademoiselle Sergent, as she looks at her watch and then signals that they can go check the scores. At the school, using a candle in the dark to read the lists, Claudine goes over the initials to determine who has passed the preliminary exams and made it to the next level (Colette 1984a, 147). After the oral exams on the following day, the same series of events are narrated in the same fashion, indicating a ritual that the students of all the schools assembled are following (Colette 1984a, 163).

The postliminal stages include the description of the train ride back to Montigny (Colette 1984a, 164–65) and the reintegration with the school and family community. In contrast to the drunken and impertinent comments that they received on their departure, there is a welcome from the students and other teachers at school, the inhabitants of Montigny, and even from Claudine's absent-minded father, who had actually noticed her three-day absence and had been wondering what had happened to his daughter (167). Van Gennep states that those members of the community who have been initiated are endowed with a "magico-religious" status for the rest of the group. Claudine and the other students are greeted by townspeople waving to them from windows during their triumphant return to the school (166). Their status has been raised in the eyes of the citizenry, and they are treated with a new respect and honor.

Several other women's education novels include similar rites of passage concerning the final exam or the entrance exams to a new school, including Reval's *Sévriennes* (1900) and *Lycéennes* (1901), Compain's *L'Un vers l'autre* (1903), and Babin's *Pharmacienne* (1907). For several heroines, their entire teaching career could be viewed as one long rite of passage. For example, the teaching career of Compain's heroine, Laure, spans the period of time when she is separated from her overbearing husband and their home. The preliminal stages include the detailed description of her train ride to the new school and her incorporation into the new setting with her supervisor. The liminal stage is represented by her yearlong experience as a teacher, including the trials, experiments, and decisions that she makes. Her return to her home and husband at the end of the novel indicates the postliminal

---

6. "on nous met dehors, enfiévrées et bruyantes à l'idée que nous viendrons lire ce soir, sur une grande liste clouée à la porte, les noms des candidates admises à l'oral du lendemain" (Colette 145).

stages of reintegration with the community, but with a new, more elevated status vis-à-vis her husband and their marriage. The rite of passage, traditionally found in novels of development, is thus often a part of Belle Epoque women's education novels, whether they discuss the rites of passages of female students or those of new women teachers.

Because each novel centers on a women's or girls' school, there are traces of the classic utopian island, isolated or separated from the harsh realities of the world. Each narrative develops the portrait of a women's community that exists in a state of semidetachment from the outside, and the arrival scene is therefore a primary element for all of the heroines in these women's education novels. Whether the protagonist will be studying or teaching, the texts include the details of her travel to and arrival at the new school, her first impressions of the town and school, and her initial difficulties with the new environment and strangers.

In Esther de Suze's novel *Institutrice,* the heroine, Marie Thérèse, describes in detail the stages of her transition from student to teacher. First, she notes the anxious wait for the letter containing the governmental assignment to a girls' school (common also in Reval's novels, including *Sévriennes*). For Marie Thérèse, this period is prolonged; she does not receive a teaching assignment until January. The train ride to her new school is experienced as a mixture of apprehension and excitement, but it soon turns into a disaster as she mistakenly gets off the train too early, thirty minutes before her station. Since there are no scheduled means of transportation for five hours and it is already six in the evening, she realizes that she must walk the last miles to her new village in the snowstorm by herself. At first it appears that she will not be able to survive the cold and dark. She stops to cry on a frozen bridge, feeling sharply her loneliness and the indifference of the train officials and the villagers who could not arrange some kind of transportation for her. Yet as she contemplates the beauty of her natural surroundings—the stars, the snow, and the mountains around her—she regains confidence and presses on alone. The protagonist in *Institutrice* thus finds her inspiration in nature, a trait harking back to the classic eighteenth-century bildungsroman and to texts from the Romantic era of the nineteenth century.

During the transitional voyage from a known way of life to the new school, the heroine often undergoes a trial of moral character and a new opportunity to test her fortitude. The journey to the new school may also be uplifting and encouraging, serving as a moment of reflection that reinforces the new teacher's ideals. Laure Deborda, in *L'Un vers l'autre,* after reading her subscriptions to "des revues féministes" and "*L'Eve nouvelle*" during her train trip to her new school, explains that she feels "a powerful feeling of communion with unknown women pursuing, by diverse means, the same work of emancipation, for themselves at first, and for their sex" (Compain 1903, 167).[7]

In contrast to the voyage section, the arrival scene in these women's education novels usually involves an initial disappointment with the physical housing arranged for the new schoolteacher: Laure in *L'Un vers l'autre* and Marie-Thérèse in *Institutrice* are both disheartened by the severe and unadorned rooms they are assigned to live in. In Reval's second education novel, *Un Lycée de jeunes filles* (1901), the protagonist cannot find a place to rent. The townspeople harbor such strong hostility toward the public girls' high school that they refuse to rent their rooms to its teachers. It is only through the ingenuity of a Sévrienne alumna, Berthe Passy, who has been teaching in the town for several years, that the newcomer is able to find a place to stay.

The initial contact with the town's mayor and priest and the school's headmistress provide one of the moments of greatest tension for the new schoolteacher. In *L'Un vers l'autre,* Laure is fortunate to find that the headmistress, Germaine Lachaud, is friendly and supportive. Marguerite Triel, in *Sévriennes,* however, finds her headmistress, Mme Jules Ferron, to be icy and distant. In *Institutrice,* Marie-Thérèse's introduction to the mayor is deferred: he is not available to greet and welcome her, as she had hoped. Instead, the mayor's maid shows her around the schoolteacher's humble living quarters and the rudimentary classroom that she will be using. The mayor and priest in her new town are initially supportive of Marie-Thérèse, an exception in the novel of education, where generally such people are skeptical of the unmarried and independent women who have been sent to teach or practice in their towns.

For students, in contrast, the arrival is usually marked by awe and excitement. In Reval's third education novel, *Lycéennes* (1902), the protagonist, Françoise Tréveray, is pleasantly surprised by the beauty of her new high school in Paris, the Lycée Maintenon. Fresh from the provinces, she writes to her sister in a naïve, but appreciative, voice: "I made my entrance at the Lycée Maintenon yesterday. God, a high school is a beautiful thing! That, a high school! No, a palace."[8] Her lengthy description of the exterior

---

7. "un sentiment puissant de communion avec des femmes inconnues, poursuivant, par des moyens divers, la même oeuvre d'affranchissement, pour elles-mêmes d'abord, et pour leur sexe" (Compain 1903, 167).

8. "J'ai fait hier, mon entrée à Maintenon. Dieu! que c'est beau un lycée! Ça un lycée! Non, un palais.... Notre lycée porte très haut, vers le quatrième ou le cinquième, une coiffure de géraniums

demonstrates her favorable impression, but it also contains an unusual organic simile, as she compares the urban facade to a small waterfall or stream from her native countryside. As she continues her acclamatory description of the building's interior and her new headmistress and teachers, she marvels repeatedly at the expense the state has gone to in order to provide such sumptuous facilities for her and her peers (Reval 1902, 30). Claudine, usually cynical and faultfinding, is similarly impressed by the clean classrooms and updated furniture in her new school building in *Claudine à l'école* (Colette 1984a, 89). Thus, all of the plot elements that constitute the arrival scene in these novels—the voyage, the new school, the first meeting with new peers and supervisors—play an important role in confirming the notion that the women's community will be remote from mainstream society. These elements are useful for establishing the novel's setting, but they are also employed as a means to separate the heroine, to place her in an isolated educational space that is only partially connected to mass culture and her previous life. Once she has become detached from the "real" world, the protagonist is free to engage in intellectual activities in a purely female environment.

This opportunity to live in a stimulating intellectual female community is one of the great changes that this particular genre brings to French literature. Previous representations of the women's community in French literature had mainly been "unofficial," as feminist theorist Nina Auerbach describes it: "Women in literature who evade the aegis of men also evade traditional categories of definition. Since a community of women is a furtive, unofficial, often underground entity, it can be defined by the complex, shifting, often contradictory attitudes it evokes" (Auerbach 11). In contrast to the "unofficial" women's community so typical in French literature before this era, the educational establishments in these particular Belle Epoque novels have been founded by the French government and are therefore not "furtive" or "underground" communities. As publicly funded schools, they do have some restrictions regarding curriculum and final exam guidelines, for example, which are determined by the national Ministry of Education, an all-male office of bureaucrats and educators. In addition to the laws and requirements set by male academicians, these women's classes are sometimes interrupted or invaded by male intruders: suspicious local officials, inspectors,

---

roses; ses murs ont un revêtement de briques bleutées, si pâles, si nuancées par l'éclat adouci du soleil, qu'on croirait voir couler, tout doucement, du grenier au trottoir, un filet d'eau vive, l'eau d'un ruisselet de Moselle. J'ai envie de faire la girafe, et de lêcher, amoureusement, cette eau imaginaire, qui me met, à la bouche, la fraîcheur des eaux de chez nous" (Reval 1902, 29).

regional superintendents, members of the boys' school staff, or guest lecturers from the local university. The women, however, do live, teach, and learn in a mainly female environment, and the individual directors and professors have some authority to lead their students according to their own personal philosophies. The women's communities that they construct therefore result in a diversity of learning and living environments specifically aimed at educating women. These utopian women's environments may not be described explicitly as a future world of happiness and equality or some isolated island of paradisiacal beauty.[9] Women's education novelists often employ their critical views of the school system and its dystopian or negative aspects as a springboard for their more hopeful dreams of a better education and a better future for students and teachers alike.

There exists, of course, many different types of communities of women, including some that are organized in a familial structure, some in a businesslike structure, and others still in a romance structure; being located in schools, these communities are usually intellectual as well.[10] The variety in the form of the community is equal to the complexity of each, for every one of these schools contains a network of women: directors, teachers, staff, and students of various ages, personalities, and abilities, all of whom contribute to the community in assorted ways. In the following close readings of the four novels, the focus will remain on the development or "emergence" of the main protagonist, to use the Bakhtinian term. But this larger community of women constantly shapes the heroine's thoughts and molds her system of values, and thus it will be important to refer to the community often as well.

Colette's *Claudine à l'école* (1900) is probably the best-known female education novel from this era in France, and it is the only one of the four discussed here that is still in print today.[11] The eponymous Claudine, from a bourgeois family in the tiny village of Montigny, gives a cynical but at the

---

9. Frances Bartkowski explains, "Few feminist utopias . . . take on a total revision of the world women might make; the social planning of earlier utopias is instead transformed into an extensive social critique which exposes and makes use of the dystopian as well" (Bartkowski 12). Bartkowski is speaking of feminist utopian novels from the 1970s, but the education novels that we will be studying here contain similar features.

10. I am borrowing here from some of Nina Auerbach's categories (familial, businesslike, and romance structures) for communities of women.

11. Excerpts from Louise-Marie Compain's *L'Un vers l'autre* have been published in English translation (see Hause and Waelti-Walters, *Feminisms of the Belle Epoque* (Lincoln: University of Nebraska, 1994).

same time affectionate description of her last year in the local public schools. Her critique covers both the subject matter taught at the school and the behavior displayed by her teachers, but her argument against the academic program is shaded differently than her attack on the dubious morality of her elders.

On nonacademic issues, and specifically the behavior of her superiors, Claudine's diary observations do not hide anything or protect anyone. One of her greatest sources of amusement involves uncovering the incredible corruption, scandal, and politics that she finds rampant in her school. Typical of most protagonists in novels of educational development, Claudine may have sought a mentor figure at her school. All her female "role models," however, are involved in various intrigues, usually sexual. Claudine tries to remain an aloof outsider to their activities even as she chronicles them with great detail in her journal. The beautiful new instructor, appropriately named "Aimée" Lathenay, becomes the center of school gossip, as she simultaneously engages in a love affair with the headmistress, Mlle Sergent, and accepts a proposal of marriage from the boys' teacher, Armand Duplessis. The powerful district superintendent, M. Dutertre, rather openly initiates a sexual relationship with Aimée, when he asks her to leave her classroom in the middle of the afternoon in order to "verifier une fissure" (check a crack) in the walls of the headmistress's new bedroom in the new school buildings (Colette 1984a, 74–79). When Aimée's fiancé finds out about this "crack checking" episode, he spends the night wandering in the woods, returning completely disheveled and exploding in a violent fit of rage in front of the students the following afternoon. Claudine narrates his attack on Aimée, Dutertre, and Sergent: "He shouted: 'Filthy little bitch! Ah, so you let yourself be fumbled for money by that swine of a District Inspector [Monsieur Dutertre]! You're worse than a streetwalker but *that* one there [Mademoiselle Sergent] is even worse than you that damned redhead who's making you like herself. Two bitches, two bitches'" (Colette 2001a, 78–79).[12]

These two disruptive classroom invasions by male outsiders result in the closing of the school for a week and the transfer of Duplessis to another school by the "cochon de délégué cantonal," Monsieur Dutertre. The teachers' dubious behavior takes yet another twist when the headmistress and

---

12. "Il crie: 'Espèce de petite rosse! Ah! tu vas te faire tripoter pour de l'argent par ce cochon de délégué cantonal (M. Dutertre)! Tu es pire qu'une fille de trottoir, mais celle-ci (Mlle Sergent) vaut encore moins que toi, cette sacrée rousse qui te rend pareille à elle. Deux rosses, deux rosses'" (Colette 87).

Dutertre are caught by surprise in bed together during the end-of-the-year school dance. The comportment promoted by government officials for women schoolteachers, "exemplary in conduct, avoiding local disputes and gossip, and keeping a distance from men" (Clark 16) is ripped to shreds in the local Montigny school system. Our heroine Claudine is able to laugh at these hilarious scenes specifically because she has not become directly implicated in them.

Claudine is not exempt from their seductions, however, as she also found Aimée attractive and enjoyed her intimate moments with the young schoolteacher during private English lessons at her home. Yet Aimée cannot serve as a mentor figure for Claudine because she is too young and inexperienced to be a role model. Rather, she turns into a romantic interest for Claudine. The idea that the headmistress, Mlle Sergent, might serve as a mentor for Claudine is also improbable. Sergent, jealous and possessive, forces Aimée to cancel her private English lessons with Claudine and then pettily jubilates over this victory against Claudine, as if she were a rival to compete with rather than a student in her school. The result of this confrontation is a lack of respect for Mlle Sergent on Claudine's part that verges on animosity, all of which she cleverly cloaks as a form of harmless adolescent rebellion. The farcical and occasionally subversive actions of the characters in Claudine's school may tend to confirm the popular image of the Belle Epoque woman. That is, she is sexually perverse and ludic. The portrait of Claudine, however, does not remain static or stereotypical. In her search for a possible mentor figure, she offers an image of a developing modern heroine: independent, intelligent, sensitive, and highly aware of her elders' misdoings.

In her critique of the academic side of things in her novel of educational development, Colette depicts in exacting detail the "technical" side of being a student, in great contrast to the men's novels studied in the previous chapter. She includes numerous descriptions of coursework, exams, and school activities. What is intriguing in this narrative is that Colette elaborates the socialization process the students must undergo by linking that process to a variety of technical or academic tasks they must perform.

For example, Claudine's middle-class background gives her a general advantage over her classmates, who come mainly from working-class and farming families. Labeled an "assistant" to the imported male music professor, Claudine is the one who teaches the required class to her peers since she is the only one in the school who knows how to play the piano and read music (Colette 1984a, 50–53). In this scene, Claudine actually takes on the role of mentor to her working-class peers. Her extensive reading and her critical mind also enable her to write excellent compositions, for which she receives the near-impossible grade of 19 out of 20 points on the brevet exam (162). She is not aloof from her working-class friends, however, and realizes that her classmates have skills that she does not possess. For example, Claudine comments that she finds arithmetic problems very difficult and looks to her peers for help in that subject area: "Most of these little daughters of grasping peasants or shrewd seamstresses are gifted for arithmetic to an extent that has often amazed me" (Colette 2001a, 133).[13] Claudine's tone concerning her classmates and their parents may appear condescending and critical, but she does admire their abilities and openly seeks their help in math. In fact, most of the students in her class help each other with their weaker subjects, with the exception of the humorless Jaubert twins.

Claudine's class status is without doubt bourgeois, yet she did not learn the traditional activities taught to girls of her class, in part because she did not have a mother or governess to teach her these "feminine" skills. As a result, she prefers climbing trees and playing marbles to embroidering handkerchiefs. In school, this lack of feminized training becomes obvious: Claudine's disdain for and disinterest in the required needlework and drawing classes are shown both directly and indirectly, through cheating and bribing other students to do her assignments for her (Colette 1984a, 60, 68, 94–95). In the novel, Claudine is the only student who, at age fifteen, continues to use physical force to retaliate when insulted or embarrassed. In several scenes, she slaps or punches classmates who have made particularly humiliating remarks about her. Whereas her working-class school friends struggle to acquire those ladylike talents deemed prerequisites for a young bourgeoise of the leisure class, Claudine has already acquired some of them (music, writing) and belittles others as old-fashioned and boring (needlework, drawing). The socialization process is of secondary importance for Claudine, but it is key for her working-class schoolmates.

Claudine is capable of engaging in a spirited critique of the school's academic curriculum because of her family's intellectual background. Since her youth, she has had open access to her father's library and has read

---

13. "La plupart de ces petites, filles de paysans avides ou d'ouvrières adroites, ont d'ailleurs le don de l'arithmétique à un point qui m'a souvent stupéfaite" (Colette 143). It is interesting to note that Claudine associates good math skills with a particular economic class (working-class or peasant), and not with a specific gender (male). One hundred years later, of course, most educators decry the bias against girls in current teaching practices that creates a disadvantage for them in math and science skills, whether they are from the upper, middle or the working classes.

everything that she could find. Unmonitored reading was considered scandalous behavior for a middle-class schoolgirl at the turn of the century, and her teachers' and examiners' reactions to her extracurricular reading activities give proof of this common attitude. During the final oral history exam for the brevet, Claudine reveals her advanced reading knowledge and her strong powers of critical thinking when she challenges the examiner to a theoretical debate on the politics of historical writing:

> "Yes, Sir, I read it in Michelet—with full details!"
> "Michelet! But this is madness! Michelet, get this into your head, wrote a historical novel in twenty volumes and he dared to call that the *History of France!* And you come here and talk to me of Michelet!" (. . .)
> "Anyway, Michelet's less boring than Duruy!" (Colette 2001a, 141)[14]

Claudine's bold rejoinder not only critiques the prescribed positivist historian, Victor Duruy, she also puts forth her idea of a better choice of historian: Jules Michelet. Underlying her disapproval, moreover, is a subtle and extended critique of the national school system for girls in general, since it was Victor Duruy who, as minister of public instruction, established the first curriculum and wrote the first proposal for government-funded secondary schools for girls in 1867. Surprisingly, after her unruly outburst, Claudine passes her history exam and her examiner even praises her independent thought, relieved to hear a critical response rather than yet another brainless recounting of historical facts. He proclaims to Mlle Sergent, "there's no harm done . . . we see so many dull ones!" (140–41).[15]

This exam scene provides an example of the dual emergence of the main character and the academic world in which she lives: as the powers of critical analysis of the Claudine character become more refined, we find a simultaneous emergence of examiners who appreciate original ideas and strong

---

14.
 —Oui, monsieur, je l'ai lu dans Michelet, avec des détails!
 —Michelet! mais c'est de la folie! Michelet, entendez-vous bien, a fait un roman historique en vingt volumes et il a osé appeler ça l'*Histoire de la France!* Et vous venez me parler de Michelet!. . .
 —Michelet est toujours moins embêtant que Duruy! (Colette 152)

15. "il n'y a pas de mal. . . . On voit tant de dindes!" (Colette 152).

opinions in young women. Similarly, when asked to take over the class while Mlle Sergent is busy helping another class, Claudine decides to dictate to her peers a poem by the Symbolist Gustave Kahn, rather than the bland examples provided in the school manual. When Mlle Sergent discovers the switch, she is angry that Claudine disobeyed her, but Claudine can see that she privately enjoys the poem and admires Claudine's knowledge and spirit: "But there was no conviction behind her scolding, for in her secret heart, she's rather amused by these hoaxes" (Colette 2001a, 38).[16] Even though Mlle Sergent feels obligated to chastise Claudine publicly for testing her authority in front of the other girls, she tacitly approves Claudine's independence.

Claudine's academic experience is affected by the transitional stage in French pedagogical history, when attitudes about the reasons for and the goals of women's education were changing significantly. These changes influence her last year of classes in very concrete terms as construction of the new Montigny school during the academic year forces Claudine and her classmates to continue their education during a period of actual physical change. As a result, the plot and the characters are part of "the landscape," as Bakhtin labels it in his essay on the bildungsroman. They "do not enter it from the outside, are not invented to fit the landscape, but are unfolded in it as though they were present from the very beginning" (Bakhtin 49). In numerous scenes, Claudine's class is asked to interrupt its lesson to help move the schools' books and furniture, the professors' private property, and themselves from one temporary classroom to the next. Throughout the novel, her class is held in the elementary school, in the town hall, and in both the old and the new high schools. The chaos created by each move is an excuse for distractions from the academic program: pranks, spying, and games. But each new setting usually brings with it new books, new desks, new classroom activities, and sometimes even new students. On the final day of Claudine's formal education, when she receives her certificate and graduates from school, the new school is also "certified," as elected officials arrive in Montigny to publicly dedicate the new building. The symbolic emergence of the heroine is thus accompanied by the physical emergence of the new permanent school building.

After Claudine's critique of her teachers' behavior and the restrictive school system, it would be preposterous to expect her to find maternal or intellectual role models in her provincial school. The women's "community" is more of a farce than a utopian subculture in *Claudine a l'école,* and we do

---

16. "elle gronde sans conviction, car, tout au fond, ces fumisteries ne lui déplaisent pas" (Colette 45).

not find familial-like structures here. Yet Claudine is no lost orphan, even though she has neither teacher nor advisor nor parent to whom she can turn for help and counsel. Rather, she takes on an identity that reflects her changing surroundings, and unhampered by specified feminine roles or constraints, she develops her own counterauthority to the school.

Colette is therefore not simply criticizing the Third Republic school system in her farcical portrayal of Claudine's village school. She is also creating an alternative to the rigid definitions that government school reforms offered: an alternative space and time in which her Claudine character could express her own thoughts freely. After school, during a long illness, and on school vacations, Claudine engages in activities that allow her to build her own identity. Her private English lessons with Aimée (Colette 1984a, 14–16, 26–27, 38–41), her long strolls in the Montigny woods with her friend Claire (8–9, 98, 109–10), and her days spent reading and writing alone in her father's library (113) are described in her diary as moments of significant value to her. She complains that she is bored with classroom work, often assigned to pass the time and leave her professors free to gossip and caress each other in the hallways. She claims that she attends school only to keep herself informed of (and entertained by) the latest scandal. Claudine's heavy cynicism serves as a cover for her idealized visions of a school where girls would thrive, and where teachers might actually be passionately interested in teaching and could provide strong role models for their students. Such an ideal school would include a curriculum that allowed students the freedom to read extensively and think critically, rather than simply memorize facts and test well. And probably most important for Claudine, girls would be allowed to run free; one of her greatest dreads is the idea of being enclosed or imprisoned inside the walls of a convent school or a lycée boarding school. Thus, by way of negative or dystopian examples, Colette points to a possible utopian women's space in French culture.

Like Claudine, Gabrielle Reval's heroine, Marguerite Triel, also critiques an eminent pedagogue of the Third Republic. Rather than Victor Duruy, Reval's target is the first director of the Ecole Normale Supérieure de Sèvres, the prestigious teacher training school for women, located in the suburbs of Paris. Mme Jules Favre directed the school at Sèvres for fifteen years, from its inception in 1881 until her death in 1896, and left her mark in a number of ways. A devout Protestant, she believed in intellectual liberation and freedom of movement for her female students. She allowed her Sévriennes to come and go from the school grounds as they wished, because she felt that, as adults, they were responsible for their own actions. She also held formal dinners with her students in her apartment on Wednesdays, to encourage critical thought and debate, and every evening before bed, each student came to spend a few minutes with her and discuss her progress, both moral and intellectual. Although most Sévriennes applauded Favre's efforts to liberate her students' minds, there remained a certain disagreement over her treatment of students' emotional and moral development (Margadant 88–92). In the novel *Sévriennes,* the director is named Mme Jules Ferron, a thinly disguised transformation of the last name Favre, but with an interesting "iron" (*fer*) connotation added. The fictional director has all the characteristics of the original Mme Jules Favre, and the heroine Marguerite engages in a two-part critique of the school, from both a pedagogical and a personal viewpoint. Marguerite's conclusions, however, are the opposite of those of the Claudine character. Marguerite confesses in the diary sections of the novel that she has been seeking a mentor figure at the school, but she is disappointed in her professors and the headmistress of l'Ecole Normale Supérieure de Sèvres. This is not because they are all involved in multiple love affairs with one another, as was the case at Claudine's school. On the contrary, Marguerite believes that her professors are too aloof, too cold, and generally too dispassionate in their rapport with their students, thus rendering a true mentor-disciple relationship impossible. After her first official meeting with the director, Marguerite feels that the director was "glacial" and "engulfed in her armchair, looking me over with her gray eye." She asks Marguerite a few dry questions and dismisses her after only five minutes (Reval 1900, 27).[17] Marguerite's main problem with the teacher training school at Sèvres is the fact that the women in authority do *not* take her into their arms, comfort her as a mother would a child, and guide her through difficult times. While she knows that the professors are all deeply committed to their "mission" (l'apostolat), as the teaching profession is often labeled throughout the novel, and they do provide a certain intellectual mentorship to the students, they simply do not exude any warmth, charm, or maternal qualities. This last trait Marguerite finds especially wanting in the women's community at Sèvres, but at the same time, particularly crucial to the Sévriennes' student experience.

Instead of giving them maternal support, Mme Ferron wishes to instill the values of independence and responsibility in her students. As Marguerite reports in her diary, "[she wants] to prepare us to live on our own, to

---

17. "engouffrée dans son fauteuil, me fouillant de son oeil gris. D'une voix sèche, elle s'est brièvement informée de la famille que je n'ai plus, de mon humeur, de mes projets. En cinq minutes ce fut fini; sans un mot bienveillant, me voilà congédiée" (Reval 1900, 27).

be self-sufficient, so that a failing will not stop our teaching mission" (Reval 1900, 29).[18] Ferron also insists that they are "responsible and free beings" (29). The primary advisor and tutor for the first-year students, Mlle Vormèse, confirms this approach when she states the dual goals of the school: "Learn to think, Learn to act."[19] On the methods used to achieve this end, Vormèse repeats Ferron's official ideology: "The greatest tolerance reigns at the School. You are free. A system of compression would only produce weakened individuals, without resilience, submissive from fear, incapable of acting with vigor in difficult circumstances. . . . Madame Jules Ferron has too much respect for your freedom to require spiritual advising for you. You are free, responsible for your actions."[20] In almost every passage concerning the official goals of the Sévrienne education and the values implicit in the education of young women, the words "free" (libres) and "responsible" (responsables) appear. Academically, Marguerite and the other students praise this emphasis. The women's community at Sèvres encourages students to question each other and their textbooks. They are actually required to go beyond a simple memorization of the facts for the final exams. Several scenes in the classroom, library, and residence halls indicate that the women held lively debates, not only on academic subjects, but on their professors' pedagogical methods and their own. Such academic freedom proves to be the key to Marguerite's intellectual and spiritual development throughout her years at Sèvres. Further, these values are essential ones for the young professors who would be sent alone to teach in the provinces, which were often hostile to or suspicious of the new teachers of the Republic. The personal emergence of the main characters of Reval's novel thus proceeds simultaneously with the development of new pedagogical goals for women at the postsecondary school level and a refreshingly modern view of women's capacities and rights.

---

18. "Elle veut nous préparer à vivre par nous-mêmes, à nous suffire, sans qu'une défaillance arrête notre mission de professeur. Elle veut que Sèvres nous donne cette force virile sans laquelle on s'aventure désarmé . . . nous sommes des êtres responsables et libres, nous ne devons attendre d'elle, qu'un mot d'estime ou de blâme" (Reval 1900, 29).

19. "Apprendre à penser; Apprendre à agir" (Reval 1900, 76).

20. "La tolérance la plus large règne à l'Ecole. Vous êtes libres. Un système de compression ne produirait que des êtres affaiblis, sans ressort, soumis par la crainte, incapables d'agir avec vigueur dans les circonstances difficiles . . . Madame Jules Ferron a trop le respect de votre liberté, pour souffrir qu'on vous impose une direction de conscience. Vous êtes libres de votre choix, responsables de vos actes" (Reval 1900, 78–79).

As in other novels about women's educational development, we find in *Sévriennes* the utopian label. Mlle Vormèse calls Sèvres a utopian oasis or "paradise" (Reval 1900, 77) for these young women; it is a "port" (76) they have been struggling toward for years, a "propitious refuge" (75) they will be able to recall for moral support after they depart. She recommends that they take advantage of their brief stay in this sheltered haven to prepare themselves for a future life of hardship and service. During her brief inspirational talk, Vormèse, who is named "the soul of the school" by the first-year students, indicates that Sèvres's basic pedagogical tenet is that it does not follow a single ideology. Each student will be encouraged to find her own path and develop her own system of thought. Her speech indicates clearly to the reader that the students' professional lives will form a type of quest plot. Once they leave the sanctuary of Sèvres, they will seek new experiences and reach new goals in distant provinces, using the skills, both technical and social, acquired at the school.

But Vormèse also notes that this new class of Sévriennes is much younger than her own class from several years ago. Since the school's creation ten to fifteen years earlier, the average new student has become younger (entering directly after high school) and more naïve. Although the director, Mme Ferron, does not appear to have adjusted for this change, Mlle Vormèse is aware of the girls' difficulties and encourages them to seek support in each other and with her. Her advice thus indicates a change from the official Sévrienne pedagogical guidelines of freedom and responsibility to one of community and mutual support. The women's community at Sèvres thus begins to resemble the conventional and patriarchal nuclear family, in which Vormèse takes the role of maternal nurturance and support while Ferron takes the distant and rational role of father figure. The school's unofficial pedagogy begins to evolve in the same general direction as Marguerite's developing pedagogical opinions. The official ideology of Sèvres, however, as stated by Mme Ferron, remains pointed in a direction precisely opposite to the thoughts of Marguerite.

On the nonacademic level, the new liberty and self-sufficiency can be intimidating for first-year students, especially after years of living in the restrictive world of boarding schools. Marguerite comments that she is worried about so much independence of movement and thought: some of the Sévriennes are too young and prey to frivolous behavior (Reval 1900, 38). In response to this glut of freedom, Marguerite and other new students are occasionally confused or lost. As Marguerite's friend Berthe Passy comments,

"Today I'm just as dumb as six months ago, and I'm less calm!"[21] Adrienne Chantilly, who entered Sèvres at the top of the first-year class, is given an indefinite leave of absence from the school when it is discovered that she is involved in an affair with a philosophy professor from the Collège de France (249–54). After three years at Sèvres, of course, each student will have developed her own rules of conduct, but at first they express their confusion, stray down undesirable paths, and look to others for indications of a system of values to embrace. It is through these "false starts," so typical of the classic novel of development, that the women characters begin to build their own identities, even though they never leave the safe haven of the school while conducting their explorations.

In Marguerite's case, the values she begins to embrace as essential to her new identity are maternal ones: her desire to find a mother figure in her professors uncovers a hidden set of goals in the Sévrienne education. The dominant rhetoric of independence and intellectual freedom espoused by Sèvres' leaders may camouflage this unspoken aspect of the educational mission, but even the most stoic and virile of the first-year students, Victoire Nollet, picks up the underlying message and believes that her goal as a teacher will be to shape the hearts (as well as the minds) of her students (Reval 1900, 179–80). Unstated but clearly a factor in the educational goals of Sèvres: teachers-in-training were expected to be capable of molding their future students' values and to act as "a little mother" (une petite mère) to them, in addition to increasing their knowledge of facts.

In response to this hidden agenda, Marguerite not only searches for a maternal role model at the school, she and her fellow students seek opportunities to develop their own maternal skills. In a surprising scene, Marguerite and a number of close friends race to her attic room after class to "baptize" a doll given to them by their literature professor, M. D'Aveline, because he thought that they were all working too hard. Following the baptism, they debate D'Aveline's merits and faults and, more generally, the quality of their education at Sèvres. The discussion is typical of the spirited exchanges that these intelligent women engage in every day. What is notable about the scene is the fact that the doll offered to them in jest is taken seriously and without question. Not only is it passed around for all to hold and cuddle, but Marguerite, who appears to have designated herself the primary caretaker, clothes the doll and sings a Schubert lullaby to it while the others

---

21. "Aujourd'hui je suis aussi bête qu'il y a six mois et je suis moins tranquille!" (Reval 1900, 118).

debate heatedly around her. At the close of this episode, an older student, Renée Diolat, remarks on the importance of Marguerite's quiet maternal gesture for these young women: "There's that wisdom that you were searching for so far away . . . and it's d'Aveline who has sent it to us."[22] D'Aveline's gift, meant as a joke to raise the students' spirits, simultaneously relegates the maternal or missionary values of the Sévrienne education to a level of secondary importance, since it is a toy and a prank. Nevertheless, the students find comfort and wisdom (cette sagesse) in maternal values, whether in their professors at Sèvres (Mlle Vormèse, for example) or in themselves as future schoolteachers.

In the real world outside of Sèvres, citizens and school directors do not always appreciate those values. The tragic suicide of Isabelle Marlotte after a difficult first year as a high school teacher provides the Sévriennes with an upsetting example of the complexities of adjusting to small town expectations. A superior student at Sèvres, well balanced and high-spirited, Isabelle began her new job by working foremost on her maternal qualities and quickly won the affection of her students ("I insisted on being their little mother").[23] She is immediately mistrusted by the town, labeled "a dangerous woman emancipator, a revolted woman, a nihilist" by her director, and given a public reprimand from the regional inspector (Reval 285). Unwilling and unable to accept these false accusations, a job demotion, and a miserable existence without friendship in the provinces, Isabelle decides to end her life. The importance of the official values of Sèvres, responsibility and freedom, prohibits Isabelle from seeking help from Mme Ferron or other professors with influence at the Ministry of Education. She writes to her friends who are still studying at Sèvres only when it is too late for their aid. In her farewell letter, her critique of the school's emphasis on principles and independence is mixed with a fond nostalgia for her years there.[24]

---

22. "La voilà cette sagesse que vous cherchiez si loin . . . et c'est d'Aveline qui nous l'envoie" (Reval 1900, 120).

23. "j'ai voulu être leur petite mère" (Reval 1900, 284).

24. "The School has a soul. Something binding attaches us to Sèvres. You will see, you will miss it. . . . And yet, it's just that, it's the overly ardent life, it's the habit that Sèvres forms in us too young of generalizing, of applying the logic of an ideal system to the abundance that submerges us, that makes us so unhappy. But I love it even more for being so beautiful and so dangerous." (L'Ecole avait une âme. Quelque chose d'indénouable nous attache à Sèvres. Vous le verrez, son regret vous suit. . . . Et pourtant, c'est Elle, c'est sa vie trop ardente, c'est l'habitude qu'elle nous donne trop tôt de généraliser, d'appliquer, au fourmillement qui nous engloutit, la logique d'un système idéal, qui nous rendent si malheureuses. Mais je l'aime encore plus d'être si belle et si dangereuse.) (Reval 1900, 283).

Isabelle's inability to reach a compromise with her new director or to work out a deal with the inspectors who want to relocate her is thus blamed on the idealistic training at Sèvres. Her story also offers a prime example of the contrast between men's and women's novels of educational development. In *Les Déracinés* the high school students returned to their mentor Bouteiller for encouragement and help during difficult moments in their first year in Paris, but Isabelle refuses to contact her former professors and mentors, driven by their insistence on independence and self-reliance.

Marguerite's critique and praise of the Sévrienne education point to her views for the ideal teacher training school. It would obviously include professors who had a passion for teaching and who were highly capable academics. But it would also include more professors who were interested in developing the emotional side of their students. They would act in more caring, maternal ways to better prepare their students for the isolated and difficult life of a provincial schoolteacher by emphasizing cooperation and adaptation rather than independence and competition. Her utopian vision of the schoolteacher's world also includes supervisors and townspeople who appreciate a young teacher's situation as a lonely newcomer and support her.

Reval's description of student-professor relationships thus contributes to her portrait of a school whose intellectual and emotional atmosphere is the polar opposite of the climate found in Colette's fictional school. Yet, in both novels, the authors create heroines who long for some sort of positive affective relations with their female mentors and their peers at school, in addition to someone who will challenge their intelligence. Because both Marguerite and Claudine have difficulties finding women in positions of authority whom they could emulate, they must develop their own definitions of the *femme nouvelle*.

The heroine of Louise-Marie Compain's *L'Un vers l'autre*, Laure Deborda, is unusual by comparison, as she is able to find positive role models in her school and her critique is directed at French society more generally, rather than at the French public schools. After less than a year of marriage, Laure decides to leave her comfortable bourgeois residence in order to escape a suffocating marriage with a dominating husband who does not allow her to pursue any activities outside the home. Her decision to study for a teaching degree, so that she may live as she chooses, is an act so daring that it produces panic and consternation in her conservative, middle-class family. The benefits of her education and her new career, however, outweigh the negative criticism that Laure receives both from her parents and her in-laws.

At the beginning of the novel, Compain presents us with an emerging heroine whose world is static and stifling. But in reaction to her decisions, her world is roused from its dormant state and begins to emerge along with the main protagonist.

In great contrast to Colette's and Reval's emphasis on students and student concerns, Compain spends less than one paragraph on her heroine's studies and exams. Instead of focusing on these traditional student rites of passage, the novel examines Laure's initiation into life as a teacher and her interactions with other professors and with the citizens of the town where she has been assigned a teaching post. This new location, Villebelle, is in the midst of turmoil and debate, reflecting Laure's personal situation. While Sèvres and Montigny are relatively calm towns, Villebelle's citizens, on strike at the local factory, are questioning the status quo in the same way that Laure Deborda is. Her school, while providing an oasis for Laure, does not entirely escape the general feeling of upheaval prevalent in Villebelle.

In another contrast to Claudine and Marguerite, Laure admires the women teachers at her new school for their openness and concern for students and colleagues alike. She sees in these women the utopian image of the future; the modern woman who will be considered an equal to man, not his servant or possession. And she has colleagues at the school who are positive and sympathetic role models, people whom she labels "generous" and "enthusiastic," rather than, as she had feared, "unconscious of the greatness of their task."[25] The literature professor, Mlle Charlotte Ringuet, who comes from a peasant family, holds strong beliefs about the teaching profession and the goals of the regional teacher training school where they work.[26] Mlle Germaine Lachaud, the school's headmistress, comes from a family of educators and knew early in life that her vocation would be in the field of education. Her professors had provided her with positive encouragement, and she appears to Laure to be one of what she calls the

---

25. "Elle avait trouvé en cette ville lointaine des femmes généreuses et enthousiastes de leur oeuvre; non, comme parfois elle l'avait redouté avec terreur, des êtres inconscients de la grandeur de leur tâche" (Compain 1903, 178).

26. "To give to the children of the French people devoted and enlightened guides. Shouldn't the country be regenerated by these chaste and educated young girls who would go out to the far away countryside to fight against ignorance, vice and superstition?" (Donner aux enfants du peuple français des guides dévouées et éclairées. La patrie ne devait-elle pas être régénérée par ces jeunes filles instruites et chastes qui s'en iraient, dans les campagnes éloignées, lutter contre l'ignorance, le vice et la superstition?) (Compain 1903, 187).

"new nuns" (religieuses nouvelles), women who will use education to provide a social emancipation of the people.[27] Germaine became a headmistress at age twenty-four, and seven years later, when Laure Deborda first meets her, she is still enthusiastic about her life's "mission." Although Laure had not planned on becoming a teacher as these women did, she finds encouragement and guidance from the strong role models they provide for her.

Unfortunately, Laure's utopian visions for her new vocation are undermined by the jealousies of one colleague at school, Mme Vergnier, and by her political alliances with hostile citizens of Villebelle. Vergnier disrupts the community of women that the headmistress had established in the school because she covets her position and power. After the fall of the republican ministry, she decides to launch her attack (Compain 1903, 217). Vergnier is also jealous of Laure's friendship with the headmistress, and to injure both women's reputations, Vergnier quizzes her niece, who is a student in both Laure's and the headmistress's classes (200–202). Based on her niece's reports of their lectures, Vergnier accuses the professors of atheism and internationalism, and rumors begin circulating around town that Laure and the headmistress are indulging in "a Jacobin and libertarian education" (204).

Although antipathetic, Mme Vergnier is a significant character for this education novel because she provides the important link between the isolated and utopian school for women and the public spheres of the town and of the Ministry of Education. She commences a chain of inquiry in the education department when she notifies her cousin Deriou, who notifies the *inspecteur d'académie* (the regional superintendent), who in turn notifies his superior, the *recteur* (rector), to investigate Laure's, Charlotte's, and the headmistress's teaching. She also stirs up gossip in the local paper *La France Progressiste* (whose editor is also related to her) about Laure's and the other women teachers' attendance of a meeting of socialists to support the strike of a local union of factory workers. The published article addresses the intentions of the professors, implying that they were drawing inspiration for their classes from the "declamatory diatribes" of the "atheist" socialists speaking at the rally (Compain 1903, 219). The rector, of course, can find nothing inflammatory in either the teachers' lectures or their students' compositions when he comes to inspect the classes. The newspaper article, however, is a threat not only to Laure's and the other teachers' personal reputations, but also to the "standing" of the entire school. To make amends,

---

27. "sans espoir de récompenses futures, se donnent à la grande oeuvre d'émancipation sociale par l'éducation" (Compain 1903, 189).

the rector requires that Laure and the other teachers apologize to the editor of *La France Progressiste* for having attended a political meeting during their free time, the implication being that their jobs were on the line should they refuse (230–34). It becomes clear that the teachers' liberty outside the utopian space of the school is severely limited.

The rumors spread by Mme Vergnier, along with her potent political connections, almost ruin Laure's reputation, but even worse, they force Laure and her colleagues into a position of powerlessness that proves too difficult for Laure to bear. Even though the truth about the scandal is finally revealed, Laure is devastated by the tension and humiliation of having to please the all-male juries of town authorities and regional school superintendents in order to keep her teaching position. The intrusions by male investigators into her school's sheltered women's community finally result in a recurring nightmare about male administrators physically assaulting her in her classroom, where she is rescued at the last minute by her husband (Compain 1903, 239).[28]

The novel creates two separate spheres: the tumultuous political and social world of the provincial city of Villebelle and the relatively stable educational world of the teacher training school for women. On one hand, Laure, Germaine, and Charlotte are interested in the city's political meetings and the factory workers' strike, and in a peripheral way, they become involved in the debates that are circulating around these issues. But when they do venture into the world outside their women's community, restrictions and hostilities rain down on them, invading their classrooms and their personal lives. If the regional inspector chooses to demand an explanation from the teachers, they must present a point-by-point justification of every one of their lectures for his approval. And they must deny any personal political leanings.

On the other hand, their stable school environment is, in fact, shown to be rigid, and they are powerless to make any changes in the curriculum or in the educational structures mandated by the state. Laure is disappointed to find that her classes must be closely monitored, not only because of the unannounced inspections by suspicious superintendents but also for the

---

28. In Belle Epoque history, we find that there were very few *inspectrices*, or female school inspectors, in France, so the fact that all the regional inspectors are male in both *Claudine à l'école* and *L'Un vers l'autre* is historically accurate, and not only a plot element used by the authors to create conflict for the women schoolteachers. For more on the fight to authorize *inspectrices* in the public education system, see Linda Clark's 1988 article "A Battle of the Sexes in a Professional Setting: The Introduction of *Inspectrices Primaires*, 1889–1914."

students' sake. They are required to pass exhausting exams at the end of the year and therefore cannot spend time in class discussing ideas, but rather must memorize facts and figures. Because students must learn so many facts for the brevet supérieur exams, the aspect that Laure had believed would be most challenging in teaching young girls—"the development of their minds"—is almost completely set aside. "How can we develop the originality of each individual with such a method that tends to make of each young girl's brain a drawer filled with the same knowledge imposed by the identity of the programs."[29] The curriculum requirements of the national pedagogical system thus place considerable constraints on the academic freedom that Laure and her students might have enjoyed. When Laure decides to offer a course on English literature, in addition to the required English language courses, the students are less than enthusiastic, explaining that the subject matter will not appear on the final exams and is therefore a waste of time (Compain 1903, 197). No one openly criticizes her efforts, but Laure discovers the real academic goals of her students when she overhears a conversation where one of them says of her literature course, "What's the use?" ("A quoi bon?" Compain 1903, 216). So Laure decides that she must conform her lesson plans to student needs, spending less time on ideas and more time on factual information. The narrator concludes, "Thus even in her teaching she did not find the freedom that she had dreamed of."[30] What Laure had hoped would be a liberating and intellectually stimulating career set in a quiet refuge far from the injustices of the real world reveals itself to be an imprisoning and discouraging environment where freedom of thought and action is almost as impossible as it was in her marriage.

L'Un vers l'autre thus offers an alternative perspective of the educational system: on the affective level, the main protagonist finds that her headmistress and most of her fellow teachers do provide an emotional support system for their students and each other, in contrast with Colette's and Reval's heroines. Thus the strong mentor-disciple relationship typical in the male bildungsroman is not only desired but achieved here. What is interesting with Compain is that the heroine never demonstrates feelings of disappointment with her role model, as was often the case in male novels of development. Rather than faulting the mentor, Laure Deborda

---

29. "Comment développer l'originalité de chaque nature avec une pareille méthode qui tend à faire, de chaque cerveau de jeune fille, un tiroir rempli des mêmes connaissances imposées par l'identité des programmes" (Compain 1903, 197).

30. "Ainsi, dans son enseignement même elle ne trouvait pas la liberté qu'elle avait rêvée" (Compain 1903, 216).

finds shortcomings with the institutional structures of the public education system for girls. Thus Compain's novel also diverges from the viewpoints expressed by Colette and Reval on such traditions as final exams. Whereas Colette and Reval considered exams to be an unpleasant rite of passage, but a necessary fact of student life, Compain points out in her novel that the exam-based structure of the educational system placed severe limits on the curriculum and on the students' opportunities to develop and learn. And while both Reval and Colette found that the major source of negative influences came through the administrators of the education system, Compain underlines the damaging affects that outsiders may have on the morale and the educational possibilities of the women's school. Through her critique of the system, we can understand that Compain's idealized version of the girls' school would include cooperative and supportive men: townspeople, politicians, and superintendents would be helpful and encouraging, instead of the disbelieving and petty individuals who harass the women professors in her book. She would also place a stronger emphasis on critical thought and emotional development in the women's classroom, rather than on memorizing materials for the required brevet exams.

Esther de Suze's *Institutrice* (1902) also includes a protagonist, Marie-Thérèse Romane, who begins as a stranger to the world of teaching, as did Laure Deborda. After recovering from her miserable arrival and shabby welcome, Marie-Thérèse comes to feel that the tiny alpine village school of Chavoux fulfills her dreams of isolation and devoted work (de Suze 84). In contrast to some of Claudine's wily and willful antics, the students of this village school are innocent and good-natured country folk: "The sweet little faces with round contours, the fresh good cheeks, leaned studiously over their open notebooks. I dictated slowly."[31]

In contrast to Laure Deborda in *L'Un vers l'autre,* Marie-Thérèse does not undergo any initial hostility or suspicion from the citizens of her town. On the contrary, during the first months of her stay, the curé and the villagers of Chavoux appear to love the new schoolteacher. At his speech before the annual prize distribution ceremony in July, the curé gives his praise and thanks to Marie-Thérèse for her first six months of teaching, stating that the whole town cherishes her, just as she cherishes their children and mountains (de Suze 178). Marie-Thérèse's easy integration into this new village is a stunning exception to the rule for the novel of women's education, where

---

31. "Les doux petits visages aux lignes rondes, les bonnes joues fraîches, se penchaient studieusement sur les cahiers ouverts. Je dictais lentement" (de Suze 100).

most teachers are treated as suspicious outsiders who have been imposed by the state. From de Suze's initial treatment of the townspeople in the novel, one might assume a new twist on this genre, yet her heroine's success with the general public does not last long.

Marie-Thérèse is satisfied with her activities and situation, and she is publicly applauded by her students and their parents. Yet even at the beginning of the narrative, everyone around her constantly bemoans her "lonely" and "isolated" fate. Victorou, an old woman who shows her to the mayor's house on her first day in Chavoux, tells her that schoolteachers are "too young" and "too alone" to serve as role models for younger girls, and she blames the administration for these errors (de Suze 54–55). Marie-Thérèse hears the same worries from a variety of people about her potential need for companionship and love, and the implicit dangers that those desires entail for a young, unmarried instructor. Not only Victorou, but also the mayor's maid (Phrasie), the mayor himself (M. Raibert), the curé of Chavoux (M. Broardel), and the curé of the nearby village Saint-Romain (M. Chavard) warn her, telling her tales of woe about other young schoolteachers who have been seduced, abandoned, and sent away in shame. Phrasie narrates the story of the stoning of the Gréoux schoolteacher, who "sinned" and left the village to give birth to her illegitimate child in the city of Gap (120). These pessimistic voices underline de Suze's main critique of the educational system: the women teachers are too inexperienced and are not defended properly by the Ministry of Education, whose mission they are performing, nor by the local citizens, whose children they are educating. Esther de Suze thus echoes Reval's comments on Sèvres and the lack of protection and preparation the Ministry of Education offered for young schoolteachers. De Suze's commentary is particularly grim because of the problems of isolation: unlike the other education novels studied here, *Institutrice* does not include a community of women. The elementary school children whom Marie-Thérèse teaches are too young to form part of a women's community, and the village is too small to warrant more than a single professor.

In typical bildungsroman fashion, however, the novel offers a series of encounters where Marie-Thérèse might find possible solutions to this dilemma for the single woman in the provinces. To counteract the effects of such negative warnings and sad stories about other young schoolteachers, Marie-Thérèse goes to visit her friends Monsieur and Madame Albert, a married couple who both teach in the village school of Pinet. Their life and work together conform to Marie-Thérèse's model of happiness in the education system, as they are both intelligent, they work together well, and they are full of life and joy (de Suze 94). This happy couple appears to be one type of arrangement that de Suze proposes for the disheartened teacher, and Marie-Thérèse believes that their situation is ideal: it appears to be a harmonious linkage of the quest plot and the romance plot for a woman schoolteacher. Yet Monsieur Albert complains that they will never be able to afford to have children because of their poor teaching salaries. He rages indignantly that schoolteachers, both men and women, would be wonderful parents but are not given the chance to raise their own children given the poor salaries the government offers.[32] His indignation is even greater for the unmarried woman schoolteacher, who, being well educated but extremely poor, has almost no hope at all for a good marriage and family. In the words of Albert, de Suze reiterates her open critique of the teaching career for single women professors and gives a glimpse of her idealized version of the national education system in the form of a married couple that teaches together.[33]

The author de Suze also presents us with Mlle Morin, a contented schoolteacher, even though she is isolated and unmarried, from the nearby village of St-Romain. Mlle Morin urges Marie-Thérèse to go to confession often and to become a spiritual being, since it has brought so much joy and meaning to her own life. After visiting Mlle Morin's curé, Marie-Thérèse begins to understand why Morin benefits so much from her religious faith. The curé Chavard and Mlle Morin have an extremely strong spiritual bond between them, and, contradictory to the standard stories about schoolteachers and local men, there is never a hint of sexual attraction between them. The Morin-Chavard couple is thus presented as another ideal choice for women schoolteachers, because their love is spiritual and intellectual. But the text repeats constantly that Mlle Morin and M. Chavard are two unusual and exceptional beings who have miraculously found each other

---

32. "France dreams of a regeneration. . . . Is it not in the home of the schoolteacher that the child should flourish with the most abundance? The government does not want to see that. It abandons us without an honorable remuneration. . . . If it were not for the solid faith in the beauty of our mission, which keeps our spirits high, where would we fall, in the esteem of others and our own self-esteem" (La France rêve d'une régénération. . . . N'est-ce pas au foyer de l'instituteur que l'enfant devrait fleurir avec le plus d'abondance? . . . Le gouvernement ne veut pas voir cela. Il nous abandonne sans une rétribution honorable. . . . N'était-ce la solide foi en la beauté de notre mission, qui nous maintient haut, quand même, jusqu'où ne tomberions-nous pas, dans l'estime des gens et la nôtre propre.) (de Suze 136).

33. In this, de Suze concurred with popular opinion during the late nineteenth-century. In *L'Ecole, L'Eglise, et la République, 1871–1914*, Mona Ozouf comments on this situation as evoked in both republican and conservative publications during the period: "l'accent sera mis sur la

in this world. Marie-Thérèse tries to emulate Morin's purity and religious devotion, but with a less interesting parish priest, she has less successful confessions and goes back to wandering in the beautiful alpine scenery for spiritual inspiration. These indications lead the reader to believe that the Morin-Chavard example may not provide a practical or common solution to the young woman teacher's fate either.

As her situation of isolation progresses, Marie-Thérèse writes less and less in her diary of her school tasks but more and more about her struggles to remain a passionless and pure individual. She does not reproach students who daydream in class, frequently joining in herself. As if in response to her wandering mind and soul, Sylves Moutet, the village drunk, asks her to marry him, threatening suicide if she responds negatively (de Suze 160–64). Given the fact that he is uneducated, an alcoholic, and very poor, Marie-Thérèse does not consider his request seriously, but his pleas strike a chord in her. Finally, she begins to live her seclusion in the alpine country in a negative way, as everyone had been predicting she would. A few days after the closing ceremony for the school year, the mayor, Pierre Raibert, comes to save her from Moutet, then confesses his own love for her (190–96). After platonically exchanging books and notes with her during the summer vacation, the mayor makes another confession of love to Marie-Thérèse, they are seen together, and Marie-Thérèse's reputation is immediately destroyed. The village turns against her overnight, making even the five-minute walk to the local market a frightening gauntlet to cross.

Esther de Suze's novel demonstrates most clearly the difficulties of combining the quest plot with the romance narrative in a novel about women's professional development. Marie-Thérèse's professional interests in her school are quickly undermined by the villagers' constant worries about her personal life, and in the end, these same villagers force her to leave her teaching position to find work somewhere else. The hints that de Suze proposes for possible solutions to these conflicting plotlines include married schoolteachers who could aid and comfort each other, women teachers who could support each other, and local villagers and clergy who could praise

---

situation misérable de l'institutrice. Le "ménage d'instituteurs," qui, vingt ans plus tard, sera une figure essentielle des constellations villageoises, est encore l'exception. Pour le moment, la solitude de l'institutrice, avec son dénuement matériel et moral, est donc le thème essentiel" (Ozouf 1982, 137). (The accent will be placed on the miserable situation of the woman schoolteacher. The "teaching couple," which twenty years later will be the essential figure in the village constellations, is still the exception. For the moment, the solitude of the woman schoolteacher, with her material and moral penury, is thus the essential theme.)

and encourage their young teachers. Yet de Suze's novel also stands out against the other examples of the women's education novel studied in this chapter because *Institutrice* deals the least with the curriculum requirements and educational structures for girls' schools during the time period. Her silence on this subject could perhaps be interpreted as a sign that the author found the educational goals of the national school system sufficient, which would place her in direct opposition to the three other novelists. Further, *Institutrice* is the only novel in which both the town and the school appear locked in time, eternal in their attitudes about and their goals for women and education. During her months in Chavoux, Marie-Thérèse learns a great deal about the education system and the position of the village schoolteacher, but neither the school nor the village changes or develops along with the heroine.

In spite of their different views on education for women, all four novels discussed above include an idyllic vision on the part of each heroine as to her future role in society and the part that her school and its learning environment would play in creating that future. Each utopian vision may be quite different, but the common thread that links the novels, as a genre, is that they all contain such idealized structures.

These structures are similar to Rita Felski's notion of the feminist "counter-public sphere," where author and reader share a common ground both within and in opposition to mass society. In these women's education novels, the heroine establishes a counterpublic position where she may voice her criticism of patriarchal society (the national school system, for example) while at the same time define a position for herself within that society that corresponds more closely to her own worldview. Because the subject matter, women's education, was a common historical and cultural experience for authors and readers of the Belle Epoque, we can assume that the counterpublic position that the heroines held may have been shared by author and reader.[34]

The most surprising feature of these women's education novels is the final location of the heroines' counterpublic positions within mass society, at least in the context of Belle Epoque culture. One might assume that in novels such as these, the female protagonist would find her utopian

---

34. For more on Felski's notion of a counterpublic sphere, see my 1996 article in *MLN* on Colette's *Claudine à l'école* and *La Naissance du jour*, where I explain the author's creation of a "gendered collective" that would permit transgressions while remaining a part of the mainstream culture.

counterpublic sphere within the all-female community of the girls' school, especially because the school is located within mass culture, while at the same time allowing some opportunities, however limited they might be, for opposition to and changes in mass culture. Each of the novels that I have discussed presents ways to change the position of women in French society *through education*. Furthermore, each of the novels presents idyllic moments of the female community at work: Claudine in her private lessons with Aimée; Marguerite in her study groups at the Ecole Normale Supérieure de Sèvres; Laure in her discussions with her school director, Germaine Lachaud; and Marie-Thérèse in her conversations with a fellow schoolteacher, Mlle Morin.

These women's communities, however, constitute only temporary passages for the protagonists. In the final pages of each story, the heroine ceases her critique of the education system and abruptly announces her decision to withdraw completely from the field of pedagogy. Claudine claims to have no idea what will happen to her after she has earned her brevet, even though her middle-class background leads the reader to the impression that she will probably marry in the near future. At any rate, she firmly rejects all suggestions by her teachers that she might want to continue her brilliant studies by enrolling in a teacher training school during the following year.[35] Marguerite and Laure both quit the teaching profession: Marguerite leaves even before she has been given her first teaching assignment, announcing that she wishes instead to live with and take care of her lover, the sculptor Henri Dolfière. After a fifty-page section devoted to a description of the "awakening" of Laure's husband Henri, *L'Un vers l'autre* concludes with a dramatic mountaintop reunion of the couple. Laure immediately resigns from her school and returns to her newly converted spouse and their comfortable home. She wishes to return to her role as a full-time *femme au foyer* and to devote herself to her husband's wishes. Marie-Thérèse resigns from her position in Chavoux in order to escape the false rumors about her alleged promiscuity. She moves to Marseille with the old woman Victorou, who has become a caring mother figure to her. In the final pages of her diary, she hints that she will soon be marrying a young man whom she has met in Marseille.

---

35. In *Claudine à Paris* (1901), the sequel to *Claudine à l'école*, after moving to Paris with her father, cat, and maid, Claudine is completely free of school or work obligations to wander aimlessly, looking for fun and adventure. In the final pages of the book, she does fall in love and becomes engaged to a cousin, Renaud, whom she marries in *Claudine en ménage* (1902) and then leaves in *Claudine s'en va* (1903).

The counterpublic sphere that the heroines finally choose, therefore, is very often located in the home or in the private domain. That is, the protagonists actually become reintegrated into mainstream culture, in traditional bildungsroman fashion. The utopian views of the teaching world that they had dreamed of earlier appear to be easily discarded for a rather traditional solution: get married and live happily ever after. As a subgenre of the classic eighteenth-century bildungsroman, this type of conventional reintegration into society is not unusual. But as Felski has argued, the conclusion of the feminist bildungsroman does not necessarily imply a conservative return to patriarchal society. She states: "The feminist text, however, reveals a rather different trajectory; the journey into society does not signify a surrender of ideals and a recognition of limitations, but rather constitutes the precondition for oppositional activity and engagement" (Felski 137). If we understand the goals of the protagonist's education to be better self-awareness and heightened critical reasoning, rather than a form of job training, then the flight from academia is often a final proof of the successful influence that the education has had on its pupils. The years of study or teaching have provided each of the heroines with the "precondition for oppositional activity" that Felski claims, that is, they have learned the valuable skills in critical assessment and independent thinking that they did not have before they entered the school or the teaching profession. By selecting an alternative to the highly structured, repressive, and uniform tracking of the state-regulated education system, all of our heroines have in some way demonstrated their independence and their ability to opt out of a system that they did not wish to endure. Similar to Michel's decision in *L'Immoraliste* to quit the teaching profession, these women leave the educational system because they find it stifling. And although they may be choosing marriage or cohabitation in a patriarchal setting, the partners that they choose (or return to) must understand and encourage their intellectual independence and their freedom to act on their own.

Their final choices may appear to be conservative ones, and it must be admitted that the authors of these works did portray the Belle Epoque women's educational experience in a negative light: their female protagonists rejected the schools and their patriarchal structures. But their criticism of the school system was by no means a call for the cancellation of public schooling for girls in France. Their ultimate message is clear: an educated heroine may be more skeptical, more critical, but she is also, in the end, happier and freer than her uneducated counterparts. The public school system thus acts as a sort of rite of passage for these young women characters who will leave behind their educational experiences, having come to terms with their own identity and having situated themselves within French society as free, adult members of that culture. As such, these works not only continue the tradition of the male novel of development in French culture, they also provide us a new model for women characters within that literary tradition.

4

CERVELINES: WOMEN SCIENTISTS IN NOVELS OF PROFESSIONAL DEVELOPMENT

ON APRIL 12, 1898, PROFESSOR Gabriel Lippmann made a report to the Académie des Sciences de Paris about a discovery made by one of his former students: the radioactivity of certain minerals and two new chemical elements, which would later be called polonium and radium. He was announcing to the scientific world the initial results of Marie Curie's doctoral thesis. Five years later, the entire world would learn of her work when she was awarded the Nobel Prize in Physics, jointly with her husband, Pierre, and Henri Becquerel.

Marie Curie was the first woman to win the Nobel Prize in Physics, and her appearance at the forefront of scientific news became a cause for much interest in her unusual marriage and professional pursuits. Reporters and photographers flooded the Curies' home and small laboratory, along with letters, poems, and invitations to speak all over the world (Curie 224–33). Even though the Curies found all the sudden notoriety a waste of time and an annoying distraction from their experiments, Madame Curie's overbooked but balanced life as wife, mother, scientist, and teacher at the Ecole Normale Supérieure de Sèvres provoked wild curiosity and speculation in the French press (Curie 224–25). In the same year, one of the first professionalization novels focusing on the life of a woman scientist, titled *Les Cervelines,* was published.

This new genre of scientific novel brought with it the appearance of a corresponding type of intelligent female character, the *cerveline,* based on the title of Yver's first novel, translated into English as *The Brainy Women.*[1] There are three "brainy" female protagonists in that specific novel, but this character type is prevalent in several other works by Yver (*Princesses de*

---

1. Waelti-Walters gives this translation of the title in *Feminist Novelists of the Belle Epoque: Love As a Lifestyle,* p. 15.

science, 1907; *Dames du palais,* 1909), Gabrielle Reval (*La Bachelière,* 1910), and Marcelle Babin (*Pharmacienne,* 1907), among others. The hubbub that surrounded Marie Curie after she was awarded the Nobel Prize might have instigated the interest in scientific female protagonists, yet the life of the eminent scientist and the lives of these fictional women are not identical.[2] Similar to Marie Curie, the typical brainy protagonist is usually well educated and from a middle-class family in which the mother is a traditional housewife and the father is a successful professional. In contrast to Mme Curie, however, the brainy woman character is very often an only child and, frequently, she chooses to pursue her father's career, thus carrying on a family tradition in a particular profession. These character traits tend to subdue the potentially rebellious or bizarre qualities of the brainy woman: rather than portraying her as a strident bluestocking or humorless bookworm, the narrator understands her as a dutiful child, absorbed by her work and by the need to perpetuate her father's fame and fortune.

It is important to emphasize that the brainy woman character, although perhaps inspired by contemporary historical figures, is also a fictional construction based in bourgeois ideals of women and power. The novel of professional development devoted to women scientists follows the structures of the traditional bildungsroman more closely than it does the life story of Marie Curie or Doctor Blanche Edwards-Pilliet or other living women scientists from the time period.[3] The historical situation surrounding the rise to popularity of these novels remains quite important, yet the fictional protagonists' choices and the narratives' structures that the authors employed indicate deviations from the historical woman scientist of the Belle Epoque.

Comparing the lives of the exceptional women characters who populate novels of scientifc development with those of historical woman scientists will highlight some of the mainstays of the traditional bildungsroman plot in

---

2. It should also be noted that simply because a book was published in a certain year does not necessarily mean that it was written in that year. I am not arguing that Yver wrote *Les Cervelines* as a direct response to Marie Curie's fame, but that women scientists in general were of great interest to the French public and the creation of fictional women scientists around the same time period should not be a surprise.

3. Although not as well known today, Dr. Blanche Edwards-Pilliet was a pioneer during the Belle Epoque, similar to Marie Curie. She and her medical school classmate Augusta Klumpke were the first women named as *internes* in the Paris hospitals in the late 1880s, an important step toward advancing women's status in the medical profession. Edwards-Pilliet became an activist for women's rights in the first decade of the twentieth century, particularly for mothers and children's rights. Also from the Belle Epoque period is Dr. Madeleine Pelletier, who became well known for her feminist lectures and activities in addition for her work in the medical field.

these novels, for example, the search for a positive role model or mentor, the false starts and detours the young protagonist must endure, and the eventual reintegration into familial and societal structures. In addition, it will show us one of the defining characteristics of these novels about women scientists: the complex intermingling of the quest and romance plots. Although the romance narrative hovers over some of the novels about women students and teachers discussed in Chapter 3, the two plotlines are in direct conflict with one another in this new category of novel, and the protagonists find unusual and creative ways to reconcile them. As such, these novels about women in the sciences constitute some of the most polemic texts from this time period and provide us with some of the strongest examples of a new narrative form for the Belle Epoque novel.

The notion of women participating in scientific fields was highly suspect among the conservative French bourgeoisie during the Belle Epoque, but for different reasons than those concerning women schoolteachers. The church and the bourgeoisie opposed state-educated professors because they posed a potential threat to the securely established teachers and curriculum of the Catholic Church's convent schools. Women scientists, doctors, and researchers, however, posed new kinds of problems for the conservative bourgeois. Unlike public schoolteachers, women scientists were not replacing nuns in previously established positions for women. Rather, they were asserting themselves in all-male fields, and their appearance implied a major challenge to masculine domination. This challenge was especially devastating to male scientists, since one of the principle changes in the medical and scientific professions during the nineteenth century in France was the increase in power, prestige, and authority that scientists and doctors gained in the eyes of the French public. Men who worked in those fields thus had much more to lose when women began to enter "their" professional schools, "their" libraries, "their" laboratories and hospitals.

In two histories of the scientific and medical professions in France, both Toby Gelfand and Michel Foucault stress the tremendous increase in authority and power for doctors during the nineteenth century. Gelfand's 1980 analysis, *Professionalizing Modern Medicine,* underlines the transfer of power from the patient to the doctor and thus confirms certain aspects of Michel Foucault's 1962 work on the beginnings of the clinic in France. Gelfand and Foucault both claim that when the medical profession began to emphasize the importance of practical training for medical students and scientific researchers, it began simultaneously to treat its clinic patients as objects of study rather than as clients and employers. The patient who was admitted to a clinic because of his or her disease became a medical example for the student interns. The patients lost their power over the doctors and researchers, who used them objectively for their experiments. This new attitude dramatically altered the relationship between patients and doctors as well as between doctors and diseases.

The historical empowerment of practitioners and administrators in the medical field during the nineteenth century is reflected fictionally in certain aspects of the women protagonists' lives and specifically in the important shift in the relationship between patient and doctor. Descriptions in three scientific novels demonstrate patients' respect for and dependence on the women doctors' scientific knowledge and their ability to cure. In contrast to the patients' respect, in two of Yver's works, *Les Cervelines* (1903) and *Princesses de science* (1907), the women scientists treat their clinic patients as objects of study rather than as human subjects, as they seek to discover and cure diseases.[4] Their lack of interest in the people whose bodies they are studying appears shocking to some of their colleagues, although this was common practice in the medical profession by 1900. The surprise comes from the fact that women, traditionally the object of the male gaze in bourgeois culture, were now the observers. Both male and female characters in these novels, along with the narrators' subtle interventions, try to turn the tables on the cerveline-observers and reconfine them to the passive object of the male gaze. In Babin's work, *Pharmacienne* (1907), we find an overt return to conventional roles, when the woman medical student is treated as an object of study by one of her supervising professors. The institution's reaction to this male doctor's "experiment" is shock and disgust, since he has broken professional codes of respect toward a future colleague as he performs his tests on his unsuspecting student. All of the scientific brainy women come into conflicts with colleagues, clients, supervisors, publishers, and professors, who still see women as confined to roles of service, care of, and dependence on others. Both in these fictional narratives and in the historical Belle Epoque, bourgeois women were generally raised to believe that they should not seek such attributes as power, domination, and authority.

---

4. There are several examination scenes in each of these novels in which the doctors do not mention the human being before them, only the symptoms of the disease. See, for example, Colette Yver, *Les Cervelines* (Paris: Juven, 1903), pp. 51–57, and *Princesses de science* (Paris: Calmann-Lévy, 1907), pp. 58–61.

Thus the new control and prestige of the medical professional over the client would necessarily rule out the legitimate possibility of women doctors or scientists.[5]

A further trait that all brainy women characters specifically hold in common with historical women scientists is their obsession with their work. The protagonists are all intelligent, well-educated women. But the quality that places them in the special category of "brainy women" is their fascination with their studies. Whether in the field of scientific inquiry, legal studies, history, literature, or archeology, the women are driven by their desire to learn, discover, and create. They are overachievers who know only work. Leisure time is almost unheard of for these women, and their happiest, most peaceful, and inspired moments are spent at their desks or in their laboratories. But these brainy women deal with the distractions of love, home, and family in ways that are very different from historical women, such as Marie Curie. Their treatment of these topics moves us directly into the realm of fiction and into the opposing traditions of the romance and the quest plot.

The narrative structures of these particular novels of development offer the most complex interconnections of the romance and quest plots of any of the novels considered in this study. The sizable presence of the romance plot often diverts the reader's attention from the importance of the quest in these texts, and it can minimize the complicated nature of the narratives that weave together these two plot types. The original definitions of the novel of development focused on male protagonists because the main features of the story include the quest: a young person leaves behind family and friends in order to discover himself, experience new adventures, then return home as a more mature individual ready to reintegrate with society. Elements often found in the quest narrative include the older mentor figure who will act as a guide, the trials or tests of intelligence and strength that will be offered to the young protagonist, and, finally, the triumphant return home, with a reward of some kind, such as marriage. In contrast, the traditional romance plot usually focuses on a young woman and the various moments of doubt, suspicion, and final revelation that occur during her courtship and marriage. Studies of the romance generally claim that the heroine must go from

---

5. Marie Curie's timidity and general disgust with the public's gushing admiration of her discoveries fit well with this notion that women should not aggressively seek power and prestige. In her biography, Eve Curie explains that Pierre Curie shunned public recognition because of a principle to abhor all hierarchies, while Marie Curie fled the spotlight due to an instinctual fear of strangers' attentions (Curie 230).

isolation, often a state as motherless orphan, to a state of connection, usually with a caring and attentive fiancé or husband.[6] Within the specific context of the Belle Epoque, Diana Holmes's definition of the romance narrative includes three parts: it must be "driven and structured by romantic love"; the style usually varies "between realism and melodrama"; and in terms of theme, it must not only include a discussion of romantic love as a woman's "destiny," but also provide an "arena to explore female identity and desire" (Holmes 2006, 199–200).[7]

The main goal in both quest and romance narratives is the same: young men and women must mature and become adults. And the traditional conclusion is often similar: marriage. Yet the protagonist of the quest may choose a number of different paths toward becoming an adult, whereas the romance heroine has only one method of gaining maturity: find a man and marry him.

Although these novels about women scientists may include some of the basic settings or plot elements of the traditional romance narrative, the protagonists themselves are notable for their lack of almost every quality deemed "necessary" for the popular romantic heroine. The typical romance characters include a young and rather naïve woman and an older, more experienced man, who may at first appear derisive or harsh.[8] The brainy women in Belle Epoque novels are young (from eighteen to thirty-five years old) and sometimes inexperienced interns or students, yet they are not confused or innocent creatures. For example, in Yver's 1907 *Princesses de science,* the "doctoresse" Lancelevée states that women doctors' knowledge of science has stripped away the mysteries and dreams that most women grow up with. They are left "dried up; we have seen everything, heard everything, known everything. We are neither nervous nor sensitive nor modest

---

6. Janice Radway's *Reading the Romance,* although written with the 1980s American woman reader in mind, has influenced my own definitions and analysis of the romance plot in this study. Linda K. Christian-Smith's *Becoming a Woman Through Romance* also offers an excellent general view of the ideology inherent in Romance literature. For a more general study of the transformations in the ideology of love in literature and the arts during the turn of the century in Europe, see Stephen Kern's *The Culture of Love: Victorians to Moderns.*

7. Jennifer Milligan offers a lucid analysis of the Romance novel in chapter 5 of *The Forgotten Generation,* particularly with regard to the interwar period of French women's literature (1919–39). She also discusses the growth and development of the romance novel more generally in France, beginning with its "revival" in the 1880s (Milligan 149) and its revisions through the mid-twentieth century.

8. I have derived this simple outline of the romance heroine from Tania Modleski's outline of Harlequin Romances in *Loving with a Vengeance: Mass-Produced Fantasies for Women.* She in turn bases her definitions on the "mother" of popular romances for women, Richardson's *Pamela.*

nor impressionable."⁹ Her description of the female doctor as heartless, senseless, and genderless ("the woman doctor is not a woman" [la femme-médecin n'est pas une femme]) indicates her attachment to male standards of professionalization in the medical field and her rejection of female standards of emotionality and vulnerability. The brainy woman could definitely not be categorized as "naïve."

The male characters in these novels do not fit the typical romance mold either; they are never scornful or unkind and only occasionally express cynicism, usually due to a previous disappointment with another brainy woman. Rather than an older man with more experience or wealth, the male protagonists are generally the same age as the brainy woman and most often a colleague or fellow student at professional school. On the rare occasion where we do find an older, wealthier man, the results are usually catastrophic. For example, when Dr. Paul Tisserel, in *Les Cervelines,* tries to seduce his young intern, Jeanne Boerk, the traditional romance roles are reversed: he is confused and desperate, she is brutal and cynical. In the end, she flees the hospital and escapes from his love and attention, thus upsetting the classic "happily ever after" ending of the romance plot. One of the mainstays of the classic romance plot, the image of the obsessive male character, does resurface regularly in these texts.¹⁰ The conventional plot and protagonists, however, are most often distorted to fit the women scientists' quest narrative, and it is the nontraditional characters in these texts who overturn the typical romance narrative.

The quest narrative, which includes the conventionally "masculine" elements of competition and ambition, also arises in these novels of professional development, and it is ususally twisted to conform to the demands of the unusual brainy woman protagonist. Although some of the heroines deny that they harbor the typical quest plot desires for fame and success, most eventually decide to work, and they choose their particular profession based on self-interested concerns, such as personal aptitude and preference for a certain field. After becoming involved in their profession, most of the

---

9. "comme desséchées; et nous avons tout vu, tout entendu, tout connu. Nous ne sommes plus ni nerveuses, ni sensibles, ni pudiques, ni impressionables" (Yver 1907, 213).

10. As Tania Modleski comments, this male obsession with the female protagonist is characteristic of romance novels in general: "Here is a very potent feminine fantasy, common to most nineteenth-century novels and to their twentieth-century counterparts. The man, whether he is plotting the woman's seduction or, as in soap operas, endlessly discussing his marital woes with his coworkers at the hospital, spends all his time thinking about the woman. Even when he appears most indifferent to her, as he frequently does in Harlequin Romances, we can be sure he will eventually tell her how much the thought of her has obsessed him" (Modleski 16).

protagonists continue to work because they are fascinated by their career and because they take pleasure in their achievements and the public acknowledgment of their efforts, thus following typical quest plot requirements.

Although most scientific women protagonists of Belle Epoque novels chose their careers because of family tradition and the power and prestige that they bring, some pursue a particular career for its humanitarian appeal, similar to teaching characters who claimed they had a mission to change society through the education of its girls. Women teachers in education novels often expressed satisfaction with their profession because of its contributions to their vision of an improved society. A few scientific protagonists, such as Babin's pharmacist, express larger goals of improving their patients' lives, but most brainy women protagonists are motivated to practice their skills because they enjoy the personal rewards involved, including renown in the field.

Despite this drive for knowledge, power, and success, the conventional quest is sometimes discarded entirely in these texts so that the main protagonist may resume or complete the romance narrative. If the quest plot is indeed carried through to the end of the novel, often the brainy woman must avoid many obstacles and pitfalls in order to reach her goal. These impediments include sexual harassment by peers or supervisors at school, discrimination on the job from clients or supervisors, and limited access to opportunities for advancement. Barriers such as these not only reflected attitudes about the *femme nouvelle* in the traditionally male liberal professions during this time period, they were also intriguing narrative devices, employed to accentuate the unusual nature of these heroines.

Within the general category of *cerveline* (brainy woman), there are two types. First, there are the women who are so completely wrapped up in their work that men, romance, marriage, and children are not a determinant in their lives. These brainy women dismiss conventional femininity and embrace the sanctioned masculine role entirely. They may take on masculine codes of behavior for their professional roles, but they still practice feminine virtue, that is, sexual purity. The characters are pure brain, with no corporeal lust or amorous passion to distract them. Novels containing this type of "absolute" or "pure" brainy woman also develop the strongest distortions in their romance narratives, mainly because the plotlines must be altered to conform to the brainy woman's desire to work rather than to love, nurture, or mother.

Second, there are brainy women who, having been awakened or distracted from their intense focus on work by the introduction of a possible romance, marriage, and even family, are "seduced," not so much by the man, but by the idea of fulfilling traditional feminine roles at the same time as the masculine ones. These characters always fall into the difficult position of trying to maintain both roles simultaneously. In order for them to juggle intellectual, sexual, maternal, and domestic demands, they often rearrange the public and private spheres of their lives.[11] In these professionalization novels, the romance plot adheres more closely to the general definition given above, even though alterations must often be made to include the work of the brainy woman. The quest plot, however, is often diverted or rewritten to make room for the brainy woman's marriage, children, and home. In my discussion, I will focus on the distinctions between these two types of brainy women, the "pure" and the "seduced." This division will demonstrate the ways in which the character and plot development are quite different for each type and, even within a specific type, the enormous variety of possible actions for the heroine.

The Pure Cervelines

One of the most extreme brainy women in this group of scientific protagonists comes from the first novel Yver wrote for an adult audience, *Les Cervelines*.[12] Her name is Jeanne Boerk, and she is the only female medical intern and student of pathology at the municipal hospital of the city of Briois. As the novel opens, Jeanne appears completely fulfilled by her profession and her ambitions for her career. An exception even to the exceptional brainy woman type, Jeanne comes from a peasant background and her reasons for pursuing medicine are not tied to bourgeois family traditions. The reader learns in passing that a village schoolteacher in

---

11. Biographies of Marie Curie include several pages devoted to descriptions of her arrangement of domestic space to transform it into an office. Eve Curie, for example, describes their living room-office "with its bare walls, furnished with books and a white wooden table. At one end of the table was Marie's chair; at the other, Pierre's. On the table were treatises on physics, a petroleum lamp, a bunch of flowers; and that was all" (Curie 150–51). The fictional women characters, in contrast, who are trying to "have it all" could be considered a turn-of-the-century prototype for the "supermom" phenomenon of the late twentieth century, when many women of the middle class tried, with varying degrees of success and failure, joy and frustration, to balance the competing demands of raising children, pursuing a career, entertaining, and keeping house.

12. For a brief plot summary of this novel, see Appendix 2. Waelti-Walters notes, "At seventeen, [Yver] published a successful book for children entitled *Mlle Devoir* and several more between 1891 and 1900" (Waelti-Walters 188). *Les Cervelines* appeared several years later, in 1903, when Yver was twenty-nine years old.

Landrecies had discovered Jeanne's intelligence, and that "until the age of thirteen she had been only the daughter of farmers."[13] Throughout the text, the narrator repeats several times that she is a "very healthy countrywoman" (campagnarde très saine; Yver 1903, 2) and a "daughter of the people" (fille du peuple; 59). Yver describes her personality as "a mix of knowledge and rusticity; rural backwardness hovered over her intelligence."[14] Not surprisingly, Jeanne is portrayed as one of the most driven characters, and she behaves more professionally and follows masculine professional guidelines more strictly than any of her bourgeois or urbane male colleagues and supervisors. She seeks knowledge at the expense of all emotional ties and believes that duty and service to the profession come before personal desires. Jeanne Boerk is thus a clear example of the status socialization that occurred in the male professional schools of the period.[15] She is also exceptional because, at age twenty-two, she diagnoses patients more rapidly and more accurately than her supervisor Dr. Paul Tisserel, as he readily admits to his colleague Jean Cécile. He explains to Jean that he had believed that she was copying her observations from a manual but then discovered that she was the manual (3). According to Tisserel, Jeanne is on the verge of surpassing LeHêtre, the general director of the entire hospital, in her powers of diagnosis. Thus her need for a mentor, usually an important part of the traditional novel of development, appears to be less important for Jeanne. Like most brainy women, she works hard and devotes every minute of her day to research, yet the narrator describes her accomplishments as the result of some inexplicable medical genius that she possesses. It is probably this characteristic that sets Jeanne Boerk apart from the other scientific women protagonists, and it provides the reader with a plausible explanation for her ascent from a simple country girl to a phenomenal pathologist.[16]

Her modest background and strong scientific genius also account for the reason that Jeanne, unlike most other Yver heroines, is never tempted by love or by a maternal instinct for her sick patients. Jeanne has developed

---

13. "elle n'avait été, jusqu'à treize ans, qu'une fille de fermiers" (Yver 1903, 106).
14. "un mélange de savoir et de rusticité; la niaiserie campagnarde ... affleurait au-dessus de l'intelligence" (Yver 1903, 55).
15. For more on status socialization, see Chapter 1 in this work.
16. In *Writing Beyond the Ending,* Rachel Blau Duplessis, when discussing the portrayal of the woman artist as "genius" in fiction, indicates the dual implications for women: "Making a female character be a 'woman of genius' sets in motion not only conventional notions of womanhood but also conventional romantic notions of the genius, the person apart, who, because unique and gifted, could be released from social ties and expectations" (Duplessis 84–85). While Yver portrays Jeanne

the same encouraging bedside manner that her more experienced male colleagues employ. And like her colleagues, nurturance is for her merely a professional duty. She explores and analyzes, focusing on the disease rather than the invalid. Her relationship with her patients corresponds directly to the modern version of power relations between doctor and patient, where the doctor retains most of the power and knowledge and the patient is no longer the employer but the object of study. Jeanne has learned this attitude from her supervisors at the hospital. The narrator indicates that Dr. Tisserel's female patients are in awe of him and that these women have developed a loving feeling of submission to their "healer" (Yver 1903, 51). One patient's belief in Dr. Tisserel's abilities to cure her is pushed to a type of cult worship: "he was for her the all-powerful healer and the all-mighty kindness."[17]

In contrast, the doctors generally see their patients in impersonal terms, discussing them as objects of study rather than individuals. During rounds one day, the Drs. Tisserel and Cécile, along with Jeanne Boerk, join in this type of discourse about their patients: "'By the way,' cried Cécile suddenly, 'you haven't shown me your meningitis case that I came to see.' 'Too late, my dear,' said Tisserel with the gesture of a collector who is missing his most rare bibelot just when he wanted to show it; 'she died last night.'"[18] The patient is referred to first as a form of disease for Dr. Cécile to look at, a "méningitique," then as a curiosity for Dr. Tisserel, his "bibelot." But she is never named and no sorrow is indicated in either doctor's tone of voice when it is revealed that she died during the night. Their only regret is that Dr. Cécile did not have the chance to examine her disease before her death.

Jeanne Boerk also uses impersonal discourse when discussing an examination performed by a new student. Jeanne refers to the patient as "un sujet" (a subject) and "un exemple" (an example). Her comments obviously have nothing to do with the individual's health at all and are completely centered on the disease and its symptoms. Tisserel follows up her comments in an equally impersonal tone, as he praises her professional behavior as well

---

as a genius of science rather than art, her status in the medical community will exempt her from the typical demands made of women in the bourgeoisie.

17. "Il était pour elle le tout-puissant guérisseur et la toute bonté" (Yver 1903, 51).

18. "A propos, s'écria Cécile, soudain, tu ne m'as pas montré ta méningitique que je venais voir.— Trop tard, mon cher, dit Tisserel avec le geste d'un collectionneur auquel vient à manquer son bibelot le plus rare à l'heure même qu'il voulait le montrer; elle est morte cette nuit" (Yver 1903, 57).

as her diagnostic skills: "'I have rarely seen such a beautiful auscultation; I must admit that Mademoiselle Boerk is the one who revealed it to me. She diagnosed perfectly all there is there.'"[19] His phrase "all there is there" indicates that the only thing he sees before him is the disease, not the living human being. His praise of Jeanne's abilities is based in part on the fact that she concentrates solely on the illness rather than the patient.

Jeanne thus excels in her profession, as she has mastered both the required skills and the required demeanor for the scientific researcher. But because Jeanne considers her power so seriously, some of her male colleagues perceive her professional attitude in a negative light. An illuminating example of their repulsion arises when she begins to boast that she never faints at the sight of blood and has a strong stomach, demonstrated by the fact that she never felt ill during the dissection of a corpse, even during the examination of a young girl's body seven days after death. Paul Tisserel and Jean Cécile, her supervisors, are both surprised, given the fact that they had both felt faint during their first dissections. Here, Jeanne's adherence to professional standards of impartiality goes too far. Her amorous director, Tisserel, joins in Jeanne's boasting, however, reminding her that she "used" the little girl for twelve days, not a week. ("Twelve days, you used the little girl with the phlegmon twelve days.")[20] Tisserel's words—"vous vous êtes servie de la fillette" (you used the little girl)—are more perverse, and perhaps more upsetting, than Jeanne's discreet claim. But Dr. Cécile remains horrified only by Jeanne's confession, specifically because it originates from the mouth of a beautiful twenty-two-year-old woman and serves to demonstrate her lack of traditionally feminine emotional sensitivity. According to Dr. Cécile, who is the inventor of the term *cerveline,* Jeanne is a perfect illustration: all brain and no heart, feminine in appearance, but inwardly inhuman.

Indeed, underlying Jeanne's conventionally feminine exterior (blond hair, bright eyes, curvaceous body), the narrator notes, there exists an extremely inquisitive mind, whose mission is to find cures to the diseases, mainly tuberculosis and diphtheria, that kill off all of her patients one by one. She does not perceive her work in the hospital or the laboratory as a burden, but rather as an intellectual diversion, even an amusement ("Elle *s'amusait* à l'extrême d'être médecin"; Yver 1903, 67). The narrator's words frequently support Jeanne's love for science and are meant to inspire awe in

---

19. "J'ai rarement vu d'auscultation aussi belle; c'est mademoiselle Boerk qui me l'a découverte, je dois l'avouer. Elle a parfaitement diagnostiqué tout ce qu'il y a là" (Yver 1903, 56).

20. "Douze jours; vous vous êtes servie de la fillette au phlegmon, douze jours" (Yver 1903, 53).

the reader, as in the following passage describing her examination of Paul Tisserel's sister Henriette: "Her force and her authority radiated now; she was no longer the country girl nor the boyish and rough student nor the uncouth girl that one loves in vain nor the exceptional woman whose eyes have seen all human misery; she was Science."[21] The narrator advocates Jeanne's love of her work and does not reflect negatively on her quick dismissal of obstacles that lie in her way. Jeanne therefore deviates from the typical bildungsroman protagonist, who often makes mistakes and errs down misleading paths while discovering his true calling in life. Jeanne never strays from her goals and always seems to know exactly what she wants from life.

And Jeanne does confront obstacles, almost on a daily basis, at her workplace. When her classmates taunt her with practical jokes and derisive humor, she ignores them, professing to be completely unmoved by their foolish behavior. On the rare occasion when she allows her emotions to surface, it is in private, away from the jeering faces of her peers. In public, she maintains a cool and collected expression, which sometimes only incites her male peers to further insults. For such a pure brainy woman, it is important to preserve a distinct barrier between her professional activities and her private emotions, never mixing the two.

The strict divisions between her professional and personal life are obvious when she deals with her supervisor's attempted courtship. Tisserel fails to win her heart after several desperate requests and humiliating actions in the public sphere of the hospital. Jeanne refuses his offer of love for a number of reasons. She is concerned with her reputation as an unmarried woman, which of course must remain irreproachable for her to continue her studies and establish a medical practice. She also refuses him because his position, as a simple provincial doctor and her intellectual inferior, would embarrass her. She confesses this feeling to a friend and fellow brainy woman Marceline (Yver 1903, 68). A marriage to Tisserel would also be an obstacle to her career, since she would not to be able to continue her studies in Paris under the guidance of more advanced pathologists if she settled down in Briois. Marceline agrees with Jeanne's reasoning and understands that Jeanne is on a different mission than that of the typical bourgeois woman of the time period (175, 179).

---

21. "Sa force et son autorité rayonnaient maintenant; elle n'était plus ni la campagnarde, ni l'étudiante garçonnière et fruste, ni la fille rude qu'on aime en vain, ni la femme d'exception de qui les yeux ont tout vu de la misère humaine; elle était la Science" (Yver 1903, 109).

Although Marceline Rhonans does not pursue a scientific career in *Les Cervelines,* she still may retain a place in the same category of pure brainy women. As a history professor in the prestigious girls' high school in the city of Briois, Marceline has a career in teaching. But the school and her work there are mentioned only in passing in the novel, with references here and there to grading or class preparation. In contrast to many education novels, there are no classroom scenes and there are no encounters with her students or teaching colleagues throughout the entire text. A women's community is not developed at the girls' high school. Instead, Marceline is portrayed as a pioneer in her field, and she finds support and encouragement with Jeanne Boerk, a fellow pioneer. Their friendship may be "without tenderness," as the narrator describes it, but it serves as a strong and equal association that helps them to survive difficult experiences in their work, similar to certain women's relationships that we find in educational institutions. Instead of the educational sphere, however, the narrative focuses mainly on Marceline's two extracurricular interests: first, the public lectures she gives every week on the history of the costume, mainly ancient Greek and Roman dress, and second, her research for her book manuscript, a monumental history of antiquity, combining archeological and historical studies. She thus has an extremely busy schedule and a varied set of occupations that fall outside of the standard teaching, grading, and lesson planning that occupy most teaching heroines. Marceline is a complex protagonist because her dreams for the future do not include marriage or even a long life of service as a schoolteacher, as she states clearly to her close friend, Jeanne. Yet she does not engage in the more power-conscious activities of the typical scientific heroine. She does not share Jeanne's ambitious dreams of working in a prestigious Parisian institution or of advancing to the top of her field. Rather, Marceline's aims are more closely molded to fit her particular research interests in history: "'My dear, ten more years and I will be almost rich and at the same time armed for the definitive studies that I plan to do. Then I will resign and I will travel. It is on site, on the same ground where they passed, that I will get to know well those nations that interest me, the Phoenician nation especially.' There was in her enthusiasm something sacred that Jeanne's indifference profaned, and her vision ended secretly."[22]

22. "'Ma chérie, encore une dizaine d'années et je serai presque riche et en même temps armée à point pour les définitives études que j'entends faire. Alors, je démissionnerai et je voyagerai. C'est sur place, sur la terre même où elles ont passé, que je connaîtrai bien ces nations qui m'intéressent, la phénicienne surtout.' Il y avait dans son enthousiasme quelque chose de sacré que profanait l'indifférence de [Jeanne], et sa vision s'acheva secrètement" (Yver 1903, 72).

Marceline's long-term goals include independent travel and research, not service to the community or teaching, and she already foresees her future resignation from the high school, not for marriage, but when she has earned enough money for her research trip. Her interests and efforts are focused on the distant lives of the Phoenicians, not a contemporary social problem or the young girls whom she is teaching and mentoring. Yet the narrator supports Marceline's unusual dreams, claiming a certain "sacred" quality in her enthusiasm. Her future life of research and discovery is described as a potentially prosperous and happy one: "Her existence seemed luminous, full and rich, like a beautiful river that offered itself up to her. All she wished for was waiting for her in the future. Her current life, made of success, kindnesses, cerebral pleasures, contented her already. She was young, admired, independent; she was surrounded closely by friendships."[23] In fact, Marceline appears to have achieved a perfect balance in her life at the young age of twenty-eight, filled with intellectual rewards and friendship. The problem of power relations never arises in her professional world, as it does in the medical profession, since her position as an independent researcher allows her to avoid a complicated hierarchical administration. The few colleagues with whom she has regular contact are not the bitter or juvenile medical students whom Jeanne combats, but other women teachers at school and certain scholars in her field with whom she maintains some correspondence. During her daily routine, Marceline appears to sail through her obligations without any personality conflicts or struggles for power. During her evening lectures, she takes complete control of her audience, entrancing them with her fluid lecture style and stunning examples of costumes. She happily balances domestic and teaching duties, and she manages to allot some time to work on her major research project as well. Thus she appears to be another exceptional bildungsroman protagonist with clear goals and a direct path ahead of her.

In order to explain Marceline's success, Yver focuses on her work habits and the fact that Marceline combines her intellectual and domestic activities. In a typical rearrangement of domestic space, one of Marceline's most important rooms in her home is her study. Its utilitarian aspects are underlined in the paragraph describing it, where Marceline is described as a sort

23. "Son existence apparaissait lumineuse, pleine et féconde, comme un beau fleuve qui devant elle se serait offert. Tout ce qu'elle souhaitait l'attendait dans le futur. Sa vie actuelle, faite de succès, de sympathies, de jouissances cérébrales, la contentait déjà. Elle était jeune, admirée, indépendante; elle était entourée de très près d'amitiés" (Yver 1903, 73–74).

of "little man" in her "cold sanctuary of science." The The narrator uses opposing adjectives to describe her bedroom, surrounded by a mystical aura of "intimacy, mystery, and femininity" (Yver 1903, 63). These separate but coexistent spheres in the home denote two distinct sides of Marceline's personality. Brooding within her orderly, intellectual, "masculine" mind is a latent "feminine" mysticism, bordering on religious fervor, that drives her to seek comfort in the Catholic Church, in ancient religions, and, finally, in love. The reader is thus not surprised to learn that this brainy woman is seriously tempted by the idea of marriage and family later in the novel, when she falls in love with Dr. Jean Cécile. The conflict between the romance and quest plots for Marceline form the central dilemma for the text.

In contrast to her domestic sphere, which was altered to accommodate her professional interests, Marceline's work environment is not permanently modified by romantic activities. Although Jean first meets Marceline in a public setting, at the weekly lecture series that she gives, their brief romance is fairly conventional and remains confined to traditionally private locations. They become acquainted as he walks her home from her lectures or through conversations in her salon, thus confining their private discussions to private spaces. When the expected demand is made—abandon your work for me—Marceline actually agrees that this is a reasonable request for a woman who is not a pure brainy woman. But she also realizes that she is not capable of making such a sacrifice. Instead Marceline decides to depart on a long research trip to Beirut, thus returning to her original status of pure brainy woman, in spite of the fact that she was moved temporarily by her romantic relationship with Jean.

La Bachelière[24] (1910) by Gabrielle Reval provides an example of a third type of pure brainy woman, one who has the same drive for power and knowledge as Yver's characters and who distorts the romance plot to fit her professional goals. Like Marceline, Gaude Malvos is tempted by marriage, but not for love or the desire for children. Rather she sees marriage as a potential source of funding for the research project that she is engaged in with her father, the famous archeologist Pierre Malvos. Gaude believes so strongly in their work that she feels no regrets about giving her body to a man in marriage in exchange for financial support for their research. Even when her father asserts that she would appear as a dead woman to him, she insists on the marriage. With this radical announcement, Gaude manipulates traditional romance plot requirements to conform to her career

---

24. For a brief plot summary of this novel, see Appendix 2.

goals. Unfortunately, this unusual proclamation initiates a major detour from Gaude's professional plans, creating misunderstandings and unhappy results both in her professional quest and her personal life.

In contrast to Marceline and Jeanne, who worked independently, Gaude Malvos follows closely the teachings of a major mentor figure: her father. His statements about Gaude, however, recall advice that Marceline and Jeanne give to each other. For example, he states forcefully that it should be clear to Gaude that her sole path in life must be the intellectual one: "You are not made for a vulgar destiny. Leave to others, your inferiors, maternity and love. You will birth ideas. You know well that intelligence and energy make up individual greatness."[25] Pierre's claim that Gaude will "give birth to ideas" echoes the opinions of Jeanne and Marceline that they will work for a larger social goal rather than raising their own children and taking care of a private household, and he thus establishes Gaude as a pioneer figure. In spite of Pierre's strong show of support of his daughter's intellect, he uses her mental abilities in a secondary way: she acts as his secretary, transcribing his notes, his dictation, and his thoughts. Confirming this idea, Gaude's mother tells the confused and frustrated fiancé that Pierre's anger is not so much due to Gaude's apparent desire to be a wife and mother, but to Pierre's own selfish fear of losing a prized secretary (Reval 1920, 43). Gaude is blind to this exploitation by her father and insists on continuing to help him at all costs, believing that his professional goals are her own.

The twisted romance plot is also misunderstood by Gaude's fiancé, who demands that she abandon her work and devote her life to him. He thereby makes the typical male appeal in these novels: give up your life for mine. His request is stronger than most because he requires that they move to a town far away from the city of Sarlay and Gaude's family, so that she will not be able to keep in touch with her father on a regular basis. Gaude surprisingly accepts her fiancé's requirement because it will guarantee the financial security her father needs, even if it means he must continue their research without her aid. Her sacrifice, of course, backfires and becomes the partial cause for her father's heart attack and death.

Reval develops in her fictional character Gaude the consummate brainy woman: she is serious, hard-working, obsessed by her research, and she will not let any sentimental notions, whether men's or women's, distract

---

25. "Tu n'es pas faite pour un destin vulgaire. Laisse à d'autres, tes inférieures, la maternité, l'amour. Tu enfanteras des idées. Tu sais bien que c'est l'intelligence et l'énergie qui font la grandeur de l'individu" (Reval 1910, 40).

her from her pursuit of knowledge. Her family situation also conforms to the typical brainy woman mold: her mother, Rachel, is a quiet, patient, and obedient woman. Her father, Pierre Malvos, has raised his daughter to follow in his footsteps, pushing her to pass the baccalaureat exam at age sixteen and to accompany him in his classroom and on archeological digs. Unlike many other scientific heroines, Gaude does not encounter raw prejudice from her male classmates, all of whom respect her and her father's wisdom. Her one goal in life is to help her father finish his research on "la cité Gallo-Romaine."

After her father's sudden death, Gaude moves to Paris with the hope of continuing her quest. This move from provinces to Paris, so typical of the male bildungsroman, remains an exception in female novels of development from the Belle Epoque. But Gaude follows the outlines of the traditional male model in a number of ways. In order to finish her father's incomplete manuscript, for example, Gaude must take several major detours and overcome a number of important obstacles, seeking a strong mentor figure along the way.

At first, she lives with her Polish cousin Thaïda, a possible female role model for Gaude in the all-male world of Parisian research circles.[26] This new mentor figure teaches Gaude some important lessons about the real world, and teases her young cousin that she has been living "on a mountain" for too long (Reval 1910, 92). Trained as a doctor, Thaïda has instead become a modern "scientific" beautician. Her medical examination room has been transformed into a modern "beautification" laboratory with electric baths and other unusual equipment. Similar to other brainy women, Thaïda has transformed part of her home into a laboratory in order to be able to continue her career. She diverges from the pure brainy woman model, however, since her mixing of spheres comes with an interesting variation: Thaïda has given up "formal" or professionally approved research, and she openly acknowledges the charlatan aspects of her new career: "I abandoned medicine and embarked on an old boat which still works. They call it *Illusion*. I, who had respected truth, a passion for research, diagnosis, analysis, I threw those bothersome companions overboard and I chose

---

26. The reference here to a Polish woman in the sciences is most probably a nod to Marie Curie, who had moved to Paris from Poland in her twenties and who made her major discoveries while living in France. The reference also draws the reader to conclude, however, that foreign women may have been allowed more freedom to work outside the traditional expectations for middle-class Frenchwomen; Mary Louise Roberts notes that we find both English and Russian "new women" in a variety of Belle Epoque texts, including Yver's *Princesses de science,* Tinayre's *La Rebelle,* and both volumes of Marcel Prévost's *Vierges fortes* (Roberts 2002, 259).

for assistants: trickery, bluffing, play-acting."[27] In her statement, Thaïda still refers to institutional standards of professional scientific research (truth, analysis, and diagnostic research), even though she realizes that she cannot continue to uphold them and still earn enough to make a living. Her new career, although a scientific compromise, has been a great financial success, and during the eight years she has been working in this new field, her reputation has spread all over Paris.[28] While relinquishing certain rights to "pure" scientific research, Thaïda is able to live independently and to donate funds to the school for orphans, which she has had constructed in Poland with her earnings. Gaude, who remains a purist about science, is shocked by Thaïda's confessions.

Reval has structured the quest plot of this particular professionalization novel in a traditional series of progressive steps away from Gaude's protected family life in provincial France. Her first job in Paris, as a private research assistant for Gilbert Luceram, is arranged through her cousin Thaïda. Gaude's second job, as a teacher in the elite private boarding school Le Chrest, is completely removed from family and friends. She obtains that position through a job placement agency that she picked at random.

As her quest takes her further from home and family, Gaude finds it easier to separate public and private spaces and becomes better prepared to finish her father's great historical work. In the first section of the novel, she acts merely as her father's secretary in their home, taking notes that he dictates and working out problems together with him at the dinner table or in the living room. When she moves to Paris, she at first encounters open sexism when she tries to find an editor to help her to complete her father's book. Her father's editor dismisses her request and explains condescendingly that her "woman's brain" (cerveau de femme) does not have the capacity to do this work, no matter how intelligent she might be (Reval 1910, 114). Although she has moved away from home, she is still relying on her father's circle of colleagues and therefore is held back by their prejudices.

After this discouraging encounter, Gaude decides to work on her own in the public libraries, thus beginning her new path of independence. After Gaude has separated her work and her home, she begins to make great strides

---

27. "J'abandonnai la médecine, et m'embarquai sur un bateau très vieux, qui marche toujours. On l'appelle *l'Illusion*. Moi qui avais le respect de la vérité, la passion de la recherche du diagnostic, de l'analyse, j'ai jeté par dessus bords ces compagnons gênants, et j'ai choisi pour auxiliaires: l'esbrouffe, le bluff, le cabotinage" (Reval 1910, 92).

28. See Magali Larson's *Rise of Professionalism* (1977) on the importance for a new group of professionals to corner a market for their skills.

in her research. In the main reading room of the Bibliothèque Nationale of Paris she feels more at ease with the material but still has difficulty writing. She expresses her doubts about her own abilities—not to do research, but to gain sufficient general knowledge of her subject. In the third section of the book, when she is at Le Chrest boarding school and completely isolated from all family and Parisian acquaintances for nine months, her writing explodes. She writes to her cousin, "I'm making progress Thaïda, I'm making progress! I have the immense joy, the unsuspected joy to find, almost word-by-word, the thoughts of my father."[29] In typical brainy woman fashion, the pioneer must be completely isolated from familial or sentimental influences to become most productive and creative.

The progress in Gaude's maturity as a scholar and writer corresponds to a paradoxical movement in Reval's novel, from an entirely male environment where she was surrounded by her father, his male colleagues, and his male students; to a mixed male-female environment when she spent all her mornings with her employers, Odette and Gilbert Luceram; to a completely female environment at the girls' boarding school. Although Gaude complains about the atmosphere of immorality and the lack of discipline among her female students, she herself blossoms as a scholar when she no longer has male colleagues with whom to discuss her work. Her community of women is not comparable to the women's environments that we find in other education novels (by Reval, Compain, or Colette, for example). In fact, there is no "community" at all at the Le Chrest School, only competition and alienation. Yet Gaude's abilities do not come to the fore until she is separated from men in her field.

This need for separation is due in part to the fact that, whether her father, her fiancé, or her employer, the men whom Gaude deals with are all irrationally and irresponsibly fixated on her. Following classic romance plot requirements, these men are obsessed with the object of their affection and cannot bear to live without her, even if it means that they must stamp out those qualities that they find most attractive in their brainy woman: her engaging intellect, her passion about her work, and her independent thought. As *La Bachelière* concludes, Reval's protagonist, one of the purest brainy women created during the Belle Epoque, leaves for Poland on her own in order to continue her pursuit of knowledge unrestricted.

---

29. "J'avance, Thaïda, j'avance! J'ai la joie immense, la joie insoupçonnée de retrouver presque mot par mot la pensée de mon père" (Reval 1910, 259).

These examples of pure brainy women are isolated loners, pioneers in male-dominated fields. In most women's professionalization novels from the Belle Epoque, there is at least one older woman who provides counsel and emotional support to the younger women embarking on a difficult career. At the least, there are other female colleagues who are struggling in the same field. Yet in *Les Cervelines* and *La Bachelière*, these pure brainy women are isolated from other women in their field, if they exist at all. Marceline and Jeanne, in *Les Cervelines,* rely on each other and spend their brief moments of leisure in Marceline's salon, smoking cigarettes and discussing their work and their goals. But they are not working in the same discipline and could never become collaborators at work. In Reval's *La Bachelière,* the pure brainy woman is also perceived as isolated from other women researchers, for the simple reason that they do not exist. As an archeologist at the Sarlay dig and a researcher at the Bibliothèque Nationale in Paris, Gaude is the only woman present amidst large groups of male scholars. Her one brief exposure to other women schoolteachers, while waiting for an interview at the placement agency, reveals a wide gulf between herself and other women educators. Even at the girls' boarding school, she has nothing in common with the two other teachers or the director and remains apart from them, never seeking advice or consolation.

These brainy women protagonists are also exceptional because they choose work and career before love and marriage, an unusual decision in the genre of Belle Epoque women's professionalization novels. Perhaps because Yver herself remained unmarried while writing *Les Cervelines,* it was the only novel that she wrote in which neither female protagonist opted for love and marriage, and where there remained a clear division between professional and domestic spheres for the heroines.[30] In her later novel, *Princesses de science,* the pure brainy woman Dr. Lancelevée is no longer a central character to the narrative, but rather acts as a negative role model for the married doctor Thérèse Guéméné. Lancelevée is aloof and distant from the other women doctors whom Thérèse knows.

These are the dilemmas of the pure brainy woman: she feels obligated to follow the male standards of professional behavior strictly, even though she is not always respected or regarded as a peer by the men in her field. And although she might be tempted by love, as in the case of Marceline

---

30. *Les Cervelines* was successful when it first appeared, and as Waelti-Walters notes, Yver's future husband, the editor Auguste Huzard, claimed that it was after reading this novel that he fell in love and decided to marry Yver (Waelti-Walters 188).

Rhonans, she renounces the romance plot in order to continue her quest for knowledge, success, or fame. These fictional dilemmas were not always present in the lives of "real" brainy women during the Belle Epoque. To return to the example of Marie Curie, she was well respected by her male colleagues and received two Nobel prizes, but she did not find it necessary to give up love, marriage, or family in order to pursue her career. Even though she could combine the private and the professional aspects of her life, her work habits and her passion for knowledge definitely place her in the category of "cerveline" or brainy woman. Readers must ask themselves why women writers during this time period felt the need to create these fictional cervelines who refused marriage and children in order to devote themselves to science. Before we can find an answer to such a question, we must explore the alternative: the fictional brainy women who followed their temptations, trying to adjust their quest, that is, their intellectual and professional lives, to admit love, marriage, and children into their private lives.

Seduced Cervelines

Yver's *Princesses de science* (1907, *The Doctor Wife* or *Princesses of Science*),[31] published four years after *Les Cervelines,* won the Prix Femina, thus establishing Yver as a well-known writer of the Belle Epoque. The main protagonist, Thérèse Herlinge, belongs to a bourgeois and fairly traditional nuclear family; her mother works at home and her father is a doctor. Thérèse's childhood training, although mentioned only briefly in flashbacks, was classical and elite, especially for girls of this era. Since the baccalaureat was not officially offered in girls' high schools during this time, the fact that she had received the prestigious diploma implies that she must have taken a special course of study or even had private tutoring to pass the exams. Further, Thérèse is an only child. Because she has no brothers or sisters with whom to compete for family affection or support, her parents allow her to pursue a professional career. She is a motivated and intelligent woman, but the unspoken comment remains that if she had had brothers who were expected and encouraged to become professionals, Thérèse may not have been able to entertain such daring notions. She also comes from a family of doctors, so in some ways she is merely maintaining a Herlinge family tradition. Thérèse soon demonstrates a certain amount of promise and ability in her young

---

31. For a brief plot summary of this novel, see Appendix 2.

career, earning the admiration of her family after she has proven herself capable of succeeding. These factors (doctor's daughter, only child, superior education), given by the author, explain why she has chosen to pursue a medical career when financial concerns did not require her to work. When they are combined with her abilities in science and her diligent studies, it is easy to understand why she is able to surpass most of her classmates and contemporaries in medicine.

Although Yver patterns her main character, Thérèse, according to the "brainy woman" mold of her earlier novel, the plot and main characters of *Princesses de science* confront unexpected detours that lead to a more melodramatic tone and more tragic events than in *Les Cervelines*. The professional development of Thérèse is interrupted numerous times by elements from the romance plot involving her fiancé/husband Fernand. In order to accommodate these intrusions, there are many more rearrangements of the domestic sphere in this novel, to allow for a woman's office, lab, or examining room in the home. And there are many more private conversations held in public spaces, either in the hospital or clinic. The characters transgress the normal boundaries between public and private spheres frequently, and the results point to a new type of heroine: the seduced brainy woman.

The opening chapter of the novel contains the first example of public and private boundaries crossed, in this case by Fernand Guéméné, a fellow student who interned with Thérèse but who has now graduated and begun a general medical practice in Paris. Thérèse has just received a love letter from Fernand, asking her permission to meet her at the hospital. Fernand's marriage proposal, in Thérèse's laboratory, is framed by the narrator's references to the harsh scientific surroundings: amid cadaver parts, boiling beakers, and rats in cages, "Thérèse was awakening to love" (la vie sentimentale s'éveillait chez Thérèse) (Yver 1907, 8). This peculiar juxtaposition of profession and romance is a shock to the brainy woman at first, and she tells Fernand bluntly that she is not interested in marriage and does not love him (9).

Despite her initial refusal, she is tempted and eventually accepts his proposal, until he reveals his wish that she halt her medical studies and career when they marry. His conservative bourgeois upbringing dictates both the type of marriage that he desires and the service-oriented career goals that he embraces. Fernand dreams of building a solid general practice based on the ideals of caring and healing, and he wants a loving wife and children, devoted to him alone. Thérèse, in contrast, reflects the more modern professional of the late nineteenth century, one who pursues technical knowledge and competence and who embraces the exploratory fields of the medical profession. When trying to explain to Fernand Guéméné why she could never abandon her medical studies to marry him, she reveals her fascination, at times lugubrious, with science. Embedded in her description is the modern scientific focus on the disease, rather than the patient, and a nascent passion for power and authority: "Oh Guéméné, Guéméné, do you not know the intoxicating trance of diagnosis, and the delight of auscultation and the triumph of predictions confirmed? . . . And what power we hold! . . . And autopsy! What a marvel, with its revelations that sanction the entire scaffolding of hypotheses produced on a mysterious case."[32] Thérèse's enthusiastic and unselfconscious description of her passion for auscultation and autopsy indicates the typical modern scientist's desire for knowledge: her curiosity about disease overshadows any impulse to heal or care for the sick. In fact, she never even mentions her patients, except when they disappointingly recover and takes their body away with them, leaving her deprived of her autopsy, unfulfilled because she is unable to discover the illness lurking within. She finishes her macabre praise of autopsy with the phrase, "Ah! There have been some wonderful times in my life, Guéméné!"[33] This image of the driven scientist is not exactly the one that Fernand had created in his mind for Thérèse. He would have preferred a woman doctor devoted to medicine for the benefits of nurturing and healing, perhaps those qualities found in the traditional definition of the nurse, but he finds in Thérèse the opposite. Nevertheless, he persists in proposing marriage, although the offer changes each time.

Following the typical path of the obsessed male romance character, Fernand's passion for Thérèse and his desire to possess such an intelligent creature overcome his disgust with her confession. Soon after, he offers a second proposal, in which he negotiates with Thérèse, agreeing to let her do laboratory work in their home, thus allowing her to continue her research but assuring him that she will never leave the house. This "compromise" allows for certain boundary crossings in one direction: the professional sphere of scientific research may enter the private domain of

---

32. "Oh! Guéméné, Guéméné, vous ne les connaissez donc pas, vous, les transes grisantes du diagnostic, et la volupté de l'auscultation et le triomphe des prévisions confirmées? . . . Et quelle puissance nous détenons! . . . Et l'autopsie! quelle merveille, avec ses révélations qui viennent sanctionner tout l'échafaudage des hypothèses émises sur un cas mystérieux! Souvent voyez-vous, j'ai frémi, pendant des auscultations difficiles, en présence de secrets que le corps vivant ne voulait pas lâcher alors que je songeais à l'autopsie qui mettrait à nu les viscères, illuminerait nos obscurités, nos incertitudes; oui, l'autopsie je l'ai quelquefois désirée fiévreusement . . . je l'ai désirée avec révolte, avec curiosité" (Yver 1907, 24–25).

33. "Ah! il y a eu de belles heures dans ma vie, Guéméné!" (Yver 1907, 25).

the home. Thérèse's activities as a modern scientist would be contained behind the closed doors of their apartment, and the general public, clients, and colleagues would not see Thérèse in the public sphere. Therefore Fernand's image of her as his own private possession would not be jeopardized. Thérèse again refuses his offer.

Tortured by the fact that Thérèse has refused him and convinced that his life will be a solitary and miserable existence without her, Fernand desperately proposes that Thérèse continue all of her work—her laboratory research, her clinical work at the hospital, and her doctoral thesis—but that she do so as his wife. Thérèse happily accepts this third proposal of marriage, even as it crushes Fernand to make it: "He offered his arms. A sadness overwhelmed him, cast a gloom over his engagement. Mademoiselle Herlinge was triumphant. It was her complete dream come true: tender tears sprung to her eyes."[34] This quotation reveals that at first the marriage was a victory for one ("she was triumphant" [elle triomphait]), defeat for the other ("a sadness overwhelmed him" [une tristesse l'accablait]), but the battle has only begun. One of the most important power relationships throughout the novel for Thérèse is the one that she maintains with her husband. Professionally, she does not appear to have any difficulties with regard to patients, about whom we read very little, or hospital administrators, since her father and his close friends are among the highest ranking officials in the hospital where she works. Even public scrutiny of her position as doctor and researcher appears to remain minimal. But her negotiations and struggle for respect within her marriage are constant and often bitter. It is in her public-private transgressions that these battles are fought.

As soon as she has finished her medical studies, Thérèse and Fernand both receive patients daily, and she begins a playful competition with her husband for clientele. On the surface, traditional public and private spheres appear to mix easily for Thérèse. Even Fernand, when speaking in public, appears to accept the "new woman" whom he has married and vigorously defends the wife's right to work outside the home when discussing the subject with his conservative uncle or his colleague Dr. Pautel. When Pautel reveals his expectation that his fiancée, Dina, a medical intern and friend of Thérèse, will renounce her studies when she marries him, Fernand gives an impassioned speech on the rights of women to pursue their career goals,

---

34. "Il tendit les bras. Une tristesse l'accablait, qui endeuillait ces fiançailles. Mademoiselle Herlinge, elle, triomphait. C'était son rêve complet se réalisant: des larmes de tendresse lui montèrent aux yeux" (Yver 1907, 82).

even when married. He explains to Pautel that they desire companions, not slaves, for wives, and that it would be odious to suffocate their wives' intellectual lives (Yver 1907, 127–28). Thus Fernand seems to have been converted to Thérèse's philosophy on the modern couple, but at home with Thérèse, the battle continues.

It becomes apparent that Yver's male characters allow public-private boundary transgressions in *Princesses de science* only at the initial stages of their relationships. The reader understands quickly that Fernand made his marriage proposal in Thérèse's laboratory only because he could not find a way to do so in a more traditional, private setting. As soon as they are wed, he begins to pressure her to give up these public-private transgressions and become a traditional wife and mother according to the strict private codes of the bourgeoisie. In a scene depicted during their second week of marriage, Fernand asks Thérèse at their intimate dinner for two if she is seriously planning on continuing her medical studies. She replies that she has already told him "twenty times" that she is, of course, going to finish her degree. The number that she gives in her statement implies that he has been hounding her with the same question ever since their wedding day (Yver 1907, 94).

The author Yver dissolves the tenuous happiness established in the first descriptions of married life by a rapid succession of events: first, Fernand's illness, which forces Thérèse to abandon her thesis experiments to take care of him, and second, her discovery that she is pregnant. Both she and Fernand agree that she must refrain from laboratory work during her pregnancy, which means that she must jettison her plans for an innovative thesis altogether. The pregnancy is viewed as a triumph for Fernand but an unfortunate accident for Thérèse. When the baby is born, Thérèse wins a small victory in the ongoing battle by hiring a wet nurse for their new son, so that she may begin her medical practice and return to the hospital clinics. Fernand understands Thérèse's refusal to breastfeed as a confirming sign that her family is less important to her than her career, something that he had always feared. When the baby dies a few months later from a disease that the nursemaid gave him through her milk, Fernand's anger and resentment turn into bitterness and sorrow. Thérèse is also devastated by the loss of her son but immerses herself in her work for comfort. Even though both Fernand and Thérèse had theoretically envisioned a way to combine professional and domestic responsibilities, neither is capable of living that dream and their battles become nightmares.

Where was the Belle Epoque reader supposed to lay his or her sympathies throughout these battles? In the case of the Guéméné marriage, the answer is clear: despite both characters' failures, Thérèse is portrayed sympathetically, while Fernand is generally portrayed as embittered, possessive, and narrow-minded. In an age when the scientific method and the cult of discovery were beginning to take on the enormous prestige that they have continued to hold throughout the twentieth and twenty-first centuries, Thérèse, even though she was a woman, is perceived as the more positive figure. She is intelligent and thoughtful, constantly wishes to learn more about her field, and aspires to new experiments and discoveries. Fernand, in contrast, is characterized as an old-fashioned and often negative figure for the medical profession. His attempts to discover a cure for cancer are pitiful and fail; the experimental immunizations that he gives to his patient, Monsieur Jourdeaux, eventually kill him.

Furthermore, Fernand is depicted as an obsessive neurotic who childishly complains that Thérèse is not paying enough attention to him. Whether at home, on vacation, in her laboratory, or on a quiet street, Fernand never misses an occasion when they are alone to remind her that he is suffering, constantly intensifying his whining and disagreeable character. Thérèse, in contrast, always responds with patience and understanding, claiming that she does not want him to suffer, but that her passion for medicine is too great for her to stop practicing. These scenes resurface until a startling moment of revelation when they are on vacation in Switzerland. Thérèse's venomous reply shocks both the reader and the pouting Fernand, as she firmly announces that he is not the only one who has been suffering or who has had to make sacrifices in their marriage:

> I sacrificed, for a maternity that you desired, a thesis that would have classified me in the ranks of Madame Lancelevée. I renounced, to be at home more often, Boussard's clinics and Artout's operations. I would have liked to study alienist medicine in Janicot's clinic: I didn't even mention it to you because Passy was too far away and you would have blamed me. . . . If I have remained a modest and ignored doctor, reduced to contenting myself with clients, that was the ransom of my love for you, because alone, without my house to take care of, without the worries of your well-being, without that pregnancy, without your exigencies, I would count for something today in the medical world.[35]

---

35. "J'ai sacrifié, pour une maternité que tu désirais, une thèse qui m'eût classée au même rang que Madame Lancelevée. J'ai renoncé, pour être plus souvent chez nous, à suivre les cliniques de Boussard, les opérations d'Artout. J'aurais désiré faire de la médecine aliéniste dans l'établissement de Janicot: je ne t'en ai pas même parlé, car Passy, c'était trop loin et tu m'aurais blâmée. . . . Si je suis demeurée une doctoresse modeste et ignorée, réduite à me contenter de la clientèle,

This fiery accusation and her long list of privations since her marriage began are blows from which Fernand never recovers and that awaken the reader to Thérèse's sacrifices.

As Thérèse appears to win the battle, both spouses flee the private sphere of the home and find comfort in their work, spending their days and evenings occupied in doctor's visits, lab work, or clinical observations. During these self-absorbed months, the quest plot dominates for Thérèse. She builds a clientele that outnumbers Fernand's, and she makes important discoveries, one of which she publishes in a medical journal. As she amasses this type of institutional recognition from colleagues and superiors in the profession, she also begins to gain power and prestige, in spite of her status as a woman in a predominantly male field. Fernand meanwhile keeps his work to himself, sharing his discoveries only with the widow Jourdeaux, a simple and attentive young woman who places her faith in the hands of the doctor. His research never enjoys the public discussion among doctors and scientists that Thérèse's work receives.

Thérèse's phenomenal success is due in part to the fact that she is completely tuned in to recent progress in medical research and to the achievements of her colleagues (Artout, Boussard, Janicot). The passage cited above indicates that she compares her own work to that of other colleagues, and in particular to another woman doctor, Madame Lancelevée, who may be perceived as a role model for her. But Dr. Lancelevée is too distant and unconventional to appeal to Thérèse. A second possible role model, Dr. Jeanne Adeline, offers an example of a seduced brainy woman, but with financial problems, too many children, and an unhappy marriage, she offers a negative example of someone whose life has fallen apart. Thérèse's classmate and friend Dina, who gives up her medical studies when she marries Pautel, disgusts Thérèse. She says to herself after a visit with Dina, that her friend has committed an intellectual suicide and has lost all dignity by presenting herself as a contented housewife (Yver 1907, 274). Throughout the book, Thérèse does seek a positive example, but she cannot find one.

Given the negative role models offered, the reader might have a difficult time guessing what Thérèse's final decision would be, especially because Yver's sequence of events regarding Thérèse does not follow typical romance conventions. In the end, Thérèse was not forced to renounce her career due

---

ce fut la rançon de mon amour pour toi, car seule, sans ma maison à tenir, sans le souci de ton bien-être, sans cette grossesse, sans tes exigences enfin, je compterais un peu aujourd'hui dans le monde médical" (Yver 1907, 295).

to her husband's demands, as her friend Dina did. In fact, Thérèse succeeded in resisting Fernand's repeated pleas to give up her career throughout the entire narrative, for about three years total. Nor did she appear overwhelmed by her work or drained by the pace of her professional activities and family responsibilities, as was her colleague Jeanne Adeline, who for financial reasons was required to continue her medical practice against her will. Thérèse's decision to become a full-time housewife is instead directly related to two surprising emotions that are never mentioned with regard to Thérèse until the very last chapter of the novel: jealousy (of Fernand's friend Madame Jourdeaux) and fear (of losing Fernand). These new emotions alter the course of her career considerably, and she abruptly decides to notify all her clients that she will no longer be practicing medicine.

Her sudden decision may appear to be a transformation into the conventional romance plot, one where love and marriage triumph over career and adventure. Yet Yver's unusual narrative does not end on a happy note. Fernand does not appreciate Thérèse's sacrifice; in fact, it might be too late for him to appreciate it: in the final scene, he is sobbing with his head in his hands because Madame Jourdeaux has written to say she is leaving him. Thérèse finds no comfort or skill in domestic activities, although she admits that she might eventually adapt and become used to them. The renunciation of her promising career in science does not bring with it the blissful family life that she had anticipated. Yver's startling conclusion thus leaves the reader of *Princesses de science* with a sense of confusion: on one hand, one might interpret the narrator's conclusions as a form of acceptance that Thérèse developed during the last part of the text, mainly through the examples she encountered in Dina and Jeanne Adeline, both of whom told her that married life and science were incompatible. On the other hand, the reader can just as easily understand the ending as a negative statement about the enforced retirement of married women from the professions due to societal pressures that ignored or denied women's interests and abilities in the medical and scientific fields.

Marcelle Babin's novel *Pharmacienne* (1907, *The Woman Pharmacist*)[36] depicts the life of a very different seduced brainy woman, Danielle Dormeuil, who does not undergo the constant badgering, or difficult demands from family and career to which Yver's characters are subjected. More similar to Reval's novel about Gaude Malvos, *Pharmacienne* reveals

36. For a brief plot summary of this novel, see Appendix 2.

a strong bildungsroman pattern, although the romance narrative does intrude to cause the heroine to take certain detours from her chosen career goals.[37]

Babin's personal experiences in medical and pharmacy school allowed her to create a brainy heroine who was not exaggeratedly exceptional. For example, after completing her coursework, the protagonist Danielle passes the Concours de l'Internat and finishes thirty-fourth: a good test result, but unlike the brainy women in other novels about women scientists, she does not score at the top of her class. In the surgical department where she interns as a pharmacist, there is not much for her to do, but instead of beginning new investigations or research, she enjoys wasting time in the hospital's *salle de garde,* playing the piano and joining in pranks with friends from pharmacy school (Babin 60). The reader thus witnesses a more "human" brainy woman in action in this novel. Danielle's attitude in school and later at work is one of acceptance, tolerance, and service to her peers and clients, similar to many schoolteachers' ethics, yet the community of women, one of the major structures in the women's novel of educational development, is entirely absent from *Pharmacienne*. Although there are a few women students in the medical school, Danielle does not develop friendships with any of them, and there are no female mentors.

Danielle could therefore be compared to Thérèse Guéméré and other scientific brainy women because she is a pioneer in her studies rather than a member of a women's community. Like them, she remains a diligent student throughout, devoting all her waking hours to the school. But she is neither a brilliant student nor an innovative researcher, and her goals are not to make groundbreaking discoveries or to develop a prestigious clientele. Danielle wishes simply to be able to support her younger brother and to earn a good living. Her reasons for pursuing a career are linked to the fact

---

37. *Pharmacienne* could in some respects belong to the genre of education novels because of the detailed enumeration of school events, including rites of passage, professors' lectures, and student pranks. During her fourth year, for example, Danielle remarks in a letter to her brother that she knows that she has become an *ancienne* [senior] in the school because the male students no longer emit catcalls and other obscene noises when she enters the amphitheaters. The description of daily harassment is supported by footnotes, almost as though Babin were attempting to inform (or warn) her female readers of the practices, songs, and jargon of medical students. Babin was herself a pharmacist, went through the same professional schools as her protagonist Danielle, and had an insiders' view of life for women in professional schools (Babin 3). These experiences contributed to the detail in her account of the difficult lives of the pioneer women who decided to attend medical school during the Belle Epoque.

that her father was and her guardians still are involved in medicine and the sciences, however her motivation is based on financial necessity rather than on personal aptitude.[38]

The first and major "detour" in Danielle's medical career comes not from a marriage proposal or financial concerns, but from a psychological experiment for which she was the unknowing subject. Danielle develops an unarticulated love interest in her professor, Dr. Clavelan, but during his "research," the reader is aware that this is not a two-sided romance and that Clavelan is merely manipulating Danielle's emotions to test his hypothesis about the relation between emotional and physical healing. Interestingly, however, the typical figures of the romance narrative are still present: the young, confused woman and the older, cynical, and brutal man. Clavelan's obsession with Danielle may also appear to fit the characteristics of a man involved in a romance plot, but the narrator explains that his fixation with her is merely part of his scientific investigation. Thus Babin makes use of some of the major elements of the romance genre in this novel, but she demonstrates how they can be employed to manipulate and hurt young women.

When Dr. Clavelan concludes his "experiment" with Danielle, she is left wounded on two levels. Professionally, her choice has been taken away from her: although she had been studying both medicine and pharmacy, she is forced to continue with pharmacy only. Emotionally, her undefined (yet growing) feelings of affection for Dr. Clavelan suddenly appear inappropriate and foolish. Here the author exposes the negative results of a doctor whose obsession with his power over both diseases and patients leads to a damaging relationship with the patient. The uneven power relations are perhaps more evident in this case because Danielle is not a nameless patient on a clinic bed but a future colleague and member of the medical profession, and therefore she should have been viewed as an active rather than passive member of the medical community and of the doctor-patient relationship. Danielle's quest plot is thus led astray by the phony romance that Clavelan created between them.

This early experience forms Danielle and her expectations for her professional career. Her initial reaction is to hide the hurt and continue her pharmaceutical studies with fervor. The narrator comments: "She felt completely different from that day on, and she felt the need to hide from

---

38. As discussed in Chapter 1, service to the community or the crown was the traditional and altruistic reason claimed for pursuing a profession. With the growth of industrial and technical professionals during the nineteenth century, however, more individuals acknowledged that financial and personal incentives motivate the choice of a particular career path.

everyone this surprise in love that had victimized her. She did not want others to bruise her soul; she became more silent than before. She concentrated on herself. She would have been ashamed to show her disappointment, the sadness of her soul. She remained inaccessible."[39] The detailed description that Babin gives of her heroine's emotional state after this romantic deception is narrated in terse, simple sentences. On a parallel, the new personality that evolves is also one that is detached, less effusive, and less enthusiastic about the profession and her schoolwork (Babin 29). The bottom line is that Clavelan's experiment has numbed Danielle, permanently changing her interactions with her colleagues. Her withdrawal from the world after this surprise denotes some of the archetypal responses of a victim of harassment or assault.

Danielle's reactions mark a distinctly different response from those of a pure brainy woman, for example, Jeanne Boerk in *Les Cervelines,* even though both characters experience male harassment. After Paul Tisserel's intrusive interruption in her dorm room, Jeanne decides that she must move to a different hospital to complete her internship, and she does show some temporary shock when Tisserel's tone turns hateful and menacing (Yver 1903, 206). But after this brush with a potentially murderous intruder, Jeanne easily reassumes her rational calm. Five minutes later, she is in control again, telling Marceline that she will never submit to Tisserel's demands and announcing to Tisserel that she is leaving the Hôtel-Dieu for another hospital. The narrator notes that Jeanne's tone is "grand calme", but it does not leave her silenced and helpless. Danielle Dormeuil suffers for a much longer period of time and blames herself as much as she blames Clavelan, never completely recovering from his experiment. Rather than simply changing hospitals to avoid further conflict with Clavelan, she changes her entire career path, from medicine to pharmacy.

As a pharmacist in the provinces, Danielle's daily occupations are rather independent and thus rarely include the power relations of the pure brainy woman in science, found in clinics, doctor's offices, or hospitals. She does not need the political or social clout that Thérèse Herlinge or Jeanne Boerk requires to continue with her career. The long power struggle that develops in the second part of the novel plays itself out between Danielle and the

---

39. "Elle se sentit tout autre à partir de ce jour et elle éprouva le besoin de cacher à tous cette surprise d'amour dont elle avait été victime. Elle ne voulait pas qu'on heurtât son âme; elle devint plus silencieuse qu'auparavant. Elle se concentra. Elle aurait eu honte de montrer sa déception, son éplorement d'âme. Elle resta incommuniquable" (Babin 28).

conservative bourgeois residents of Domfront, and it is similar to some of the contests new schoolteachers undergo in their new communities with the mayor, priest, and other conservative town members. Finally, thanks to the good will of one of the younger members of the local Fleurigny family, Danielle is able to establish confidence in these difficult customers and her business improves.

Her attempts to combine public and private activities do not meet with overwhelming chaos or failure either, mainly because Danielle does not have a husband, children, or competing demands from different public offices. She lives and works in the same building, and her life is fairly simple and regulated, similar to Marceline Rhonans's description of her life of independent research in *Les Cervelines*. Yet she is quite different from a pure brainy woman like Marceline. One of the major questions for Yver's character was whether to marry or to remain single, but that is never a choice for Danielle. Rather, her main question is, "Whom shall I marry?" After several missteps, she decides to marry the local artist Edouard Fleurigny, but as she is accepting his proposal, she asks the all-important question: "You will permit me to continue with science? And to come to the pharmacy from time to time to help my brother?"[40] Edouard, whose general philosophy is cited as the epigraph on the title page ("Reality is never anything but the inequality of the dream born from the imagination."),[41] states that since she would never think of asking him to give up his career, he would never ask her to do such a thing.

Similar to some of Yver's brainy women, Babin's married protagonist builds a laboratory attached to Edouard's studio, so that the married couple may work side by side. But in contrast to Yver's Guéméné couple, Babin's Danielle and Edouard do not have children, at least not during the first years of their marriage. Therefore, Danielle is never seriously concerned with the conflicts that Yver's heroine had to manage. Danielle can work on all sorts of experiments and occasionally help her brother behind the counters of the Twentieth-Century Pharmacy (Babin 198). For the Belle Epoque, this dénouement could be considered a satisfying compromise: the romance plot and the quest plot are intertwined, and the heroine is able to negotiate both. Danielle's careful choice of a husband who would support both her career and herself appears to be the key to a successful brainy woman seduction.

---

40. "Vous me permettrez de continuer toujours à m'occuper des sciences? Puis de venir parfois à la pharmacie seconder mon frère?" (Babin 192).

41. "La réalité n'est jamais que l'inégalité du rêve enfanté par l'imagination" (Babin 1).

Given the relative newness of fictional career women who might also be wives and mothers and the skepticism they generated among the bourgeoisie, most women's professionalization novels from the Belle Epoque evolve around the choice: either career or marriage. A look at the reception of these four novels provides us with important proof that the choices and career reversals made by some of the married female protagonists did indeed contribute to their status as polemical, highly discussed texts during the Belle Epoque. The most popular of the four novels discussed here, and the winner of the Prix Femina in 1907, *Princesses de science* could appeal to both conservative and liberal feminist readers. Thérèse's decision to give up her practice could be applauded by conservative readers of the bourgeoisie as a return to traditional mores. Yet the novel ends ambiguously, since Thérèse's sacrifice does not immediately improve her marriage nor does it bring back Fernand's love to her. Feminist readers could thus interpret the novel as an indictment of bourgeois codes that required women's retirement from work upon marriage. The fussy dependent male character Fernand, cast generally in a negative light throughout the novel, is further proof that women are sacrificing too much when they opt for marriage. The unsettled ending of *Princesses de science* allowed for a variety of interpretations of the protagonist's final actions.

Indeed, a broad spectrum of Belle Epoque readers appreciated this more contentious ending. One of Yver's contemporaries, the conservative writer and journalist Gyp, wrote in a letter to her colleague Maurice Barrès that she found *Princesses de science* "very very good" and "complex." Moreover, Yver "follows the evolution of women and she approves of it without approving it" (quoted in Silverman 198 and 282). Gyp, of course, is well known for her polemical anti-Semitic and antifeminist statements, and it may well be that her endorsement of Yver's novel has contributed in some way to the long-term view that Yver was an antifeminist and conservative writer. But this novel did not receive praise solely from conservative sources like Gyp: Yver's novel had enough support from women on the Vie Heureuse Prize jury to be awarded the prestigious literary prize that year. Many of the women on the jury were active feminists during the Belle Epoque, and their support of this text indicates that feminists could approve of the intellectual and independent nature of the main character Thérèse and of the critique of society implied by the conclusion. Thus, even though the final decisions in all these novels indicate that a choice might have to be made—the public sphere or the private—the more dramatic conclusion was obviously one where the female lead had to make the wrenching decision to give up her favorite pastime, her promising career, and her public recognition. The brainy woman whose final decision was the most ambiguous turned out to be the more critically acclaimed for the turbulent Belle Epoque era. When we compare Yver's "complex" conclusion to the "happy" ending of *Pharmacienne* or the "to be continued" endings of *La Bachelière* and *Les Cervelines,* it is clear that the latter conclusions do not have the same "punch" as *Princesses de science,* even for readers of the early twenty-first century.

5

INDÉPENDANTES:
PROFESSIONAL WOMEN WRITERS

WOMEN WRITERS WHO DISCUSSED Yver's *Princesses de science* did not give it unanimous praise. The novelist and journalist Camille Marbo wrote a fairly severe critique of the work in her article "La Femme intellectuelle au foyer" ("The Intellectual Woman at Home"), published in the August 1907 issue of the *Vie Heureuse* magazine, only one month after Yver's novel had appeared in print. Marbo not only gives a list of Parisian women who both work and have a successful marriage and family life, but she critiques Colette Yver's heroine Thérèse Guéméné and her friend Dina for abandoning their intellectual pursuits to take care of their husbands.

In her rebuttal to Marbo's piece, which appeared in *La Vie Heureuse* two months later (October 1907), Yver defends her decision and explains that she was not proposing the more "humble" woman as the ideal. Her appeal to the reader is direct: "Certain unprepared readers saw in the novel the disapproval of the intellectual woman. That is an error that could dishonor the work and that the author asks to rectify. If in this book, in opposition to a princess of science, a very simple woman rises up, one who is more apt than the first to make a man happy, one should not believe that this humble and touching creature was imagined as the symbol, the ideal proposed in conclusion."[1] Thus in her response to Marbo, Yver denies the idea that she believes all intellectual women *should* choose husband and family over career.

So the question remains: why did these authors—Yver, Reval, Compain, or Tinayre—include such conformity in the conclusions to their narratives? Were they perhaps being "practical," "descriptive" or "prescriptive?"

---

1. "Certaines lectrices légèrement prévenues ont vu dans ce roman la réprobation de la femme intellectuelle. C'est là une erreur qui pourrait le déshonorer et que l'auteur demande à rectifier. Si dans ce livre, en opposition avec une princesse de science, surgit une très simple femme, plus apte que la première à faire le bonheur d'un homme, il ne faudrait pas croire que cette humble et touchante créature ait été imaginée comme le type, l'idéal proposé en conclusion" (Yver, *La Vie Heureuse* 6, no. 10 [octobre 1907]).

While all three of these hypotheses have tempted critics, both in the past and more recently, all three crumble upon closer analysis. First, we may ask if these authors were being "practical," that is, were they hoping to satisfy the demands of a conservative editor or reading public by including a renunciation of career and public life for women at the end of their novels? Certain recent critics, such as Jennifer Waelti-Walters, have suggested this possibility (Waelti-Walters 177), but I believe that this proposal falls short, in part because written proof between editors, readers, and authors has never been firmly established. Even if such a correspondence were to be discovered, it would leave the larger question unanswered: why would a conservative reading public or a traditional editor who does not approve of professionally active women allow for a positive portrayal of working heroines throughout the majority of the text? How could the renunciation of career in the last few pages be enough to satisfy such a group? A second hypothesis is that these women writers were being merely "descriptive," that is, they were outlining the actual difficulties that women professionals faced in the current social context. But this hypothesis also falls flat, at least for women in the sciences, since Marie Curie and other prominent women scientists demonstrated clearly to their contemporaries that women did not have to renounce their careers in order to maintain a happy marriage and a family. Critics have also pondered the possibility that these writers were being "prescriptive," that is, they were suggesting that women *ought* to behave in this way. The majority of critics who have accused these writers of antifeminist tendencies probably believed this attitude to be the case, from Simone de Beauvoir to recent critics and historians.[2] This idea, however, is also not convincing. Colette Yver herself explains clearly in the *Vie Heureuse* article cited above that she is not recommending this decision for all professional women. Most of the authors considered in this book had husbands and/or children, and yet they continued to write and publish novels and other materials (plays, articles, essays, and so on). If these writers truly believed that women *ought* to give up their careers when they got married, why did they not do so themselves? Literary critic Diana Holmes has noted that such a stance is at odds for women writers who obviously had not made the choice, and who had continued as both married women and

---

2. Simone de Beauvoir dismisses Yver at two different points and Tinayre twice in *Mémoire d'une jeune fille rangée* (1958). We find the same antifeminist accusations in Diana Holmes in *French Women's Writing, 1848–1994* (1996), Jennifer Milligan in *The Forgotten Generation* (1996), and Nancy Sloan Goldberg in *Woman, Your Hour Is Sounding* (1999).

as professional writers (Holmes 1996, 53–54). How then do we explain the gap between historic living conditions and fictional portrayals of women professionals?

Given the unsatisfactory nature of these different hypotheses, I will return to my original thesis: these women writers chose these types of endings because they lent a new type of dramatic tension and complexity to the narrative structure of their novels and helped to forge a new form of literary text during the Belle Epoque. Such a premise is confirmed when we examine portraits of professional women writers in texts from this era. If a renunciation of the career were to be applied to novels containing a woman writer, such a plot device might appear to undermine the author's own professional career. But most women writers of the Belle Epoque did not embrace the abandonment of the writing career in their fictive works that portrayed women journalists, novelists, or playwrights. Without that renunciation plot device, however, how is one to make such a text interesting or appealing to the reader? What new narrative structures did they create in order to allow for romance and quest plots to coexist throughout the novel? And how did they demand more complex solutions and create a series of negotiations for their writing heroines, involving both the private and public status of the protagonist? Below, I will examine three different depictions of women writers: Eugénie Lebrun in Yver's *Les Cervelines* (1903), Josanne Valentin in Marcelle Tinayre's *La Rebelle* (1905), and Renée Néré in Colette's *La Vagabonde* (1910).[3] Each protagonist takes a different path to resolve the typical problems presented to women professionals, combining a self-sufficient attitude about their personal lives with a unique awareness of their public roles as culture producers in French society.

When compared to the female protagonists in the other novels studied so far, these characters are unusual in many ways. They are not pioneers in their field because women writers had existed for some time in France and were even occasionally represented in French literature: Balzac's Camille Maupin (the nom de plume for Félicité Des Touches) in *Béatrix* (1839) and Maupassant's journalist Madeleine Forrestier in *Bel Ami* (1885), for example.

---

3. For a brief plot summary of each novel, see Appendix 2. There were other creative works during the time about women writers, including some by male authors: the brothers Margueritte in 1899 published the novel *Femmes nouvelles* about an all-women-staffed newspaper (probably based on *La Fronde*); Roberts discusses the theatrical successes *La Fronde* (1900) by Lucien Besnard and *La Femme seule* (1912) by Eugène Brieux (Roberts 2002, 44–45). Also, in the more general category of Künstlerroman, or novel of artistic development, there is the 1906 novel by Gabrielle Reval, *Le Ruban de Vénus* about a woman artist at the Ecole des Beaux-Arts.

But women writers were still relatively rare in France during this time period, and certainly they were not included in the Académie or other exclusive circles for *hommes de lettres*. Furthermore, in contrast to the scientists and teachers studied in preceding chapters, the women writers portrayed in these novels are fairly experienced producers of culture in their society. Therefore, the plotlines focus less on the professional *development* of the protagonists than in other novels studied thus far. In fact, since there is no formal training to become a writer, we find no descriptions of classroom scenes, professors, or peers in these texts. Mentor relationships are important in *La Vagabonde* (Renée and Brague) and *La Rebelle* (Josanne and Mlle Bon), yet they remain secondary for most of the narrative. Certain major professional events do arise, such as an important publication or a critical review of a new work, but the apprenticeship phase of the career process is largely completed. Instead, the reader sees day-to-day work patterns, and the technical side of the female berufsroman comes out most clearly in these sections of each text. The reader also witnesses significant midcareer shifts that take place for these women in the arts, such as Josanne's promotion to full-time investigative reporter.

A second major difference between these protagonists and those of the education and scientific novels is that these women have already been married when the novels begin; two (Eugénie and Renée) are divorced at the beginning of the narratives, and Josanne is soon widowed. All three have had the chance to be naïvely in love, and all three have grown wary of the "charms" of married life. All three soon confront new men who will demand their attention, their love, and their lives. Thus, the romance plot is still present in all three narratives, but it is seen from the viewpoint of a more experienced widow or divorcée.

Finally, these novels about women writers and artists include a significant role for the writer's audience. The readers' and spectators' social and economic class holds a primary function in the ways that the protagonist understands her professional role and the needs and desires of her private life. Many education and scientific novels focus on the heroine's status in French society and in relation to her future peers and colleagues, but without regard for the status of her students or her patients. The three protagonists we will study in this chapter work for audiences from different social and economic classes, and each audience has an important impact on her personal and professional development. Renée Néré, in *La Vagabonde,* has switched careers from novelist to mime, and as the text begins, she is preparing for a performance in a Parisian music hall for a popular, mainly working-class audience. Josanne Valentin, in *La Rebelle,* is a journalist for a women's magazine titled *Le Monde féminin* and writes her fashion pieces and interviews for a primarily petit bourgeois audience of women who live in the provinces. Eugénie Lebrun, in *Les Cervelines,* writes her successful novels and plays for a privileged and wealthy bourgeois audience in Paris. Each one is portrayed as a marginal woman in French society, but whether she is a rebel, a vagabond, or a brainy woman, each heroine carves a different niche for herself in Belle Epoque culture, due in part to her relationship with her audience. The public and professional roles of these women shape the choices they make in their private lives. Studying the protagonists' roles both as producers and as consumers of culture allows for a better understanding of the negotiations that each novel makes between conflicting romance and quest plots.[4] Accordingly, I have divided this chapter into two sections: the first part focuses on the characters' professional roles and their relationships to their audiences; the second part will examine their private lives and the ways in which their personal decisions are shaped by their work in the public sphere.

The Writer's Career: An Art or a Living?

In Yver's *Les Cervelines,* we find a direct confirmation of the notion that members of the dominant class desire an affirmation of their values and lifestyle in the art they consume. The reactions to Eugénie Lebrun's recent literary work specifically include a reference to the upper-class audience: "That year she had a sensational success with her novel, *The Ankles.* In it, love abounded, streamed, overflowed. The spirit of the times was understood by

---

4. Pierre Bourdieu, in his 1984 study *Distinction,* claims that cultural production aimed at the dominant fractions of society (the wealthier bourgeois class) usually coincides with and confirms those groups' expectations. The dominant class in a society seeks not only "distinction," as Bourdieu labels it, but also reinforcement of its own values and practices (Bourdieu 1984, 293). In contrast, the dominated classes in a society take on two opposing attitudes, depending on their relation to the dominant class. The working class follows what Bourdieu calls "the choice of the necessary." Its behavior implies a cultural taste restricted by economic boundaries. For Bourdieu, that behavior extends beyond simple financial concerns and develops into a system of taste in itself, often in opposition to those cultural tastes deemed "legitimate" by the dominant class (374–75). Two defining qualities of this dominated working class, according to Bourdieu, are thus solidarity with the group and the "bon vivant" personality (394). The other dominated class, the petit bourgeois, follows the practice of "cultural goodwill." Bourdieu explains the difficult position of members of this class: "Uncertain of their classifications, divided between the tastes they incline to and the tastes

deciphering the enigma of the title: *The Ankles*. We knew what it was about."[5] The wealthy bourgeois audience for whom Eugénie Lebrun writes, embodied in the impersonal pronoun *on* (we), knows what she is talking about; they have a clear understanding of the "enigma" of the title, the subject matter of the novel, and the reflection that the work gave of the "spirit of the times" (l'état d'esprit de l'époque). The novel thus reinforces their cultural practices. It is interesting to note that Yver indicates indirectly that the type of reader she expects might be reading *Les Cervelines* belongs to the petit bourgeois or working classes, rather than the bourgeois sectors of French society. Her narrator states that "we" knew what the title meant, but then goes on to explain what the double meaning of *les chevilles* is (ankles/linchpins) to her readers: what they are "in the theater, for the author of a play, and what they must be in the passions of a man's life."[6] With this clarification by her narrator, Yver reveals her assumption that the readers of *Les Chevilles* might lack the necessary cultural capital to be able to understand the dual meaning of the novel's title.

This text by Eugénie Lebrun becomes a great success among the ruling classes, which would generally include the category of professional doctors and scientific researchers. The well-known Dr. Ponard, for example, demonstrates that he has read and enjoyed a number of her works, citing titles of Eugénie's past successes at the beginning of the narrative when he is explaining who she is to his younger colleague Jean Cécile. Ponard mentions her recent plays, rightfully assuming that Dr. Cécile will know of them.

---

they aspire to, the petit bourgeois are condemned to disparate choices" (326). The petit bourgeois is usually more adamant and allows for less variation in appreciation and consumption of culture.

Bourdieu also outlines two distinct positions among the producers of culture, which are usually in battle with one another to define legitimate art and culture (Bourdieu 1993, 40). Authors are divided into success and failure based not only on economic profit, but also on the type of audience to whom they appeal: "Authors who manage to secure 'high-society' successes and bourgeois consecration are opposed to those who are condemned to so-called 'popular' success—the authors of rural novels, music-hall artists, chansonniers, etc." (46). Those who produce "art for art's sake" are therefore usually considered more important than those who produce a "bourgeois" or "popular" art. Two of the three portraits of Belle Epoque women writers included in this chapter provide striking examples of a heroine's move back and forth, from a producer of "art for art's sake" to that of a "bourgeois" or "popular" artist. These fictional portraits are not only of the women as producers of culture; their positions as consumers of culture, in fact, often lead to a contradictory movement between the two poles or, at the least, the temptation to do so.

5. "Elle eut cette année-là un très retentissant succès avec son roman: *Les Chevilles*. L'amour y foisonnait, y ruisselait, y débordait. L'état d'esprit de l'époque s'entendait à déchiffrer l'énigme du titre: *Les Chevilles*. On savait de quoi il s'agissait" (Yver 1903, 38).

6. "au théâtre pour l'auteur d'une pièce, et ce qu'elles doivent être dans la vie passionnelle d'un homme" (Yver 1903, 38).

Her identity is thus directly linked to her famous works: "Who is she? ... Why it's Pierre Fifre, the author of 'Peasants,' of 'Madeleine-Capucine,' you know, last year's success at the Odeon."[7] Jean Cécile's surprise ("Pierre Fifre, a woman?") does not come from a lack of recognition, but rather from the revelation of two new facts. First, the woman whose broken ankle he has just treated is not a courtesan, as he had assumed from the demimondaine appearance of her apartment, she is instead a successful writer. Second, the true sex of the author of these theater hits is revealed abruptly, possibly changing Dr. Cécile's interpretation of the works. Eugénie's practice of taking on a masculine nom de plume, common for the time period, allowed her the role of cultural producer that might have been denied or misinterpreted because of her sex.

Yver portrays Eugénie as both a producer and a consumer of culture, although she does not place her in the same class for both roles. Eugénie has given up much of her economic privilege as a consumer of culture by divorcing a wealthy banker. She is quite content, however, with her new status and cultural capital as a writer for the bourgeoisie. She describes her feeling of liberation after her divorce, claiming that she felt intoxicated by freedom and happiness, and happier to be free at twenty-eight than she was when in love at age twenty (Yver 1903, 37). Eugénie's description of her daily routine further demonstrates her contentment with her new life: "My solitude is agreeable to me. I can pursue my internal dreams. Often I return home, walking in a golden vision, in the unreal, moved by the great Parisian scenery that has never ceased to enchant me. . . . After that I devote myself to work. Nothing disturbs me, nothing comes to offend or demolish these exquisite sensations and this illusory world that I see."[8] These declarations announce that Eugénie's divorce has provided her, as a consumer of culture, with greater cultural capital in exchange for less economic privilege. The quest element has won the battle in Eugénie's story. While the romance plot remains an important ingredient in the sophisticated plays and novels that she writes, it is of secondary importance in her personal life.

---

7. "Qui est-ce? . . . Mais c'est Pierre Fifre, l'auteur de 'Paysans,' de 'Madeleine-Capucine,' vous savez bien, l'année dernière, à l'Odéon, ce succès" (Yver 1903, 21).

8. "Ma solitude m'est agréable. J'y poursuis mon rêve intérieur. Souvent je rentre chez moi, marchant dans une vision d'or, dans l'irréel, émue du grand décor parisien qui n'a jamais cessé de m'enchanter. . . . Après je me donne au travail. Rien ne me trouble, rien ne vient heurter ni démolir l'architecture de ces sensations exquises, de ce monde illusoire que je vois" (Yver 1903, 43).

In contrast to her status as a consumer of culture, Eugénie Lebrun's status as a producer of culture retains links with the dominant economic and political class. Her literary successes indicate that she has not entirely relinquished her access to the power and prestige of this group. Dr. Ponard tells Jean Cécile that Eugénie earns money "like a man" with just a few strokes of the pen (Yver 1903, 21). In the field of cultural production, therefore, Eugénie creates literature and drama that not only appeals to but is also well compensated by the dominant class. The narrator includes details of her writer's block and various other struggles as an artist who creates art for art's sake.[9] These passages indicate the work of a writer who is not concerned with deadlines or profits, but with inspiration, creative production, and artistic talent. Yet the overwhelming emphasis is placed on the stock types that she creates, the details that she uses to reproduce a realistic image of the haute bourgeoisie, and the personalities of her friends whom she examines and imitates when constructing characters for her new works. Her habit of writing personal dramas and romances into fiction has blurred the boundaries between the fictional and the real world, leaving her too dispassionate and analytical for men, such as Jean Cécile, who fall in love with her. This is one of the main reasons why the romance narrative never advances in this section of Yver's text.

Renée Néré, in *La Vagabonde,* begins as Eugénie had begun: with a divorce, reduced economic power, and a certain critical and bourgeois success in writing literature. For several reasons, however, she moves deliberately away from her bourgeois audience, taking the opposite path, straight to the working-class music halls. In contrast to Eugénie, Renée appears to prefer her "condemned" status as a "popular" star in the music hall, as sociologist Pierre Bourdieu labeled such a position (Bourdieu 1991, 46). One of the main reasons for Renée's decision to give up writing is that she had become a writer while she was married and therefore considers the practice of writing a luxury, an activity for women of the leisure class who have hours to spend hypnotized on the couch, forgetting time and concentrating only on creating new "treasures" for the blank page (Colette 1984b, 1074).[10] Colette confirms the

---

9. "Elle le tenait au courant de ses mécomptes, de ses délicates souffrances d'artiste, de ses lassitudes, de ses cruelles intermittences de talent" (She kept him apprised of her disappointments, her delicate artist's suffering, her lassitude, her cruel intermittent talent.) (Yver 1903, 30).

10. "Ecrire. . . . C'est le regard accroché, hypnotisé par le reflet de la fenêtre dans l'encrier d'argent, la fièvre divine qui monte aux joues, au front, tandis qu'une bienheureuse mort glace sur le papier la main qui écrit. Cela veut dire aussi l'oubli de l'heure, la paresse au creux du divan, la débauche d'invention d'où l'on sort courbatu, abêti, mais déjà récompensé, et porteur de trésors qu'on décharge lentement sur la feuille vierge, dans le petit cirque de lumière qui s'abrite sous la

statement made by her contemporary Camille Pert, who believed that women did not pursue journalism or writing as a full-time career because there was not enough financial security in that line of work (Pert 298). Rather, it was a leisure-time activity that occasionally produced a bestseller.

The act of writing for Renée had also been a means of isolating herself from her surroundings, a way to avoid dealing with her crumbling marriage. She confesses to her diary that suffering and writing seemed to go hand in hand: "I settled down to suffering with an unyielding pride and obstinacy, and to producing literature" (Colette 2001b, 27).[11] Renée's literary endeavors were therefore not a planned career move but an escape technique that was temporarily soothing. Thus Renée conceives her writing more as art for art's sake, rather than as a product for bourgeois consumption.

In some ways, Renée even denies the quest element in her early writing career, dismissing her literary success as something fleeting, based on the dubious judgment of critics whose opinions were always opposed to hers. Her own opinion of her first novel indicates some condescension, related to the work's incredible success among the "tout Paris," and she calls it "a chaste *little* novel of love and marriage, slightly *insipid* and very *agreeable,* which had an unexpected and extravagant success" (Colette 2001b, 27).[12] The adjectives "little" (petit), "insipid" (serin) and "agreeable" (gentil) are mildly mocking and demonstrate Renée's lack of enthusiasm for her bourgeois hit. But she does mention that her first work's great success encouraged her to write a second and even a third novel, although they both sold less well than the first. Her second work, lacking positive public reception, had a readership mainly of other authors. Here, her audience was reduced to other *gens de lettres,* but it still carried some renown. Her third novel was neither a bourgeois hit nor an artistic success, but it remains her own favorite, and she calls it her "private unrecognized masterpiece" (mon chef d'oeuvre inconnu à moi) (Colette 2001b, 28; Colette 1984b, 1085). Renée thus indicates that writing for the sake of a reading public (whether bourgeois,

---

ampe" (Colette 1984b, 1074). ("To write is to sit and stare, hypnotized, at the reflection of the window in the silver ink-stand, to feel the divine fever mounting to one's cheeks and forehead while the hand that writes grows blissfully numb upon the paper. It also means idle hours curled up in the hollow of the divan, and then the orgy of inspiration from which one emerges stupefied and aching all over, but already recompensed and laden with treasures that one unloads slowly on to the virgin page in the little round pool of light under the lamp" [Colette, Mcleod trans. 14].)

11. "je m'étais mise à souffrir avec un orgueil et un entêtement intraitables et *à faire de la littérature*" (Colette 1984b, 1084, emphasis added).

12. "un chaste *petit* roman d'amour et de mariage, un peu *serin,* très *gentil,* et qui eut un succès inattendu, démesuré" (Colette 1984b, 1084, emphasis added).

intellectual, or artistic), and as a potential vocation, never presented itself as a viable option. She describes herself as "a woman of letters who has turned out badly" (une femme de lettres qui a mal tourné) (Colette 2001b, 14; Colette 1984b 1075). As is typical of the traditional bildungsroman plotline, circumstances in Renée's life have required her to make a detour from her initial goals, and the "false start" caused by her divorce has led her to choose mime performance as an alternative career path.

As a divorcée, Renée has switched over to the supposedly more dependable working atmosphere in the music hall, yet the idea that mime and dance performances might provide a more stable income than writing appears to be only part of the reason why Renée has changed careers, especially when we consider the many uncertainties and difficulties involved in the life of a music hall performer. This profession is also based on approval by an unknown audience but includes harsher physical circumstances: strenuous physical training and rehearsals, cold dressing rooms, uncomfortable traveling arrangements, short contracts without guarantees of renewal. Renée herself notes the pitiable example of noble suffering and rejection of one of her colleagues, Antoniew and his three dogs, who may not be invited to return for a second season: "Nothing could be sadder, more dignified, or more disdainful than this man and his three creatures, proudly resigned to their wandering lot. . . . Tenderness, like rest and security, is for us an inaccessible luxury" (Colette 2001b, 38–39).[13] The working conditions in the music halls of Paris seem to be filled with as much uncertainty and disappointment as those in the life of a writer.

Despite this precarious existence, Renée claims that she loves her new career. Her description of the audiences, popular and sometimes boisterous, yet appreciative and goodwilled, provides some explanation for her satisfaction with her role as culture producer in the industrial arts. Throwing cheap bouquets of violets and applauding thunderously, the working-class crowd with its enthusiastic bon vivant attitude gives her confidence, and it remains sympathetic and admiring throughout the novel. In contrast, the occasional solo performances that she gives at private parties of the Parisian bourgeoisie make Renée uncomfortable and edgy, especially because they throw her back into her old milieu from which she feels she has been exiled by her divorce.

---

13. "Il n'y a rien de plus triste, de plus digne, de plus dédaigneux, que cet homme et ses trois bêtes, orgueilleusement résignés à leur sort de vagabonds. . . . Comme le repos et la sécurité, la tendresse est pour nous un luxe inaccessible" (Colette 1984b, 1093).

Renée describes the black mood and feeling of dread that hangs over her all day before a private performance that her agent has contracted for her and her mime partner, Brague. In that particular audience, Renée finds sitting in the very first row a woman who slept with her husband, then another in the second row, and a third farther back in the crowd. The women are all embarrassed and surprised to see Renée performing on the stage in front of them. The men in the audience may have been aloof and uncaring when she was a married woman of the dominant class, yet they now watch with curiosity and appetite as she performs half-nude for them in their living room (Colette 1984b, 1099). Renée, in contrast, is disgusted and angry, and she renders these faces from her past nameless, even in her thoughts. Although Renée is obviously the traitor along class lines, in her mind she accuses the women in the audience of sexual treason and the men of conspiracy (Colette 1984b, 1095). Her personal reasons for separating herself from this crowd are thus closely linked to her professional decision to give up bourgeois literature for the career of a mime. Renée prefers the drunken catcalls and the fist fights of working-class music halls to the sinister silence of the private bourgeois salon or the fickle approval of bourgeois literary critics. The impact that her marriage has had on her career path is reinforced here, along with the ways in which the earlier romance plot has affected her ability to carry out her quest for an independent life.

La Vagabonde, however, is an unconfessed elegy in praise of writing, since Renée is composing a "journal intime" (private diary) of her thoughts and experiences that eventually constitute the entire text of the novel. This renewed interest in her earlier career resurfaces as hints of her returning desire to write arise throughout the work: "From time to time I feel a need, sharp as thirst in summer, to note and to describe" (Colette 2001b, 14).[14] Although Renée dismisses these desires as irrelevant or distracting to the tasks of living, paying the bills, and simply surviving, this writing activity continues to attach her to the artistic fractions of French society. In this manner, Colette re-embraces the writing profession even as her protagonist appears to spurn it.

In contrast, Marcelle Tinayre's protagonist, Josanne Valentin, embraces her career in writing enthusiastically, following in the footsteps of her father, José Daniel. Josanne directs her work toward the lower classes, but with differing results than those of Renée. The audience of her women's magazine,

---

14. "J'éprouve bien, de loin en loin, le besoin, vif comme la soif en été, de noter, de peindre. Je prends encore la plume, pour commencer le jeu périlleux et décevant, pour saisir et fixer, sous la pointe double et ployante, le chatoyant, le fugace, le passionnant adjectif" (Colette 1984b, 1074).

Le Monde féminin, consists mainly of women from the petite bourgeoisie living in the provinces. Josanne mockingly describes the carefully crafted depictions of the "elite" that the editor, Mme Isidore Foucart, requires for the articles of *Le Monde féminin:* "In *The Feminine World,* all the women were pretty, almost all were virtuous; all the men were 'talented;' the worst ones had 'children's souls.' Men and women, all were rich; they exhibited, in their suave 'interiors,' designer or couturier clothing. And their effigies, their biographies, so much fame and glory, stirred up the hearts of the little provincial women who subscribed to the magazine" (Tinayre 44–45).[15] The strict limitations of a petit bourgeois set of tastes are obvious in Tinayre's description: there can be no departures from conventional cultural stereotypes about the dominant class: all the women are pretty, all the men are talented, and all of them are rich. To maintain such a middle-brow version of culture, censure must often be imposed on writers and photographers at the magazine. In one scene at the offices of *Le Monde féminin,* for example, the editors must cancel an interview with a "Miss Brémond, great actress," because she insisted that the magazine include with its biographical article two risqué photographs of herself that she happened to find amusing. Trying to explain why the pictures are impossible, the photographer points to the *pudeur* (modesty) of the subscribers of *Le Monde féminin* (43).

Although the writers rarely enter into direct contact with their readers, a moment arises in the offices of *Le Monde féminin* that illustrates the "disparate choices," as Bourdieu labels them, of the petit bourgeois subscriber (Bourdieu 1984, 326). A woman verbally assaults Josanne and a number of other employees because she did not receive her bonus prize, a cheap handheld fan, with her annual subscription. She threatens to switch over to the newly founded *Vie Heureuse* or *Fémina* magazines in order to get her fan. As the staff passes her on from one to the other, they make disdainful remarks about her petty attitude and behavior: aspiring to a certain bourgeois ideal, yet inclining toward a working-class practice of "getting one's money's worth" (Tinayre 43).

Josanne's class status at the magazine is not entirely clear-cut. Although her father's reputation as a journalist places her in the intellectual or artistic population of the bourgeoisie, his early death has forced Josanne and her

---

15. "Dans *Le Monde féminin,* toutes les femmes étaient jolies; presque toutes étaient vertueuses; tous les hommes étaient 'talentueux'; les plus rosses avaient des 'âmes d'enfant.' Hommes et femmes, ils étaient tous riches; ils exhibaient, dans des 'intérieurs' suaves, des costumes du grand tailleur ou du grand couturier. Et leurs effigies, leurs biographies, tant de réclame et tant de gloire, allaient troubler le coeur des petites abonnées provinciales" (Tinayre 44–45).

mother into petit bourgeois or even working-class living conditions. As the novel begins, Josanne is the sole breadwinner for her own family, and her husband's lengthy illness requires expensive medicine. She is thus required to lead an extremely frugal existence: she does her own marketing every morning; cleans the apartment herself; and the impulse purchase of *The Woman Worker* (*La Travailleuse*), a book on women's rights that she found intriguing, causes her anxiety about their monthly budget and a certain amount of regret. The feelings of the two directors of the magazine toward Josanne illustrate the dual class position that she maintains. On one hand, Mme Foucart does not like Josanne's lower economic status, describing her as "poor, dressed indifferently, and very arrogant." But her husband and co-director, M. Foucart, appreciates Josanne's intellectual capital: "intelligent, courageous, exact, and proud:—a model employee and a 'brave' woman (une 'brave' femme)" (Tinayre 45–46). At the beginning of the novel, Josanne's status as a general staff member reflects her ambiguous class status. Her assignments range from clerk to secretary to copy editor, but she does not complain about arriving at the bureau earlier than all the other reporters, nor does she find the variety of tasks that she must juggle for *Le Monde féminin* to be a burden (38). Tinayre's label for Josanne, "l'employée à tout faire," of course brings to mind the more menial employment of the *bonne à tout faire*, an underpaid domestic servant position held by overworked young women in many petit bourgeois households during the turn of the century. Josanne's career and her attitudes do not fit the mold of the "exceptional" professional, such as the brainy women Jeanne Boerk or Marceline Rhonans. Nor is she well known publicly for her articles on women's rights, like her colleague at the magazine, Mademoiselle Bon. At this early stage, her work is above all a source of income, to allow her to maintain her independent lifestyle and support her husband and child on her own. Thus she produces culture in a similar fashion to Renée in *La Vagabonde*.

Josanne's first writing assignments are mainly limited to banal summaries of recent books for the book review section and to predictable forecasts about seasonal trends in women's fashion, rather than investigative reporting or interviews with celebrities. She admits openly that her editor, M. Foucart, often pressures her into writing on topics that are not of great interest to her. In a letter to Noël Delysle, whose book *La Travailleuse* she reviewed, Josanne states that the opportunities for self-expression were rare (Tinayre 81). In one ironic scene, Josanne is writing a piece on the latest clothing styles when her worn blouse rips at the seams. At first she becomes upset, weary of being less fashionable than her well-dressed colleagues.

Yet she also notes the irony of the situation: mending her frayed old shirt while sitting in the beautiful offices of the magazine writing about haute couture and next season's fashion which she herself could never afford. She even laughs as she thinks about what her petit bourgeois readers would think of her if they could see her in her tattered clothing (40).

Even when Josanne is promoted to "journaliste" and invited by M. Foucart to conduct interviews and do investigative reports for the magazine, she must still bring her writing style in to line with petit bourgeois cultural constraints. For example, when she visits the Villa Bleue, a home for unwed pregnant teenagers, M. Foucart gives her a cautionary piece of advice that contradicts the most basic tenets of investigative reporting, namely clarity, factualness, and truth: "Foucart had recommended that we 'attenuate the stomachs': 'Remember that your article will be read by young women. They must not be able to understand anything.'"[16] Instead of informing the reading public, Josanne's editor requires that she obscure the facts and keep her younger readers uninformed about the perils of unwed teenage motherhood. Mademoiselle Bon, who has encouraged Josanne to write this article and even accompanied her to the Villa Bleue, explains to the home's director that women reporters cannot always write openly and expose the misery and horrors of other women in the world around them, mainly because of editors' constraints: Foucart, for example, demands that charity be "discreet" and misery be "veiled" in his magazine (Tinayre 98–99). The subject matter of this particular article is problematic in many ways for the conservative tastes of the petit bourgeois audience. One of the only reasons Josanne has been allowed to pursue the topic is the fact that the Villa Bleue has been founded by a group of wealthy Parisian socialites, whom the readers of *Le Monde féminin* admire. The photographer for the article makes these society women the centerpiece of his portrait, along with several women doctors and administrators; the pregnant girls are included almost as an afterthought and mostly well hidden from view. He boasts about his clever placement of the teenagers' stomachs, so that only the young pretty ones are truly visible, and none really look pregnant.[17] His work thus transforms into reality Foucart's principles about discretion and obscuring the facts.

16. "Foucart avait recommendé d''attenuer les ventres': 'Songez que votre article sera lu par des jeunes filles. Il faut qu'elles puissent n'y comprendre rien.'" (Tinayre 96).

17. "Ça c'est mon triomphe! Il n'y en a pas une seule qui ait vraiment l'air d'être enceinte! . . . J'ai mis les plus grosses et les plus laides tout au fond, et devant, rien que des jeunes et gentilles. . . . C'est charmant!" (Tinayre 98).

Josanne's promotion to the position of journalist at *Le Monde féminin* thus does not give her artistic freedom. Her prose writing remains produced for and consumed by a specific class of reader. Josanne, however, does not renounce her career because of the censure or limits imposed on her writing. In fact, she professes no interest in creating art for art's sake and no urges to write a novel or play on the side.[18] In contrast to both Eugénie and Renée, who claim at least some artistic ability and originality, Josanne's self-critique firmly denies any creative genius. At the same time, she affirms her journalistic talents, including her verve, spirit, and the ability to write clearly.

The portrayals of female culture producers in these three novels highlight the conventional features of their writing or performing careers. Although each woman is creative to a certain extent, she is also portrayed as aware of and accepting the constraints imposed by her particular audience, whether they are working-class, petit bourgeois, or bourgeois consumers. Thus, in their public or professional roles, unlike their scientific counterparts, these women are not recognizably "exceptional" individuals. In their personal lives, however, their values and attitudes about romance, love, and marriage remain outside the socially accepted norms of behavior. Each heroine devises her own system of principles to live by, and for each, her "rebellious" decisions in private are determined in part by her public position as a producer of culture.

Self-Sufficient Women in Love

Each of the writing protagonists studied here is tempted by a wealthy or professional man to abandon her artistic production for the economic privilege and security of a traditional female position in the dominant class. All three reject this offer, but for different reasons.

Josanne Valentin, as we have just seen, is hardly a *rebelle* when it comes to her professional life: she appears resigned to the production of a conservative journalism for her petit bourgeois readership. But in decisions concerning

---

18. "If I had some talent, I would write books: I would tell truths, serious and sad, that only a woman can tell well.... Alas! I don't have talent.... I write an article skillfully; I have a little verve and spirit, and experience.... But I lack the gift of achieving my imagination, I lack a creative faculty.... I would be a good advisor, perhaps a good collaborator." (Si j'avais du talent, j'écrirais des livres: je dirais des choses vraies, graves et tristes, qu'une femme seulement peu bien dire.... Hélas! je n'ai pas de talent.... J'écris adroitement un article; j'ai un peu de verve et d'esprit, du métier.... Mais il me manque le don de réaliser mes imaginations, la faculté créatrice.... Je serais une bonne conseillère, peut-être une bonne collaboratrice [Tinayre 142].)

her personal life, she chooses actions that often fall outside the category of bourgeois convention, creating a truly subversive character. As the novel opens, Josanne's illegitimate child Claude is two years old, her affair with the wealthy bachelor Maurice Nattier has gone on for five years, and her husband Pierre's illness has been dragging on for eight long years. She is clearly at the end of her rope with both of these men, and as the narrator makes obvious, neither one is worthy of Josanne's attentions. Josanne faithfully tends to her bedridden husband until the day he dies. Her life of sacrifice extends beyond "decent" bourgeois convention to include her own body, which she abandons to her husband's desires, even as his diseased body disgusts and repulses her. Even in sex, Josanne feels a compulsive obligation to agree to his every demand (Tinayre 32). Tinayre's portrait of Josanne's husband resembles that of many of Yver's male protagonists, a whining, egotistical brat whose self-pity and fits of rage, combined with his debilitating disease and reliance on ether and other addictive drugs, turn him into a decaying and wretched human being. The narrator inevitably leads the reader to feel pity for Josanne in her role of sacrificial wife.

Meanwhile, Josanne has maintained a romantic and picturesque love affair with Maurice Nattier, even though the possibility of marriage or a future life together seems very remote. Their love is described initially as "a discreet and delicate love, which perfumed Josanne's dark life like violets perfume the woods in spring. It was a chaste and innocent love, very proud of resembling love that one finds in books" (Tinayre 6).[19] As the narrator indicates, their love affair is typical, even novelistic, comparable to those found "in books."[20] Josanne's attitude about extramarital sex is unconventional for a bourgeois housewife, much closer to the remarks emitted by professional courtesans, as she claims openly that she is not ashamed of

---

19. "un amour discret, délicat, qui embauma la vie obscure de Josanne comme les violettes invisibles embaument les bois, au printemps. Ce fut un amour chaste et puéril, tout fier de ressembler aux amours qu'on voit dans les livres" (Tinayre 6).

20. Several passages make reference to the "literary" quality of Josanne's life. For example, during one of her daily shopping trips through the local markets, Josanne comments that her neighborhood, in the Latin Quarter, seems to appear out of different French novels: "Josanne est bien sûre que ces gens sont des personnages de Balzac qui reviennent. Le fantôme du père Goriot descend parfois la montagne Sainte-Geneviève pour rentrer à la pension Vauquer. . . . Elle s'amuse à retrouver, après le Paris de Balzac, le Paris d'Eugène Sue. . . . La rue Mouffetard. . . . Elle achète son beurre chez la crémière au teint de lait . . . telle 'Gervaise' dans l'*Assommoir*." (Josanne is sure that these people are Balzac characters who have come back. The phantom of Father Goriot sometimes comes down the Saint-Genevieve mountain to return home to the Vauquer Pension. . . . She enjoyed finding, after Balzac's Paris, the Paris of Eugène Sue. . . . On Mouffetard Street. . . .

having an affair and is even pleased to say so. Her lover, Maurice, however, being rather conservative and hypocritical according to the narrator, is shocked by Josanne's lack of guilt (6–7). Maurice's selfish and unheroic character mutates into a contemptible portrait of immaturity and irresponsibility when he abandons Josanne as soon as she announces that she is pregnant with his child (9). When he reappears after the child's birth, Josanne and he continue to meet occasionally for a quick hour or two of physical pleasure together, in hotel rooms or hasty carriage rides (23).

Josanne's justifications for protecting her relationship, although complicated, indicate a personal philosophy to be true to herself and to her own desires and needs: "I cannot live without happiness. And the pleasure of sacrifice is not enough for me. . . . I am not a saint; I am not a heroine: I am a woman, very much a woman."[21] In surprising contrast to her humble acceptance of menial tasks and dull assignments at *Le Monde féminin,* Josanne boldly states that she has the right to satisfy her own wishes and goals in private, in addition to her obligations to care for her husband and child. She does not worry about what her petit bourgeois readers would think or what her bourgeois colleagues at the magazine would say if they knew about her affair with Maurice. Josanne clings to both men for a variety of reasons—love, responsibility, or pleasure—until Pierre's death from cancer and the news of Maurice's marriage to an engineer's daughter, which follows quickly thereafter.

From the outset, Tinayre has modeled a female protagonist who is remarkable in her personal values and relationships. The man with whom Josanne eventually falls in love is equally an outsider to bourgeois conventions: Noël Delysle, whose study of working women, *La Travailleuse* (*The Working Woman*), appears to match her sentiments about women's rights to work, love, and live as they choose. Her first contact with this man is intellectual, as she skims his text in a bookshop while waiting for a tardy Maurice to meet her. Delysle's words inspire her as they confirm her own belief system, stating that a poor woman has the right to more than the three

---

She buys her butter from the dairy saleswomen with the milky skin . . . like 'Gervaise' in [Zola's] *The Dram Shop* (Tinayre 52–53). Josanne's profession, as a literary and fashion critic for *Le Monde féminin,* obviously predisposes her to see life through literary lenses. It also indicates that she has read a variety of novels, from the realist to the naturalist traditions. Yet the narrator and other characters in the book also join in these types of remarks, which may indicate an authorial attempt to influence the reader, letting her know which types of fiction have influenced the author in writing.

21. "Je ne peux pas vivre sans bonheur. Et la volupté du sacrifice ne me suffit pas. . . . Je ne suis pas une sainte; je ne suis pas une héroïne: je suis une femme, très femme" (Tinayre 8).

basic necessities: she also has "the right to think, to speak, to act, to love as she wishes" (Tinayre 13). Her impromptu decision to buy *La Travailleuse* results in the propitious opportunity for Josanne to write a review of a text that she actually finds intellectually stimulating, and it provides an occasion for Delysle to write to her, thus initiating a long-distance correspondence.

When Josanne finally meets and falls in love with Noël, she does not immediately begin a romantic relationship with him, and she continues to write and to live independently. Her decision to refuse Noël's first offer of marriage is linked in part to her belief that women should be able to live freely, on their own. She also refuses his offer because of his brutish jealousy of her son Claude, who acts as a reminder to Noël that Josanne had a previous lover. His jealousy clearly unveils Noël's hypocritical feelings about women, since it demonstrates that his theories about women's rights to live on their own and love as they please contrast directly with his emotional possessiveness and his obsession with Josanne's past.

Surprisingly, Josanne is not offended by Noël's hypocrisy but rather is moved by it and encouraged to help him overcome his old-fashioned emotions. It is Noël's long battle with jealousy that eventually stamps out any "rebellion" or independence in Josanne's goals for her personal life. At first, she refuses to feel guilty about her love affair with Maurice, and she does not regret her past life before Noël: "She could not persuade herself that she had committed an unspeakable act, and that she would only be able to escape scorn through remorse, penitence, and humility. She felt nothing that resembled Christian contrition and she did not want to be loved out of pity or weakness."[22] During moments of lucidity, Noël agrees with her rational arguments. But he returns to his bursts of outrage and despair whenever Josanne makes the slightest mention of a past action or emotion.

Tinayre builds tension throughout the narrative with a series of scenes between the couple, alternating between angry drama and calming reconciliation, until Josanne reaches a state of emotional exhaustion and renounces her past in order to obtain Noël's complete affection (Tinayre 333). At the same time that she repudiates her past, she announces that she is no longer a *rebelle*: "Do not use that name "rebel" for me anymore. . . . I rebelled against the moral and material injustices that I had suffered, like so many women,

---

22. "Elle ne se persuadait pas qu'elle avait commis une acte infâme, et qu'elle ne pourrait échapper au mépris que par le remords, la pénitence, et l'humilité. Elle ne ressentait rien qui ressemblât à de la contrition chrétienne et elle ne voulait pas être aimée par pitié, par faiblesse" (Tinayre 260).

but not against love."²³ Once Josanne has given up her right to a past life and to her independence, Noël feels liberated from his jealousy, thus revealing his underlying conservatism. It is only after Josanne sacrifices herself that they can live happily together.

Could this be considered a "happy" ending? The couple may appear blissfully united at the conclusion of the novel, yet Marcelle Tinayre leaves enough ambiguity in her text so that the reader must decide for herself whether or not Josanne and Noël will continue to be happy together. For example, it appears that they will marry in the near future, but the marriage is never openly discussed. Instead, it is mentioned only indirectly when Noël takes it upon himself to announce to Josanne's editor that she will soon be abandoning her career in journalism in order to take care of him and their future family when they wed (Tinayre 348). The text does not contain any statement by Josanne about forgoing her career in journalism for a marriage to Noël, even though his announcement, ending with the plural *nous* ("nous nous marions"), implies that she was in agreement. It is left to the reader to decide whether or not Josanne will actually give up her writing career and her independence, if and when she marries Noël Delysle. As we have seen for Josanne, the personal and private are two separate spheres.

Much of the romance between Josanne and Noël may appear to belong outside the traditional realm of bourgeois courtship: they have sex many months before there is a mention of marriage, they both admit to previous lovers and sexual experiences, and much of their relationship is based on their compatibility as intellectuals and writers. It is only in the physical aspects of their relationship that Josanne reverts to conservative notions of the "laws of nature" about the power of men over women in love. After an afternoon of lovemaking at Noël's apartment, her thoughts silently address him as he smokes peacefully: "It is both our desire that I be your respected equal in the eyes of the world, in your mind and in your friendship. But the rebel rebelled against an unjust society, and not against nature; she did not rebel against the eternal law of love. . . . She does not reject the tender, joyous and noble voluntary servitude, which does not humiliate, because it is offered. Truly, it pleases me to call you 'my master.' "²⁴ Josanne does not believe that these physical desires for submission affect her equal status

---

23. "Ne me donne plus ce nom de 'rebelle.'. . . Je me suis révoltée, contre les injustices morales et matérielles, dont j'ai souffert, comme tant de femmes, et non pas contre l'amour" (Tinayre 334).

24. Que je sois votre égale respectée, devant le monde, devant votre raison et votre amitié, c'est notre désir à tous deux. Mais la rebelle s'est rebellée contre la société injuste, et non pas contre

with Noël as an intellectual or a friend. Nor do they reduce her feminist principles in the social and political realms. As with her affair with Maurice, Josanne believes that she can continue to pursue her intellectual and feminist goals while enjoying a submissive physical relationship with Noël. Thus she may indeed feel free to continue her career as a journalist even after she marries Noël.

Renée Néré in *La Vagabonde* draws a similar distinction between submitting to a powerful physical relationship with a man and maintaining her independent way of life. This division is made simpler for Renée because her attraction to Maxime Dufferein-Chautel is not at all intellectual, but solely physical. Max originally noticed Renée in one of her music hall performances, and their first encounter, in her dressing room after the show, is filled with his intense animal desire for her (Colette 1984b, 1079–80). After Max learns that Renée does not respond to the "wild desire" (désir sauvage) of her music hall admirers, he controls his passion but still focuses all of his attention on her body rather than on her conversation or her thoughts (1122). Max does not appear curious about Renée's ideas or activities, and he does not reveal any of his own. Renée knows nothing about Max's interest or abilities, except that he belongs to the leisure class and has no occupation, no profession. She asks herself if he thinks, reads, or works but decides that given his economic class, he does none of those things (1123). Renée insists on adjectives that emphasize the quotidian and unexceptional in Max—commonplace, adequate, so many men ("banale," "suffisant," "tant d'hommes"). He is just a typical male, replaceable and rather uninteresting. As they spend more time together, Renée's ignorance of his principles, politics, and interests remains a large gap in their relationship. She merely laughs at the fact that he spends all his time on love, thus taking the traditionally female role of the courtesan in their relationship, while she works for a living and is preoccupied with her career as much as or even more than she is concerned with their affair (1170–71).

Their physical relationship, in contrast, takes off dramatically and develops quickly throughout the narrative. Renée enjoys being swept off her feet and turning herself into a submissive object of affection. During an interlude in their lovemaking, she remarks on her obedient behavior in front of him: "Maxime has remained on the divan and his mute appeal

---

la nature; elle ne s'est pas rebellée contre la loi éternelle de l'amour. . . . Elle ne repousse point la tendre, joyeuse et noble servitude volontaire, qui n'humilie point, puisqu'elle est consentie. Vraiment, il me plaît de vous appeler 'mon maître'" (Tinayre 305).

receives the most flattering of responses: my look of a submissive bitch, rather shame-faced, rather cowed, very must petted, and ready to accept the leash, the collar, the place at her master's feet, and everything" (Colette 2001b, 127).[25] Renée's use of the dog-master metaphor recalls the same type of master-slave vocabulary that Josanne employed to describe her sexual rapport with Noël ("it pleases me to call you 'my master'" [*La Rebelle* 305]). Renée does not balk at this instinct to obedience and submission, and her old friend Hamond explains that it is because she is in love (1177). Although Hamond refers to the humiliating or degrading tasks Renée performed for her ex-husband Adolphe Taillandy when she still loved him, the lesson is the same for her acts of submission with Max, since she is beginning to love him when Hamond makes this statement. Just as Josanne dismissed her feminist principles when in the bedroom, Renée agrees with Hamond that love does anesthetize one's sense of independence and pride (1184). There are even moments when she is with Max where she contemplates giving up everything—her mime partner, her music hall performances, her road trips—in order to live peacefully in the "great shadow" of her lover (1180). But for a number of reasons, Renée must reject this dream, and in great contrast to Josanne, Renée finally decides that her humble physical servitude to this man will adversely affect her independent status vis-à-vis her career and her new way of life, which she has struggled to establish and maintain since her difficult divorce three years earlier.

Renée's new life as an independent working woman is probably the most important cause for her uncertainty about her future with Max. Although she does not have complete control over her work schedule, Renée has gained the authority to make demands of her agent, Salomon, for tour bookings, salary levels, and the type of commission she considers appropriate for his services. In an important scene in Salomon's office, Renée demonstrates her unshakeable will that allows her to get what she wants at work (Colette 1984b, 1135–37). This hard-won independence is not easily relinquished, even for the life of luxury and leisure that Max promises her. When she tells her old friend Hamond of her visions of a future life with Max, she is stunned by Hamond's obvious question about renouncing her career (1179). This first reaction indicates the extent of Renée's attachment to her work and to the independence it affords her: she will not abandon her career easily.

---

25. "Maxime est demeuré sur le divan, et son muet appel reçoit la plus flatteuse réponse: mon regard de chienne sournoise, un peu penaude, un peu battue, très choyée, et qui accepte tout, la laisse, le collier, la place aux pieds de son maître" (Colette 1984b, 1160).

Later, when she and Max playfully discuss the prospect of having children together, Renée again bolts when the idea of giving up her work is suggested. In this instance, Max expresses the pleasure he would feel when Renée's pregnancy would force her to refrain from traveling all over France without him and end her career on the stage. She is not surprised that Max wants to possess her completely. In fact, she has been telling him for days that he is a natural "père de famille" (paterfamilias), a conservative stay-at-home type. But his words, "tu serais prise" (you would be caught), reactivate old questions and concerns in Renée's mind.

Renée's decision to forgo marriage to Max indicates that she associates her personal emotions with her actions in the public sphere of work, and she cannot find a way to separate the two. If she renounces her independent travels and her public life on the stage, she will also be losing her individual character and her sense of self in her private life. When Hamond suggests that she begin writing novels again to replace her theater activities, Renée is tempted by the idea. But she realizes that she would have to be completely devoted to Max's life of leisurely pastimes, travel, and sports. Her desire to write would be smothered, just as her desire to perform and to travel on her own would have to be crushed. Thus, because Renée cannot envision herself as an active partner in a future marriage with Max, she cannot feasibly envision the revival of her writing career either.

One of the major differences between Renée and Josanne is the fact that Renée finally chooses not to abandon her own sense of identity. Although she does not invite the recurring comparisons that appear to her between Max and Adolphe, she does not deny them or claim to regret her past and her previous love for Adolphe. Renée's only regret is that she and Max do not have similar backgrounds with similar degrees of suffering, betrayal, and experience in married life. If they did marry, she would recognize all the inconveniences and problems that newlywed couples encounter, since she has already been married, whereas Max has not (Colette 1984b, 1212). But Renée does nothing to change their differences and does not pretend that she can ignore or erase her past actions and thoughts as Josanne did to appease Noël's jealous nature.

Eugénie Lebrun, the heroine in *Les Cervelines,* also keeps Jean Cécile at a healthy distance from her emotional life, but Eugénie informs her would-be lover immediately that she is not interested in a romantic relationship, as soon as he expresses his designs in a confessional letter to her. She calmly explains that it is just a passing fancy and that Jean will soon forget his passion for her. Her first marriage, like Renée's in *La Vagabonde,* has cured her of the desire for another husband. Rather, Eugénie is much happier living on her own and surrounding herself with friends and admirers rather than a demanding and authoritarian husband or lover.

Yver highlights Eugénie's distance from Jean's romantic mindset through a series of detailed scenes that are highly attentive to Eugénie's movements, in order to reveal with subtlety her mindset. Even in their first encounter after Jean has sent her his important love letter, Eugénie's tone, although kind and generous, is completely businesslike, as if she were critiquing a fictional work that had been sent to her for review rather than a love letter. Her first comments to him as he enters her apartment emphasize the style and effect of his writing instead of the content of his letter: "Truly, nothing has ever touched me like that letter. You who claimed not to know how to write! I read and reread it; it is admirable."[26] She comments that his prose is concise, direct, and devoid of flowery phrasing. Using her skills as a professional author and an expert on writing, Eugénie has immediately set the tone of their conversation and established the distance that she wishes to keep from their potentially emotional discussion. Therefore, when she moves on to the heart of the matter, Jean is already silenced and submissive to her authority. Although he manages to object to her reason, to plead that his love is "heroic" and unlike the affections that she has experienced from less ardent suitors, her calm and reserved nature remains untouched. When they return to his letter, Eugénie again avoids any mention of its content and focuses instead on her examination of Jean's handwriting. Eugénie's trendy fascination with graphology leads to a painful scrutiny of Jean's personality, based on her analysis of his capital and lowercase letters (Yver 1903, 36).

Her analytical dissections of both his writing style and his personality anger Jean, as they serve to indicate Eugénie's total lack of passion for him. They do not, however, succeed in alienating his feelings for her and his desire to make her his wife. When he finally sends his old professor, Dr. Ponard, to ask for her hand in marriage for him, she refuses, again giving clear and obvious reasons for her decision: "She did not accept; she could not accept, possessing all life's pleasures, happy, celebrated, absorbed by her art, and free. Marriage could add nothing to her happiness; it was only a way to destroy it."[27] Her successful career and her faithful friends and admirers afford Eugénie a

---

26. "Vraiment, rien ne m'a jamais touchée comme cette lettre. Vous qui prétendiez ne savoir pas écrire! Je l'ai lue et relue ; elle est admirable" (Yver 1903, 33).

27. "Elle n'accepta pas; elle ne pouvait pas accepter, possédant de la vie tous les agréments, heureuse, fêtée, absorbée par son art, et libre. Le mariage ne pouvait rien ajouter à son bonheur, mais il était seulement un moyen de le détruire" (Yver 1903, 38).

serenity as a single woman that remains in direct contrast to both Renée and Josanne, who admit to strong bouts of solitude and isolation in their single lives.

When Jean Cécile makes his final visit to Eugénie's apartment and delivers his ultimatum, love me or I will never see you again, Eugénie again finds an ingenious way to distance herself from his excessive emotional outpourings. As she responds to his demand, she remains completely absorbed in her repairs to a tiny marble statue, fragile like Jean's feelings: "She was amusing herself now by gluing together a miniscule marble statue that the valet had broken. She put together, one after the other, with much delicacy, the tiny little parts that were no thicker than her finger. 'Come now,' she said to Cécile slowly, interrupted at each comma by the difficulty of her manual task, 'don't be unjust, or crazy.' "[28] Eugénie's steady hand and level tone only serve to enrage Jean, who leaves her forever and returns to his family's home in Briois. Eugénie offers patience and understanding for Jean's difficulties, and Jean cannot tolerate his loved one's "help." In contrast to the women writers in Colette's and Tinayre's novels, Eugénie never cedes her position. In the end, her forecast that Jean would recover and forget about his passion for her comes true. Alone in his apartment six months later, he must admit that Eugénie was right after all (Yver 1903, 47).

The portraits of these three self-sufficient women are directly related to their modes of cultural production in the public sphere. The two women who are most dependent on their public for legitimacy, Renée and Eugénie, are the least likely to need reinforcement in their private lives. Eugénie Lebrun is entirely reliant on her bourgeois audience and admirers, not only for her economic survival but also for friendship and social interaction. While she also maintains connections to the artistic and intellectual spheres of French society, she openly embraces her bourgeois audience's system of values at the same time that she perpetuates it in her literary works. Renée also relies heavily on her working-class audience at the music hall, but mainly for economic survival. She enjoys their bon vivant attitude toward culture and life, but her social network excludes them. She limits her social interaction to a few family friends from the bourgeoisie and several colleagues from the

---

28. "Elle s'amusait maintenant à recoller un marbre minuscule qu'avait brisé le valet de chambre. Elle remettait l'un après l'autre, avec milles délicatesses, de petits membres fins qui n'égalaient pas en grosseur son doigt. 'Voyons, dit-elle à Cécile lentement, interrompue à chaque virgule par la difficulté de sa besogne manuelle, ne soyez ni injuste, ni fou'" (Yver 1903, 41).

music hall who place themselves in the category of the artiste. Renée is not as engaged as Eugénie is with her public role of culture producer, and she therefore has serious thoughts about abandoning that role for a private life with Max.

The position of both of these women in the field of cultural production contrasts strongly with Josanne's. She is only indirectly dependent on her petit bourgeois readership for economic survival, since her salary comes from the Foucarts' budget, which in turn relies on subscriptions. She is paid not according to the success or failure of a particular piece, but by the rapidity with which she can finish an article, the skillfulness of her writing, and by the number of articles she writes within a certain time frame. The main influence on her cultural production comes specifically from the demands of her editors, Monsieur and Madame Foucart. In social terms, Josanne does not embrace the values of her petit bourgeois readers at all. Because of her financial constraints, Josanne's material mode of living would often be considered at a level below the rigid standards set by the petit bourgeois. In contrast, her interests in political writings and objets d'art remain above the typical desires of her readers. Her friends are mainly chosen from the intellectual or artistic classes of French society: writers, journalists, and activists in feminist groups. She is therefore not strongly attached to her work at *Le Monde féminin* nor to her readers, who remain anonymous to her, and she is more inclined to consider a renunciation of her cultural production to ensure a stronger bond in her private life with Noël.

By looking at each of these female protagonists from both viewpoints, as producers of culture as well as consumers of culture, we can better understand the ways in which their relationship with their audience and their public roles as producers of culture influenced their decisions about marriage and career. These portraits also permit us to understand that the women who developed these characters (Yver, Tinayre, and Colette) did not have prescriptive or descriptive aims when constructing their novels about professional women writers, nor were they offering "safe" or "practical" endings for their editors or their readers. Instead they were creating narrative conflicts that would allow for a critique of women's oppression and a praise of the working women who sought to find ways to combine romance and quest in their lives.

THE COMPOSITE NOVEL:
WOMEN LAWYERS OF *LES DAMES DU PALAIS*

THE LEGAL PROFESSION PROVED to be one of the least popular career choices with women of the Belle Epoque, and numbers of women in this field did not increase until well after World War I.[1] Yet women were constantly in the courthouses of France, due to an increase in infamous women criminals during this period, what Mary S. Hartman in *Victorian Murderesses* calls "the French female crime wave" (Hartman 239). Toward the end of the nineteenth century, Hartman notes that, unlike their British counterparts, French bourgeois women were taking the law into their own hands, doling out a "higher" justice to husbands and lovers, often as *vitrioleuses* (women who threw acid on their husbands and their mistresses) or more simply as murderers (242). Women were the central players in several of the most dramatic and publicized trials of the Belle Epoque: the 1903 Affaire Humbert, the 1908 Affaire Steinheil, and, of course, the infamous 1914 Affaire Caillaux.[2] Two of these women, Meg Steinheil and Henriette Caillaux, were accused of murder: Steinheil appeared to have murdered her husband and mother; Caillaux openly admitted to murdering Gaston Calmette,

---

1. An article in *La Vie Heureuse*, "Débuts des femmes avocats" (27, no. 9, September 1905), states that only four women had taken advantage of the 1900 law that allow women to practice the law in France (two in Paris, one in Toulouse, and one in Perpignan). In her 1910 work *Le Travail de la femme*, Camille Pert also notes that very few women practiced law during the first decade of its legalization for women, from 1900 to 1910. After World War I, Colette Yver claimed that the number of women lawyers was constantly increasing as the number of men in law was decreasing. She cites two figures to support her claims in the 1929 text *Femmes d'aujourd'hui*: first, one-quarter of the new interns at the Paris courthouse in 1928 were women (50 women out of 200 total registered). Second, the total number of women lawyers in Paris in 1928 was 178 (Yver 1929, 4–5). Despite Yver's enthusiasm, this total number is relatively small given the fact that almost thirty years had passed since the decree to allow women to practice law and try cases became effective in 1900.

2. For a well-documented historical account of these three cases, see Benjamin F. Martin's *The Hypocrisy of Justice in the Belle Epoque* (Baton Rouge: Louisiana State University Press, 1984). For a detailed history of the Affaire Caillaux in particular, see Edward Berenson's *The Trial of Madame Caillaux* (Berkeley and Los Angeles: University of California Press, 1992).

the editor of *Le Figaro,* to save her husband's (and her own) reputation. Thérèse Humbert was accused of fraudulent business dealings that had robbed Parisian creditors of millions of francs over a twenty-year period. The press devoted many pages to stories of these scandalous outlaws of the bourgeoisie, describing these women as cunning, duplicitous, exotic, and proud. How could these married and prosperous "ladies" murder, steal, and lie? Theories based on their peasant background or their obsession with reputation and honor may have offered some explanation, but the fact that wealthy bourgeois women committed these stunning crimes left Parisian society confounded. Hartman offers the theory that French bourgeois women were too isolated from the public sphere and therefore had no organized or official outlet for protest, and no education on how to demand equal rights and power in their personal relationships, as did the British through their women's suffrage groups, for example (240).[3]

Perhaps more confounding than the crimes themselves were the final outcomes of these trials: despite obvious incriminating evidence, eyewitness accounts, and even confessions from several of the accused, few of the women were given lengthy prison sentences, and a large percentage were acquitted as women who had been wronged.[4] Of the three sensational trials listed above, only Thérèse Humbert was convicted of her crime. Her sentence, five years of hard labor, was extremely light, given the length and extent of her fraud.

Benjamin F. Martin's detailed descriptions and analyses of the trial proceedings reveal that many of these women, along with secondary witnesses, had incredible presence before the judges, the jury, and the audiences attending the trial. Thérèse Humbert, Meg Steinheil, and Berthe Gueydan (Caillaux's ex-wife) contributed grandly, even theatrically, to the lawyers' arguments: they confused the facts, caused commotion, and gained sympathy. While none of these women were actually lawyers, their abilities as persuasive advocates for their own causes demonstrated that women had the necessary dramatic skills, if not always the legal expertise, to argue compellingly for themselves. The eloquence and hysteria of these women's presentations may have been a factor in persuading judges and juries to decide on light sentences or exoneration.

---

3. I must disagree with Hartman on that point: French women's suffrage campaigns of the nineteenth century may have been less vocal than those of the British suffragists, but they demonstrated that women could participate in a political process and knew how to organize and lobby for their own causes, however unpopular they might be.

4. In 1892, for example, 52 percent of women accused of major crimes were acquitted (Hartman 241).

The official presence of women in the Belle Epoque courtroom is another matter: in spite of the new 1900 law concerning women (see Chapter 1), lawyers and the court systems were still mainly male. Women were still not citizens, had no legal rights once they were married, and could not be politicians or participate in the formation of the law. We find a similar societal resistance to the idea of women lawyers at the turn of the century.

In the fictional world of Belle Epoque novels, the number of women lawyers is also miniscule, despite the fact that women professionals often speak out for their legal right to work and to live independently. The few female attorneys who appear as characters in novels of professional development are usually depicted as convincing and articulate women who know how to juggle reason, emotion, and legal statistics, and their portraits are wide ranging, partially because they are not limited by existing profiles of women lawyers, as may have been the case with women educators (Mme Jules Favres), scientists (Marie Curie, Blanche Edwards-Pilliet), and writers (Séverine, Rachilde, among others). What happens when there is neither the influence of public opinion nor the marker of personal, autobiographical experience? If there were no basis for the plot and setting in current working conditions, would the novelist be free to invent utopian visions about women and work? If so, what would these visions look like? Given the gap between reality and fiction, would it be possible to diverge from the renunciation plot format that occurs in so many of the novels studied in preceding chapters? What would the form and structure of such a novel resemble? This type of novel about women's professional development could potentially present a completely new kind of working heroine in French fiction and a new configuration for women's conflicts and struggles in French novels.

To answer these questions, we will turn to the 1909 novel *Les Dames du Palais* (*Ladies of the Court*) by Colette Yver about women lawyers.[5] In this text, we find examples of the three types of Belle Epoque protagonists studied in the previous chapters of this book: portraits of a women's community, of pioneering brainy women, and of an independent or self-sufficient woman. These types all retain ties to the genres with which they are associated (novels about teachers, scientists, or artists, respectively), but Yver modifies them to create a coherent and expanded fictional depiction of women lawyers at work. The composite structure of this novel indicates

---

5. For a short plot summary of this novel, see Appendix 2. Yver also wrote a short story, in 1903, on a woman lawyer: "Le Cas de conscience d'une avocate" in the collection *Un Coin du voile*.

the possibilities that were available for the portrayals of women lawyers. Yet even with this freedom, certain narrative techniques, such as the conflicting romance and quest plots and the renunciation conclusion, still exist. Thus, our study of this composite novel will help to confirm further the notion that Belle Epoque women authors chose this type of narrative structure neither for its reflection of prevailing conditions, nor as a prescriptive device (what women professionals *ought* to do), but rather as an effective narrative device to demonstrate the tensions and difficult choices faced by their unusual heroines.

The Community

Les Dames du Palais presents a variety of women who all work at the same Parisian courthouse (*palais de justice*). For example, Jeanne Martinal is a hard-working widow, preoccupied with her three young children and their economic survival. Louise Pernette, a timid and beautiful young woman, is described as a diligent intern interested only in saving money from her cases so that she may marry, retire from the law early, and have a family. Isabelle Geronce, the wife of a wealthy surgeon, wears outrageous fashions and make-up to court and holds the position of the affluent and flirtatious courtesan of the courthouse. She believes that the courtroom is her stage, a place where she can perform. Madame Clémentin, whose husband was disbarred for fraud, is herself suspected of illegal activities, but she continues to practice with cunning and malice. The heroine of the courthouse, Henriette Marcadieu, is an outstanding orator whose early successes point to a glorious career in the law. Her fiancé, André Vélines, explains to his grandmother: "You must not believe that there is one type: *the* woman lawyer. There are very simply women lawyers, with as many varieties as there are personalities."[6] André's statement may have been incorrect historically, given the relatively few women lawyers practicing in France in 1909, but it is quite accurate when applied to the diversity of social and political types found within the fictional community of women who practice law in *Les Dames du Palais*. A closer look at some of the major characters reveals the outlines of an educational community within the legal system.

---

6. "Il ne faudrait pas croire qu'il existe un type: l'avocate. Il existe des avocates, tout simplement, avec autant de types que de personnalités" (Yver 1909, 231).

The eldest woman lawyer, Madame Angély, provides the principle source of inspiration for this community of women, most of whom are just beginning their law careers. Yver presents her as a neutral authority figure; she does not try cases, being content to teach law in girls' high schools and to advise to other lawyers. Angély is one of the few professional women in the novel who understands her work as a sort of mission for the amelioration of society, even though earlier in her career she may have seen it more as a source of revenue or an engaging activity. As such, she is representative of the earliest stage of women lawyers in France and corresponds to the nascent era that, in professionalization theory, requires a "missionary" or "service" orientation of its members, as sociologist Philip Elliott has claimed (Elliott 112) (see Chapter 1). Like early women schoolteachers, who were struggling to make women's education a legitimate and recognized profession in France, Madame Angély believes that women lawyers will promote the practice of law for women and children, and she pursues this end with almost religious devotion. When André Vélines sees her among a crowd of lawyers milling around at the Palais de Justice and describes her to his grandmother, the words he uses are most appropriate for an individual with a missionary or religious orientation, rather than for someone involved in the mere practice of law: she is a "fondatrice" (founder), an "oracle" (oracle), and an "ancienne" (elder). Her judgment is "penetrating" and her understanding of the law is "perfect" (Yver 1909, 9). It is interesting to note that the name Yver chose for this character derives from the word *angel* (Angély), and she lives on the street of the *chanoinesse*—a religious denomination for a highly placed nun.

While their male counterparts consult Madame Angély in secret, as André confides to his grandmother, the women lawyers openly seek advice from her in the halls of the courthouse. She is a genuine mentor figure in this novel and thus somewhat of a rarity for the female novel of professional development. Other novels in this genre usually include the search for a female mentor or the decision to do without one. In *Les Dames du Palais,* however, the traditional bildungsroman pattern of mentor-disciple relationships is quite strong. In fact, Madame Angély is the main reason why most of the women lawyers are practicing law, as she is the one who encouraged them to continue their law studies after they had taken a course with her in high school. When she enters one of the main halls, the Salle des Pas Perdus, the young women lawyers interrupt whatever they were doing to join Madame Angély, some literally running to her side (Yver 1909, 11).

Angély's influence on the young women is a combination of the two kinds of values that Mme Ferron and Mlle Vormèse taught to schoolteachers in Reval's novel *Sévriennes*. On one hand, she was their intellectual mentor, since she taught them the basics of the legal code in the lycées. On the other hand, she is a moral and a maternal guide for the young women who are entering the profession. Her main desire is close to the goals of the women schoolteachers and directors of women's schools discussed in Chapter 3. She wishes to see the courthouse filled with women lawyers who will create a better world through law, an ideal she holds dear: "In her mind, the Bar was lacking women, especially for children. She would have liked, not eight or ten young women apprentices, but fifty or one hundred, ready to plead cases for her dear abandoned children, and her generous heart bore maternal women lawyers, capable of being moral tutors for their young clients, as well as legal counselors."[7] The specific verb used here (*enfantait*, which translates literally as "gave birth to") highlights the maternal quality found in Angély's teaching style, and that she seeks to promote in her lawyers. This feature echoes many of the fictional schoolteachers' desires to become "maternal" guides and role models for their students. The young women lawyers revere Angély in a saintlike manner, and her utopian visions for the law profession are copied by her young protégées. Angély's pupils not only learn to argue for children's rights, but they also act as moral guides who would teach the children important lessons, thus enabling them to lead productive lives in the future. Angély's influence is widespread: many of the women lawyers in the novel spend some or all of their time as court-appointed defenders, representing children or adolescents who have committed petty crimes. Thus the quest narrative of the text includes an idealized vision of a better society through the law. The charitable nature of the cases these women lawyers take on extends to a more benevolent conception of the practice of law, as both a means of defending the poor and defenseless and a way of gently correcting youthful offenders and placing them on a more fruitful path before they have the chance to become hardened criminals. The women practicing law thus bring traditionally private concerns, the moral education of children, into the public sphere of the courthouse. While the goals are more closely connected to those of women schoolteachers, the means for

---

7. "A son sens, la femme manquait à la barre, près de l'enfant. Elle aurait voulu, non point huit ou dix jeunes filles stagiaires, mais cinquante, mais cent, prêtes à plaider d'office pour ses chers déshérités, et son coeur fécond enfantait véritablement des avocates maternelles, capables d'être aussi bien que légistes, les tutrices morales de leurs jeunes clients" (Yver 1909, 50).

reaching them are more similar to those employed by women scientists and researchers, who often made interesting exchanges in their private and public lives.

Not all the women lawyers in *Dames du Palais* hold the same convictions as Madame Angély, however. Like the different personalities and theories on women's social and professional roles that emerge in *Sévriennes* or *L'Un vers l'autre,* the characters of *Les Dames du Palais* enumerate a variety of viewpoints on the role of women in law and in French society generally. During an afternoon tea that Madame Angély holds in her home, their discussion at first remains rather theoretical and general, as they discuss the rights and duties of women in marriage. Always the advocate for children, Angély proclaims that a married woman must accept her husband's infidelities for the sake of their children; this maternal duty outweighs a woman's right to justice or to a point of honor with her husband. In contrast, a more "modern" feminist lawyer, Madame Surgères, promotes women's rights to accuse and punish their husbands for infidelity, just as men have always had the power to publicly shame and ridicule their unfaithful wives, to remove children from the homes of these women, and even to kill their wives, if found in *flagrant délit,* as mentioned in the Napoleonic Code.[8] She further proclaims the individual rights of women to pursue their own interests, against the duty to sacrifice themselves to marriage and procreation: "The individual is an end in itself and cannot be considered as the means of another individual. In a society as I understand it, love and maternity will be an episode in the life of a woman; they will no longer be her whole life."[9] A number of the women assembled speak for one of the two opposing sides, creating a heated debate with many nuances. The widow Jeanne Martinal, for example, supports Madame Angély's view of marriage and sacrifice, pointing to her personal experience of hard work and dedication for the benefit of her three boys. In contrast, Isabelle Géronce supports Surgères's view for women's equality with men, while the novel's narrator adds an insinuating comment that Géronce's own numerous "histoires sentimentales" (sentimental liaisons) probably account for her endorsement of the feminist's position (Yver 1909, 193).

---

8. Hartman gives a succinct account of this clause in the Code (Hartman 244–45).

9. "L'individu est fin en soi et ne peut être considéré comme le moyen d'un autre individu. Dans une société comme je la comprends, l'amour et la maternité seront un épisode dans la vie des femmes, ils ne seront plus son histoire" (Yver 1909, 195).

When the discussion proceeds to the more particular debate about the role(s) of women lawyers in French society, three positions are clearly enunciated on this topic, and more voices join in to build from these starting points. In her efforts to dissuade a young intern from quitting the profession, Angély claims that women must join the legal profession in greater numbers in order to help children who are in need of defense. Again, her traditional feelings about women's maternal powers motivate her side of the argument. Jeanne Martinal offers a second position, claiming that since she must be a provider as well as a mother for her own children, she does not have the time to plead cases for other children and must consider the legal career as a way to earn money, taking only those cases that will be most profitable for her. Surgères protests that women lawyers should stay in the profession to exercise their rights as intelligent beings and to establish justice for women. While Henriette Vélines can see valid points in all three positions, Isabelle Géronce declares that women should become lawyers only to defend women against men (Yver 1909, 200–204).

Their debates and differences of opinion do not detract from their unity as a group and their feelings of solidarity with one another. Jeanne Martinal, the most practical of the group, laughingly explains to Géronce that if a man came to her with an important case, she would be crazy not to accept it. But she also reaches out to the most militantly feminist lawyers, the "guerrières" (women warriors), as she calls them, and explains that she appreciates their actions and understands that she herself may benefit from them, even if, for financial reasons, she cannot participate herself (Yver 1909, 204–5). After numerous interruptions, cries, exclamations, and generally heated discussion, the narrator describes the meeting of women as one of "kindness" and "warmth." The community of women, much like the one described in *Sévriennes,* holds strongly opposing beliefs, based on their social class, economic status, marital status, and age. And, as a community, the women also value the open communications that exist and appear to learn from each other. The narrator notes the novelty of such a congregation of female minds but also underlines the naturalness with which the women engage in their group discussions: "This women's meeting was truly a new tableau, devoid of all frivolity, they studied conscientiously the most modern social problems with as much simplicity as their mothers would have discussed the latest fashions."[10]

---

10. "Et c'était un tableau vraiment neuf que cette réunion de femmes, à l'esprit dégagé de toute frivolité, qui étudiaient consciencieusement les plus modernes des problèmes sociaux, avec autant de simplicité que leurs mères en eussent mis à raconter leurs toilettes" (Yver 1909, 205).

There is, however, some curious gossip circulating about several of the women lawyers. Within the community, for example, Isabelle Géronce's extravagances are often the subject of mockery. Louise Pernette, Jeanne de Louvrol, Marie Morvan, known as the "stagiaires inséparables" (inseparable interns), and Henriette Marcadieu all joke about Isabelle Géronce's excessive make-up, oversized skirts, and her "cols de guipures" (lace collars) which were "légendaires, considérables et scandaleux" (legendary, considerable, and scandalous). In the tone of a juvenile high school student, Louise confides to her companions that the long trains on Géronce's dresses forced all the other lawyers to stand back and let her pass by when she entered the hall (Yver 1909, 14–15). Along with this adolescent gossip, women also exchange theories on Henriette's remarkable successes in her early career; these comments range from admiration to bitter and jealous criticism (188–92). But the group is unified around the concept that women lawyers have the right and the duty to practice alongside men in the courthouse.

Despite some of the parallels that this community ethic of mutual support creates between women lawyers and schoolteachers, there remain several strong differences in the legal career for women. They are, as Auerbach claims, an "unofficial community," and their assembly as a group is often arranged in an ad hoc manner (Auerbach 11). While women schoolteachers attended state-authorized training schools established for women and formed a state-sanctioned intellectual community of women, the women lawyers in *Les Dames du Palais* all attended law school as pioneers; some struggle with financial difficulties or homesickness, and all struggle with sexist biases. In this way, they reflect more closely the educational experiences of women scientists, who usually did not have female mentors or colleagues with whom to learn and grow. Their ties to each other may not appear as strong as those of the schoolteachers studied, perhaps because of this lack of an official community structure.

The absence of an authorized organization may create looser ties between the women lawyers, but it also affords the women a certain freedom to develop their own style and manners, both in and out of the courtroom. Schoolteachers, as we saw earlier, are often reprimanded for the slightest signs of deviation from the prescribed behavior for professors in the classroom, the bedroom, or the town square. In contrast, women lawyers appear to have more freedom to live their lives as they choose in the private sphere: Isabelle Géronce is married to a surgeon but maintains a professional career of her own and several lovers on the side; Jeanne Martinal is widowed and spends most of her time away from the courthouse with her three children and her aunt; Louise Pernette, single, poor, and without family, spends all of her free time memorizing the civil code. Many of the women lawyers are wives, mothers, fiancées, or lovers, and they have complicated personal lives that do not permit full-time participation in a purely female and professional community such as those of the women schoolteachers. Yet the narrator makes it clear that their private lives do not detract from their abilities as professionals or from public opinions of them. In this way, they have more parallels with women writers and artists than they do with women teachers and students. Indeed, women lawyers are free to create their own personal style in the public sphere of the courtroom. Among the women lawyers most skilled at presentations are Isabelle Géronce, who puts on a spectacle in front of her audiences, and Henriette Marcadieu, who employs a mélange of emotion and reason to persuade her judges.

Outside their own group, the attitudes toward women lawyers also vary and do not follow a strict set of moral codes or societal prejudices. Most of the elder men attorneys in *Les Dames du Palais* look upon the young women with either "mansuétude" (indulgence) or "bienveillance" (generosity), while the younger male characters find that women pose a potential menace to their future career, especially if they had been planning on a mainly female clientele (Yver 1909, 17). There is, however, no overt hostility or prejudice against the women, unlike the behavior of male scientists or medical students in novels about women in science. Male and female characters discuss upcoming cases together in the busy main hall of the courthouse, and in appearance at least, women's opinions are equal to those of men.

The book contains no backstabbing colleagues or any plots to get rid of potentially dangerous thinkers from the courthouse, yet a sort of benign paternalism reigns throughout the professional ranks of *Dames du Palais*. For example, when Isabelle Géronce whimsically adds Maurice Servais to her troop of lovers (another young lawyer at the Palais and the fiancé of Louise Pernette), both Madame Angély and the president of the Barristers Order of Paris, Monsieur Fabrezan, step into a parenting role to reunite the young couple and to keep Géronce at a distance. Angély appeals to Fabrezan's more traditional and paternalistic view of the Barristers Order in order to move him to protect the two younger lawyers. He takes this event as an excuse to launch a heated attack against women lawyers and the scandals he feels they have created in "his" order: "A few chignons under the lawyers' caps and the brotherhood abandons its virile character, disorder is born, confusion begins. . . . What need did we have for all these women?"[11] His outburst is softened by Madame Angély's presence, as she reminds him of the brilliance of Henriette Vélines, the devotion of Jeanne Martinal, and the charitable works of wealthy women lawyers. He himself must finally admit that Angély is a saint and that most of the women in his order make excellent contributions to the legal profession.

The Barristers Order in the novel thus acts as an extended family structure that nurtures and protects the younger members. More established lawyers regularly pass on cases to those who are only beginning their careers and need to build up clientele. The elders also keep an eye out for potential troublemakers, such as Monsieur Clémentin and Madame Géronce, and they try to maintain harmony among the association's members as much as possible. Unlike the rigidly hierarchical system of inspections and reports required by the Ministry of Education, which produced anxiety and imposed restrictions on the characters in all of the women teachers' novels, in this novel, we find a more subtle method in the lawyers' association that discretely aids and quietly corrects the problems in its ranks.

It is perhaps due to this encouraging attitude by the professional legal organization in the novel that female characters appear to have gained acceptance in the public sphere of the Palais de Justice. The Parisian public appears interested in, but not appalled by, the idea of women lawyers in the novel: spectators who come to watch trials are often amused or surprised by the sight of women in the traditional cloaks of the lawyer, yet they are neither horrified nor offended by it. Instead, the women are a curiosity, and their courtrooms are often packed with inquisitive onlookers. Women from the upper classes turn to women lawyers for support and understanding in divorce and child custody cases, and women and children from the working classes, who cannot afford expensive attorneys, rely on the good will of these new women lawyers to defend them in front of judges. On the whole, then, this community of women lawyers practicing in Paris does not undergo severe surveillance by their colleagues nor threatening restrictions by the citizens who hire them or who come to watch them try cases. Their plight thus differs significantly from that of women schoolteachers, although they do gather strength from their work as a fellowship.

---

11. "Pour quelques chignons sous la toque aussitôt la confrérie abandonne son caractère viril, le désordre naît, le trouble commence. . . . Qu'avions-nous besoin de toutes ces femmes?" (Yver 1909, 241).

The Cerveline Lawyer

Among the community of women at the Palais, one particular lawyer, Henriette Marcadieu, stands out, and provides the text with a brainy woman heroine similar to those protagonists found in novels about women scientists. She is the only daughter of Judge Marcadieu, whose reputation as wise elder in the Palais de Justice of Paris is well known. After pleading with her parents, Henriette receives permission to study law and to practice in the same courthouse as her father, thus carrying on a family tradition. Henriette receives aid and counsel from her father, her father's colleagues (all of whom are well-established attorneys), and from Mademoiselle Angély. These connections help her to excel in law at the early age of twenty-three.

It is difficult, however, to firmly plant her in either the category of pure or seduced brainy woman. She may appear to be the typical seduced brainy woman, for two reasons. First, she is very happy to fall in love with and marry another promising young lawyer at the Palais de Justice, André Vélines. After she marries, her dreams of a fulfilled life as lawyer, wife, and mother come true. Second, she does not abandon her "feminine" values when practicing her law, as most scientific brainy women are willing to do, in order to conform more completely to masculine standards of professionalization. This becomes clear when Henriette's career soars after an important child custody case, which she argues perfectly against her father's peer, the venerable president of the Barristers Order of Paris, Monsieur Fabrezan. Her friend, Suzanne Marty, chose Henriette to represent her in the trial because of her exceptional abilities as a lawyer, even though she is young and inexperienced: "You are still a little girl who is unaware of her abilities, but that does not prevent you from having a great talent, Henriette, a surprising talent that does not resemble anyone else's; you have deep, mature, and virile ideas and you state them with your simple grace."[12] Madame Marty's praise emphasizes the typical pure brainy woman qualities in Henriette: unusual talent, insight, and maturity well beyond her years. But Suzanne Marty also chose Henriette for this significant case in part because she believes the gendered stereotypes that claim that women lawyers are better suited than men to argue for mothers and children. She continues, "This case must be argued by a woman. I have been oppressed too much

---

12. "Vous êtes encore une petite fille qui s'ignore, et cela n'empêche que vous avez un grand talent, Henriette, un talent surprenant, qui ne ressemble à celui d'aucun autre; vous avez des idées profondes, mûres, viriles, et vous les dites avec votre grâce simple" (Yver 1909, 75).

by men. . . . They all work together; they have between them an occult solidarity to subordinate us. While you, my little Henriette, you will be my other self, you will make heard my own voice at the bar."[13] Suzanne is of the opinion that Henriette's femininity, sincerity, and heart will triumph over Fabrezan's eloquent and experienced speech. Her trust in Henriette's abilities is thus based both on her "male" talent and on her "female" emotions and confirms Henriette's status as a seduced brainy woman.

The Marty trial itself, and Henriette's presentation, is chronicled in detail by the narrator to demonstrate the well-constructed strategy that Henriette has chosen, demonstrating this mixed use of feminine and masculine elements: she begins with some spiritual opening remarks that put the judges at ease and allow her to compliment the esteemed Fabrezan who has just spoken, all without detracting any strength from her own presentation. She then launches an emotional, and partially spontaneous, opening argument. Following this section where she lets her emotions "talk" ("la petite Vélines laissait causer son émotion"; Yver 1909, 176), she presents a well-prepared series of dry, factual evidence that reinforces her defense of Suzanne Marty. Finally, she concludes with a concise résumé.[14] During her presentation, several lawyers comment to her husband André on her abilities, using such adjectives as "épatante," "renversante" (amazing, astounding) to describe her abilities. Their words may appear to indicate mere surprise or amazement but when Fabrezan comes over to offer his praise after her closing statement, the narrator signals to the reader that Henriette's argumentation is of a superior persuasive and technical quality, authorized by the president of the Barristers Order himself (181).

This detailed description of Henriette's first important argument demonstrates the difficulties of trying to classify Henriette as a pure or seduced brainy woman. The elements essential to the portrait of a pure brainy woman are mixed in with the more emotional or feminine side of Henriette's case, and her legal genius is presented clearly during the trial as an innate quality. When Henriette decides to make some impromptu changes to her strategies after hearing Fabrezan's defense of Suzanne Marty's husband, the narrator claims that she is using her intrinsic legal abilities as she improvises her impassioned speech as compared to his traditional presentation (Yver 1909,

---

13. "Il faut que cette cause soit plaidée par une femme. J'ai été trop opprimée par l'homme. . . . Ils s'entendent tous; ils ont entre eux une solidarité occulte pour nous asservir. . . . Tandis que vous, ma petite Henriette, vous serez une autre moi-même, c'est ma propre voix que vous ferez entendre à la barre" (Yver 1909, 74).

14. "clear, almost arid, but which pleased the judges and which the professionals appreciated" (net jusqu'à la sécheresse, mais qui plut aux juges et que les professionnels apprécièrent) (Yver 1909, 180).

176). Henriette has a dazzling effect in the courtroom, and not only because she has prepared long and hard for the case using traditional methods and has assembled all the necessary items to prove without fail that her client is the better guardian for the child. The narrator claims that Henriette is a "born" lawyer (véritable avocate-née) and thus has these inexplicable abilities to improvise so brilliantly before the judges and the crowded courtroom audience. Both Yver and Reval also employed this notion of an "innate" ability in their novels when discussing the inexplicable powers of diagnosis in their pure brainy women scientists.

Among law colleagues, the initial reaction to Henriette's excellent defense of her client is praise and admiration for her adroit combination of emotional and rational arguments. No mention is made of Henriette's gender in public spaces, such as the main hall of the courthouse. But during the private gathering of the women lawyers at Madame Angély's home, mentioned above, the fact that she is a woman arises in their conversations. The adamant feminist, Madame Surgères, proclaims Henriette's victory as a victory for the entire feminist cause, whereas Isabelle Géronce, the jealous social climber, claims that all the fuss and admiration are simply due to the fact that Henriette was a woman. She feels that when women demonstrate even the slightest bit of competence, everyone shows amazement, thus belittling both Henriette's performance and women lawyers more generally.

The other women assembled all protest that Géronce is wrong, but several admit to some jealousy, awe, and even "a certain malaise" (un singulier malaise), due not only to Henriette's verve, assurance, and creativity at the bar but also to the intense attention she is receiving from the male-dominated Palais de Justice (Yver 1909, 188, 190). Following her successful defense, Henriette herself begins to believe in the sex-based argument; that is, that women lawyers, because of their intimate knowledge of mother-child relationships, defend women remarkably well in cases of divorce and child custody.

Later in the novel, the narrator reconfirms the importance of the lawyer's sex in the child custody case when Henriette's husband, André, takes over the case for the appeal while Henriette is on pregnancy leave. The same players are involved in the appeal: the same divorced couple and child, the same lawyer for the father (Fabrezan), and the same evidence that Henriette used to win the child for the mother. André is repeatedly described as a bright lawyer who, just a month earlier, succeeded in winning an impossible trial: the case of a notorious swindler who had taken nearly 250,000 francs illegally from the pockets of credulous Parisians (Yver 1909, 255). His persuasive rhetoric earned André this coup, and although he is becoming better known in legal circles, the general public has not yet discovered his talent. Isabelle Géronce, in her tirade against Henriette mentioned above, states that André is a better lawyer than Henriette and that if he had been in Henriette's place, he would have easily won Suzanne Marty's case with a more substantial set of arguments.

In principle, then, André should be able to argue the appeal and win easily, given Henriette's precedent and his own general talent. Yet André inexplicably loses the case, and Suzanne Marty is forced to give up her child to his father (Yver 1909, 263). The loss is a terrible blow for André and simultaneously reinforces the notions that women lawyers argue better for women in domestic cases and that Henriette is a "born" lawyer, more skilled and persuasive than her husband, even though much less experienced than he is. When Suzanne Marty decides to appeal the decision a year later, she returns to the Vélines household, but asks specifically for Henriette to represent her, thus reconfirming the notion that the practice of law by women will yield more comprehensive lawyers who will be able to argue their female clients' cases more persuasively. This particular case thus highlights Yver's portrait of the pure brainy woman in this novel.

In many ways, though, Henriette is also a seduced brainy woman. She works hard to balance her domestic and professional duties, and she is not the only woman lawyer who is shown both in and out of the private sphere. Yver presents the practice of law as an activity that is completely compatible with traditionally female enterprises in the home, in contrast to her portrayal of women doctors in *Les Cervelines* or *Princesses de Sciences*. Yver depicts the life of the typical lawyer as perfectly suited for married women who also want to spend time doing domestic work. Whether for male or female lawyers, we find a fairly routine pattern in the novel: mornings spent at home preparing cases in the study until lunch, early afternoons spent at the courthouse either trying cases or meeting colleagues, then late afternoons are spent back at home receiving clients before dinner. Whether the narrator is describing the daily schedule of the wealthy and successful lawyer Henriette, who has a nursemaid for her baby, a cook, and a butler, or of the impoverished Jeanne Martinal, who has only a poor aunt to help her with her three young boys, the tone is the same: one of general predictability that allows the mother to spend some time each day at home with her children. Indeed, André's conservative grandmother, when she first meets Henriette, mentions that one of the reasons that she has changed her mind about women lawyers is the fact that they can be near their families while pursuing domestic activities: "You are not those scientific women whose brutal and absorbing studies can dry out the soul. You have your home office where you work near your mother or your husband, depending on the situation. You barely spend three hours a day at the courthouse."[15] Here, via the voice of André's grandmother, Yver shrewdly defends the negative comments that she had made about the heartlessness of women scientists in her earlier novels. Yver had received public criticism for her unkind and often exaggerated portrayals, and this later portrait of a brainy woman who could "have it all" served, in a way, as Yver's response to those critics. The attorney Henriette, both as unmarried young woman and as a married wife and mother, appears to balance with ease her professional duties and her traditionally feminine private activities in the home and on the job. When she marries André Vélines, she does not stop practicing law but merely moves her office from her parents' home to her new home with her husband.

As with other brainy women portraits, Yver gives close attention to her description of the "domesticated" workspaces that these professionals create. The narrator of *Dames du Palais* describes in minute detail the arrangement and decoration of the interior of Henriette's and André's future home so that both of them will be able to continue practicing law after they are married (Yver 1909, 86). The lengthy description of the house indicates Henriette's initial priorities: two of the main rooms are reserved for the two law offices, separated by a common waiting room. The living quarters are smaller, but they are decorated with intimacy and security in mind. Offices located in the domicile may be an accurate reflection of the historical practice of this era, and such a pattern is described in *Les Dames du Palais* where Henriette's father and one of his colleagues, Fabrezan, both have their offices in their private homes. But male professionals did not usually establish their workplace at home so that they could attend to child care responsibilities and domestic staff supervision; it was merely a convenience or a convention for them. Yver never describes either of these male lawyers in domestic situations or involved in domestic work, and neither one demonstrates any concern or anxieties about combining professional and private duties, in contrast to the descriptions of women lawyers throughout the novel.

Henriette is a distinct personality among brainy women because she is concerned with the arrangement and furnishings of her home. In contrast to the women doctors of Yver's earlier novels, who find domestic concerns tedious and distracting, Henriette enjoys making decisions about

---

15. "Vous n'êtes pas des femmes de science, dont les études brutales et absorbantes peuvent dessécher un peu l'âme. Vous avez chez vous votre cabinet où vous travaillez, selon le cas, près de votre mère ou près de votre mari. A peine passez-vous quotidiennement deux ou trois heures au Palais" (Yver 1909, 26).

her new home. André appears to be the perfect spouse as well, agreeing to Henriette's sensible management of household affairs and to her equally logical arrangement of their work environment.

Like many seduced brainy woman scientists, Henriette mixes public and private activities within her home. In one of the turning points of *Les Dames du Palais,* Henriette returns home from the courthouse, and with her hat still on her head and her briefcase still in hand, she rushes to the nursery where she believes that the baby recognizes her and speaks her first word, "Maman" (Yver 1909, 313–14). When she brings the baby into her husband's office to celebrate, the portrait of the traditional nuclear family is complete, with a slightly modern twist: father, mother, and child are united, with the additional presence of Henriette's secretary. The father tenderly kisses the mother on the forehead and babbles to the baby as she nurses from her mother's breast, while the mother heatedly debates a convoluted point of inheritance law with her secretary. This scene superficially depicts one utopian vision for the modern woman of the twentieth century, a combination of tender familial devotion with intelligence and professional interests (314).

In contrast to these depictions of professional work located in the private sphere, Henriette also enjoys usually private moments in a young woman's life in the throes of the very public domain of the courtroom. When André first reveals his love for her, it is not in a typical bourgeois private space. Nor is the couple under the watchful surveillance of a chaperone. Rather, André begins to express his intentions and launches the entire courtship at the back of a crowded courtroom during an important divorce trial. At first, Henriette tells him that the court is not the place to make these types of statements, but she lets him continue and eventually accepts his proposal of marriage there, at the same moment that the judge is announcing his decision in favor of a divorce.[16] The dialogue between André and Henriette is interrupted by the judge's speech, in italics within the text.[17] The contrast is strong: on one hand

---

16. There are, of course, the etymological connections between court and courting/courtship, which exist both in French and English (*faire la cour, la cour de justice*), which Yver undoubtedly was exploiting in this scene.

17.
    —Ah! We would be happy!
    At the back of the tribunal, the voice of the presiding judge rose up,
    monotone, indistinct, listing the clauses:
    —*Whereas the Madame d'Estangelles introduced on 17 January an action for divorce against her husband; that he, on his side, filed a counterclaim for divorce;*

there is the judge's solemn decision to separate the husband and wife and parcel the four children out to different parties because of the "most demoralizing spectacle" (le spectacle le plus démoralisateur) provided by these unhappy parents. On the other hand, there is Henriette's joyful decision to marry André and to join their dreams, ambitions, and lives, making a mutual promise to respect and honor each other's wishes. The somber atmosphere in the courtroom no longer has any effect on Henriette because she has become "blasée," as the narrator notes, having already seen too much pain, betrayal, hate, and ruin in the court (Yver 1909, 46). The comment here recalls the impersonal and detached attitudes that brainy women scientists often maintained in front of their clients: the patients were seen as experiments, not as human beings. In a similar fashion, Henriette listens attentively to these divorce decrees but is detached from the suffering of the human beings in front of her. Instead she takes joy in focusing her attention on her fiancé's words and on thoughts of her happy life with him.

During the important Marty child custody case, where Henriette makes her stunning argument, we find another instance of public and private boundaries crossed. Henriette must interrupt the trial for a fifteen-minute pause due to sudden fatigue. The crowded courtroom suspects that, being a woman, she cannot withstand the pressure of pleading such an important case, and the judge asks if Henriette would like to postpone the proceedings for a week to prepare better. Henriette refuses his offer, continues her presentation valiantly, and leaves the courthouse two hours later in triumph. After hearing the important decision in her client's favor, she reveals to her husband that the trial was exhausting for her not because of the importance of the case and the fame of the prosecutor but because

---

—*Whereas, life together having become intolerable, the d'Estangelles spouses presented the most demoralizing spectacle to their children.* . . .
—Yes, we would be happy, replied the young man."

(—Ah! Nous serions heureux!
Au fond du prétoire, la voix du président s'éleva monotone, indistincte, enfilant les attendus:
—*Attendu que la dame d'Estangelles introduisait le 17 janvier contre son mari une*
instance en divorce; que celui-ci a, de son côté, formé reconventionnellement une demande en
divorce;
—*Attendu que, la vie commune étant devenu intolérable, les époux d'Estangelles donnaient à*
leurs enfants le spectacle le plus démoralisateur. . . .
— Oui, nous serions heureux, reprenait le jeune homme.) (Yver 1909, 40–41)

she is pregnant. Thus, at the end of a wrenching family drama in the courtroom, Henriette lightheartedly announces to André the beginning of their own family (Yver 1909, 183). Once again, Henriette reveals private concerns in public without causing scandal or upset and even provides a happy counterweight to the misery and sorrow produced by the trial. Henriette is constantly consoling wives who want divorces or divorced mothers who want to maintain custody of their children, yet these aspects of her career that constantly attack the institutions of marriage and family do not appear to affect her blissful understanding of her own marriage and of the institutional boundaries between private and public that she transgresses.

Henriette, and women lawyers generally, appear to be the protagonists most capable of living a dual life in both the private and the public domains because they are able to adapt the two environments to fit their work needs. Yet even these heroines confront bitter and jealous husbands, colleagues, and parents. Underlying the tender family scene cited above, for example, we find jealousy, mourning, and resentment. Henriette's secretary, Jeanne Martinal, acts as witness to the nuclear family's embrace; she was hired when Henriette's Marty victory brought with it an overwhelming number of new women clients. While fame and success increased the demand for Henriette's services, they turn out to be negative forces in the lives of her colleagues; her glory diminishes the reputations of other women lawyers and reduces the number of cases they receive. Jeanne Martinal, recognizing that she will not be able to survive with a small number of clients, insists that Henriette hire her as her secretary, even though this means a demotion for her, from promising lawyer to humble secretary. Jeanne claims that her ultimate mission in life has shifted to that of family provider, so that the subservient job is not difficult to endure. But the tender family scene between Henriette, André, and their baby daughter brings tears to Jeanne's eyes; it reminds her of her happiness with her husband before his death and of the contrast between her previous life of ease and of her new life of hard work and sacrifice (Yver 1909, 316).

Jeanne Martinal's presence as Henriette's secretary also brings out sharp feelings of jealousy, as it forces André to fully recognize that his wife is more successful than he is. From the beginning of the novel, André is depicted as an ambitious and power-hungry individual. After ten years of law practice, he is not content with his minor reputation, given his "appetite for authority" and his desires to "dominate" the courthouse.

This portrait of a driven professional is reinforced by the narrator's insinuation that André was originally attracted to Henriette because of her father's power and reputation: "Two years earlier, when he had noticed at the courthouse that pretty girl, so seductive, the idea of allying himself with the high judges had not been for nothing in his resolution to marry Miss Marcadieu."[18] By the time they marry, of course, he claims to love her for other reasons, but he was initially interested in Henriette for the prestige and connections that her father would bring to his career. This passion for authority never dies.

André's disappointment and bitterness are revealed to be enormous when he realizes that his wife's career is surpassing his and that her legal skills continue to grow while his remain merely adequate. He already had heard himself referred to at the courthouse as "the husband of Madame Vélines" (Yver 1909, 255) and had suffered humiliation when he lost the case that his wife had won several months earlier. Madame Mansart, his grandmother and only remaining relative, encourages his egotistical pursuit of fame and his embittered jealousy of Henriette's success during a two-month stay at their apartment. Her condescension toward Henriette's "stupid" Parisian clients indicates her naïve pride in her grandson at the same time that it emphasizes her sexist beliefs in male authority and superiority. When she questions André on this incomprehensible behavior by Parisian clients, he brushes off her indignation, claiming that it is just a fad and that the truly serious clients still request his services rather than Henriette's. The narrator, however, undermines the truth of André's remarks by showing how serious and perceptive the intelligent Suzanne Marty character is, and how at the same time she is insistent that Henriette, rather than André, represent her. The narrator's portrayal of Henriette's clients is thus the opposite of "stupid Parisian women" (les Parisiennes sottes). André often appears to laugh at or casually dismiss his grandmother's patriarchal value system, yet underlying his nonchalant attitude we find his growing impatience and resentment with Henriette and his return to his grandmother's traditional views.

To find that his wife is so busy that she needed a secretary while he has only a few cases of his own triggers jealousy and simultaneously a lack of ambition or enthusiasm for his work (Yver 1909, 207–8). André's wounded

---

18. "Deux ans auparavant, quand il avait remarqué au Palais cette jolie fille, si séduisante, l'idée de s'allier à la haute magistrature n'avait pas été pour rien dans sa résolution d'épouser mademoiselle Marcadieu" (Yver 1909, 68–69).

pride and its effects on his productivity are real, but at the same time the narrator underscores the fact that they are mostly a result of his own fears and paranoid perceptions: What do his colleagues think of him? What do his clients think? What will his one-year-old daughter think of him when she grows up? These questions haunt André and paralyze his ability to work.

The Self-Sufficient Woman

In the midst of André's jealousy and Jeanne's sadness, Henriette appears not to notice, or perhaps purposefully ignores, the effect her success is having on those around her. Her focused attention on herself and her own concerns follows a pattern announced at the beginning of the novel and, surprisingly, is not criticized by Yver as an egotistical, nonfeminine characteristic. In this regard, Henriette falls into the category of the self-sufficient woman, who appears most often in the novel of the writer or performer.

In considering whether Henriette is self-sufficient, the first question to ask is whether or not a legal career can be considered an "art" or, at the least, comparable to the career of a writer or performer. In the case of Henriette's work in the law, the answer is definitely "yes." The narrator conspicuously notes several ways in which Henriette endeavors to develop a personal style of her own, paralleling the narrative voices found in descriptions of other Belle Epoque women artists in such works as *La Vagabonde* or *Les Cervelines*. But in contrast to the well-established producers of culture found in those two novels, at the beginning of *Les Dames du Palais* Henriette is still an intern, and as such she attends a variety of trials (in the civil court, divorce court, criminal court, and the assizes court) and follows the argumentation of some of the great lawyers of her time, almost as an apprentice would study the works of great painters, with the intention of learning their techniques. She hires a retired actress to give her diction lessons at home during the afternoons, and she reads every night in the *Causes Célèbres* about astute maneuvers by different attorneys or about the defense strategies of judges and clients, to better prepare herself for future cases (Yver 1909, 63). Although Henriette's intention to mimic well-established male lawyers and her adherence to male professional standards in her field do indicate her status as an Yverian "cerveline," one who follows the masculine rules and seeks to triumph in a male-only field, her achievements eventually go beyond the typical arguments and the standard defense speeches. After overcoming her initial tongue-tied fear during her first trials, her manner and style become apparent, and, according to the narrator, her zeal and the tone of her defense speeches (l'accent de ses plaidoiries) place her work well above the banalities usually committed by young lawyers in training (65). Through the voice of André, we learn of Henriette's growing ability to construct a well-crafted argument that displays a creative element in addition to merely well-organized facts. After he has heard Henriette participate in one of the legal association's Saturday morning debates, he makes the following complimentary observations on her work: "You are no longer the child who dodges her defense speech by imploring the indulgence of the court for her client."[19] André comments on her "personal thought" (pensée personnelle) and her "skill" (habileté), which demonstrate that Henriette's creative flair for argumentation is slowly evolving.

André continues to act as a guide for the reader on Henriette's development as an artist in law. After several months of married life, he begins to recognize the evolution of an independent and artistic system of thought in his wife's practice, and his thoughts indicate that Henriette is not simply a brainy woman who does anything and everything to follow male patterns of professionalism for a successful career. He even believes that she should follow a more traditional approach in preparing her cases and wishes to impose this, his own method, on her (Yver 1909, 125). The description of the "manière classique" is rather deprecatory, especially when we consider the terms "vieux bureaucrate" and the "puérilités" and "formules" that André employs to prepare his cases (125). Similar to the narrator's description of Fernand Guéméné's medical research in *Princesses de science,* the discussion of André's work reveals an old-fashioned and tedious methodology.

The narrator's discussion of Henriette's work patterns, in contrast, lends to the interpretation that her preparations for a trial, and the performance itself in the courtroom, are the equivalent of an artistic activity. Just as the novelist Eugénie Lebrun, in *Les Cervelines,* discussed the problems of writers' block and Renée in *La Vagabonde* noted the problems of constructing a well-turned phrase, Henriette struggles with different ways to present a persuasive and well-written defense for her clients, especially for Suzanne Marty. André does not understand her methods or her "work mode, which was sort of impressionistic and made her excite herself, hypnotize herself

---

19. "Vous n'est plus la gosse qui escamote sa plaidoirie en implorant pour son client l'indulgence du tribunal. Vous savez développer une pensée personnelle avec beaucoup d'habileté. C'était très bien" (Yver 1909, 66).

over a case, overexciting her tranquil brain, intoxicating it, heating it up, to the point where she worked out her defense in a trance-like state, in a cerebral shiver, in a nervous burst."[20] In the courtroom, her dramatic abilities are enthralling; she has the power to engross an entire room of people (Yver 1909, 177). She is able to juggle drama with facts, creating an engaging presentation for spectators and judges alike. The fact that Henriette enters a sort of trancelike state at the bar, and that she can immobilize a crowd with her performance, reflects the artist working in front of an audience, similar to the attitudes of the mime performer Renée Néré, in *La Vagabonde,* when she is on stage at the music hall or in front of a private salon audience.

One of the traits that most firmly establishes Henriette as a self-sufficient and artistic protagonist is her defiantly independent attitude about her work. She consciously seeks to invent her own system of thought, and, on the eve of her marriage, she announces that she will prepare her cases on her own, without consulting her husband, whose ten years' experience may have helped her. When she refuses his help, he believes that she is acting in an infantile manner but does not object to her wishes, thinking that her foolishness will teach her quickly that she needs his advice and wisdom. Given this freedom, Henriette chooses to prepare her defenses according to her own methods and following her own style, and it becomes a habit for her to refuse his help, rarely even telling him which cases she has accepted or discussing strategies for upcoming trials. Like the women writers discussed in Chapter 5, Henriette does not seek advice from either men or women colleagues (Yver 1909, 124). Henriette's budding independence continues to make its mark throughout the novel—when she chooses to hire a secretary without consulting her husband and when she decides to leave him rather than sacrifice her career. Even though she eventually returns to their home in order to reconcile their personal problems, Henriette's initial departure is definitive at the moment, and it is a true mark of her status as an independent woman.

Above all, Henriette falls into the category of the independent professional woman because she is unaware of or remains aloof from others' emotions. She creates an artificially determined happy ignorance, comparable to Eugénie Lebrun's glow when she arrives home from her solitary promenades

---

20. "son mode de travail, en quelque sorte impressionniste, qui la faisait s'exalter, s'hypnotiser sur une affaire, surexciter son cerveau tranquille, le griser, le chauffer, au point qu'elle élaborait sa défense dans un état tout particulier de transe, de frémissement cérébral, d'emportement nerveux" (Yver 1909, 124).

through the streets of Paris in *Les Cervelines*. We see Henriette's blissful innocence both in the scene discussed earlier, where she did not suspect the resentment of both her secretary and her husband as she nursed her baby girl in front of them, and in an important dinner scene where André and his grandmother are seething with impatient jealousy while she blithely recounts all the important clients who have sought her advice during the day. After this dinner scene, the narrator describes Henriette's complete satisfaction with her family, work, and life, thus underlining how oblivious she is to André's grief and his grandmother's resentment.[21] A few moments later, Henriette is astonished to discover André crumpled in a heap in the vestibule where he has been nursing his discontent by paging through the numerous newspaper clippings about his wife's successful career. His confession of fear and jealousy is staggering for the unsuspecting Henriette, comparable to Josanne's amazement when she discovers Noël Delysle's jealousy of her son in *La Rebelle*. Yet Henriette quickly recovers from this shock and appears to forget his unhappiness as she continues to practice the law independently.

Just as Eugénie Lebrun could write continually about unhappy romances in her novels and plays while never understanding or recognizing Jean Cécile's pain, Henriette practices mainly divorce law, yet she never glimpses the possible unrest in her own household. Her grandmother-in-law, Mme Mansart, is uncomfortable with Henriette's knowledge of so many "indecencies" in bourgeois households and cannot believe that Henriette is able to remain unaffected by so many twisted avowals from the upper-class women who come to her for advice (Yver 1909, 224). Even as Henriette is patiently explaining to Madame Mansart the kind of equality that exists between André and herself, she has no idea that André is devastated by her refusal to become his secretary.

The narrator portrays Henriette's actions and emotions as directly opposed to those of her surroundings. Most often she is able to ignore the tragedies playing out around her, and when they are finally revealed, she cannot believe that her husband's, her secretary's, and her grandmother-in-law's thoughts have been so different from her own. Yet the narrator never portrays Henriette's lack of intuition about their feelings as a flaw in her character. Rather, the narrator constantly reminds the reader of Henriette's delicate

---

21. "Henriette slowly undressed in her room. She considered herself lucky, counted her joys, thought of her child, of her husband's love, of her nascent glory. Everything smiled on her. She had chosen the most beautiful life, useful, laborious, intense, and the day's consultations coming back to her, she thought with pride of the women of high society, uncertain, like minors, whom she had counseled, guided, directed with the authority of a spiritual advisor." (Henriette se déshabillait lentement dans sa

feminine charm and her rare balance of reason, intuition, and understanding. Her shock at André's outburst is therefore read as understandable and her decision to flee appears rational.

Given the composite structure of this unusual novel, a variety of conclusions might seem possible, but in the end the renunciation plot prevails and Henriette decides to abandon her career to take care of her husband. Even though the community of women in which she works and her independent status as an artist are important for the novel's narrative structure, the option that she finally takes points to the dominance of the seduced brainy woman portrait. Yver's dramatic "renunciation" conclusions provided a controversial ending in her novels (see Chapter 4), and the ending in *Les Dames du Palais* is no exception to that rule.

In this particular novel, however, disappointment and disapproval come from a much more intimate source for the main protagonist than for the teachers of education novels or the writers of the novel of artistic development. Teachers were hounded by town citizens, local superintendents, or rigid government mandates, but Henriette Vélines's utopian vision of her role as lawyer, mother, and wife is undermined by her own husband in her own home. When she finally realizes that her idealistic notions of combining family and career are crumbling, she decides to renounce her professional activities. The results are thus diametrically opposed to those of women's education novels. The teachers chose to escape the various oppressions caused by the inflexible teaching system by leaving the system itself and by marrying and having a family. Henriette, in contrast, appears to embrace the cause of her oppression rather than fleeing it: when she gives up her career, which has provided her with nothing but positive reinforcement, in order to assist André as his secretary, she is not only choosing her family over her career, she is confirming her husband's right to dominate and oppress her. Thus, in this example, the renunciation plot brings with it very negative repercussions for the pursuit of a legal career by women. Furthermore, as a producer and consumer of culture, Henriette comes from a class background similar to that of her clients. Suzanne Marty, for example,

---

chambre. Elle s'estimait heureuse, comptait ses joies, songeait à son enfant, à l'amour de son mari, à sa gloire naissante. Tout lui souriait. Elle avait choisi la plus belle des vies, utile, laborieuse, intense, et les consultations de la journée lui revenant en mémoire, elle pensait avec orgueil aux femmes du monde, incertaines, pareilles à des mineures, qu'elle avait conseillées, guidées, orientées avec l'autorité d'un directeur spirituel [Yver 1909, 246].)

is a family friend whom she has known on a personal basis for years before she decides to represent her as a client. Her senior colleagues are also her father's friends, whom she has known since she was a child. It is therefore surprising that she feels the need to give up her career for marriage, rather than continue independently as did Eugénie Lebrun or Renée Néré, whose situations and class status were most comparable to Henriette's. Her temporary separation from André, when she goes to live with her parents for several weeks, is narrated as a positive experience, yet she decides surprisingly that it is her duty to return to her oppressor and face the difficulties with her husband that she has been ignoring for months.

It becomes clear, then, that many different portraits of women lawyers were possible at this time in France and that Yver could have invented a variety of scenarios for her main protagonist's concluding decision. Therefore her choice to turn Henriette into another seduced brainy woman is specifically that: a choice. Her preferred dénouement implies a marker or boundary for Belle Epoque literary history: while fictional characters could act in manners similar to their real-life counterparts (such as Reval's teachers or Colette's vagabond), those characters that did not have actual historical equals seemed doomed to a conservative ending, at least in the case of Yver's protagonist Henriette Vélines.

In spite of this negative ending of renunciation, I hesitate to label Yver an "antifeminist," in contrast to several critics who have written about this Belle Epoque author in recent years.[22] Although she concludes her text with the decision to bring her protagonist back to the fold of a conservative bourgeois household, Yver's portrait of Henriette throughout the novel has been of an active, intelligent professional. It is not because her protagonist is incapable or incompetent that she abandons her career, but rather because her husband and his grandmother have such conservative leanings and remained blind to the rich fulfillment that Henriette receives from her work. With a more supportive husband and family, it is almost assured that Henriette could have continued to successfully balance career activities and intimate family life. I believe that Yver's message is thus not strictly antifeminist, but rather that it can be interpreted as an indictment of the social pressures that forced women to choose between family and career

---

22. In particular, I am thinking of Jennifer Waelti-Walters in *Feminist Novelists of the Belle Epoque* (1990), Diana Holmes in *French Women's Writing, 1848–1994* (1996), Jennifer Milligan in *The Forgotten Generation* (1996), and Nancy Sloan Goldberg in *Woman, Your Hour Is Sounding* (1999).

during this time period. There were several French authors who wrote about female professionals in an aggressively misogynist manner. I prefer to reserve my label of "antifeminist" for those who truly did not respect women as intellectuals or as professionals, rather than for Yver's portraits of professional women who succumbed to societal pressures to return to motherhood and marriage.

7

AFTER THE WAR

IN THIS BOOK I have concentrated on women writers from the first decade of the twentieth century because that is the time period when novels featuring women professionals first blossomed and enjoyed both critical and popular success. When World War I began, the tone and topic of women writers' texts changed, often dramatically. Nancy Sloan Goldberg, in her literary history *"Woman, Your Hour Is Sounding": Continuity and Change in French Women's Great War Fiction, 1914–1919,* demonstrates that books written by some of the same women (Yver, Tinayre, Colette, for example) during the war years (1914–18) were often diametrically opposed to their Belle Epoque productions. In her survey of more than forty novels, Goldberg reveals the emphasis on the Republican Mother image and on the ideal of service to others that became so prevalent in women's wartime writings. Although many female protagonists in these fictional texts found themselves working outside the home, some for the first time in their lives, most often these were not career women but rather mothers who had transferred their nurturing and caring abilities to the role of nurse in a hospital.[1]

One of the most striking changes in tone during this transition period can be found in two works by the Swiss author Noëlle Roger: the prewar novel *Le Docteur Germaine* (1912) about a woman doctor practicing in working-class London, and the wartime novel *Carnets d'une infirmière* (*Notes of a Nurse,* 1915) about a nurse working during World War I. In the first text, the author portrays the doctor as a hard-working and spirited professional who combats social prejudice against the poor and destitute. In the later novel, the protagonist is a devout nurse who seeks to ease the pain and suffering of wounded soldiers. Both characters are, in one sense, healers, yet their

---

1. For a detailed analysis of this type of storyline, see chapter 2 ("Republican Mothers All") in Goldberg's text. Although most of the texts included in her study are not "career stories," their rewriting of women's goals and possibilities, albeit within the narrow context of a major national crisis, is remarkable. Goldberg's explication of the innovative features of the "shero" (chapter 3) in these works is likewise fascinating.

understanding of their roles and their belief in their work contrast strongly. In the Belle Epoque novel, Germaine, the doctor, sees her role in society not only as a member of the medical institution, but as a social worker; she becomes involved in her patients' lives and takes an interest in their general well-being as well as their physical health. As such, she does not follow the strict socialization codes of the medical profession. As we have seen in earlier chapters, the "modern" doctor treated his or her patients as nameless objects of study. Germaine's professional status, however, is an important, even essential, part of her identity, and it causes many serious issues when she marries her childhood friend Guillaume Evoles. When Germaine explains to Guillaume's mother why she hesitates to marry, she describes herself as "two beings pitted against each other": the wife and the doctor (Roger 1912, 21). As in many Belle Epoque novels about women scientists and doctors, Germaine is drawn ineluctably to her career, and it is the professional doctor, rather than the devoted housewife, who prevails during most of the narrative.

In contrast, the nurse in Roger's wartime novel believes that women's roles in the hospital are secondary to those of both the soldiers and the male doctors. The novel opens with words that convey a feeling of service and effacement, rather than of professional goals or career. In her description of the protagonist's goals, the author writes about her heroine as "an obscure and useful gear" (obscur rouage utile) whose "personality disappears" (la personnalité s'évanouit), and as "this anonymous person who obeys" (cette anonyme qui obéit) (Roger 1915, 13), indicating Roger's shift away from the modern medical institution's practice of prioritizing the professional's control over the patient. Instead, in the context of wartime crisis, the patients, all male, have names, families, and prior histories, and they are not seen as mere objects of study for researchers. The nurses, all women, in contrast, are rather bland and anonymous figures whose names and family histories are mentioned only briefly in passing (23–28). Most wartime texts, while intriguing, are not novels of professional or educational development and thus fall outside of the general boundaries of this book, even though their transitional presence between the literary worlds of the Belle Epoque and the interwar period remains an important and, until Goldberg's study, forgotten marker of change.

After World War I, the women writers considered in this book continued to publish, but many abandoned the heroines and plotlines that had been one of their central focal points, and in some cases, they made a rather dramatic switch. Colette Yver, for example, remained interested in the dilemmas and progress of working women, publishing documentary-style texts on the current status of feminism, *Dans le jardin du féminisme* (1920, *In the Garden of Feminism*), and on the status of women in the professions, *Femmes d'aujourd'hui: enquête sur les nouvelles carrières féminines* (1928, *Women of Today: A Study of the New Feminine Careers*). In the decades following the war and through the 1940s, however, her fictional works included many novels devoted to the lives of saints or stories set in a variety of historical settings, focusing only rarely on contemporary women professionals. The antifeminism for which she is now so famous came to the fore after World War I and continued to escalate in her writings of the interwar period.

Gabrielle Reval also wrote a series of biographical portraits of Belle Epoque women artists and writers—*La Chaîne des dames* (1924, *The Chain of Women*) and a memoir about early graduates from the Ecole Normale Supérieure de Sèvres, *La Grande parade des Sévriennes* (1935, *The Great Parade of Sèvres Women*)—but her fictional works no longer focused on professional women protagonists. Even Colette, who had developed the profile of a working divorcée in her 1910 *La Vagabonde,* switched to a different tone in the 1920s, with her novel *Chéri* (1920) and her semi-autobiographical texts *La Maison de Claudine* (1922, *Claudine's House*), *La Naissance du jour* (1928, *Break of Day*) and *Sido* (1930) that focus on interactions between lovers and mother-daughter relationships.[2]

Such shifts in narratorial emphasis can be explained in part by historical shifts in France's political views of women during the immediate postwar period. The French government made immediate efforts in 1918 to pressure women into relinquishing the jobs they had taken during the war, and they were laid off in massive numbers only three months after the war ended.[3] Along with direct government action to force women back into the home, the Senate voted down the bill to allow women's suffrage. New laws were passed to reinforce women's duty to reproduce, including strong antiabortion and anti-birth-control legislation (Milligan 12). These heavy strictures on women's rights to work and live independently came as a general backlash, after women had made important gains in freedom during the war.

---

2. I have argued, however, that even a text such as *La Naissance du jour,* which critics have discussed for years in terms of its important mother-daughter relationship, also includes a not-so-hidden narrative about fame and success that Colette, the established author, wishes to impose on her readers. See Rogers, "Addressing Success: Fame and Narrative Strategies in *La Naissance du jour*" (1996).

3. Jennifer Milligan in *The Forgotten Generation* (1996) notes that the minister for employment began to announce these policies only two days after the peace treaties were signed (Milligan 12).

Marcel Prévost's epistolary text, *Nouvelles lettres à Françoise ou la jeune fille d'après-guerre* (1924, *New Letters to Françoise, or the Postwar Young Girl*), mentions several times that young women of the bourgeoisie had become used to freedom of movement during the war because they were needed in the hospitals and clinics and other public places and learned to move about without chaperones. Because of their exposure to wounded soldiers in these hospitals, many young women of the middle and upper classes lost their modesty, according to Prévost. They remained pure, but they were no longer uninformed, and those who in the 1920s wanted to restrict their daughters' knowledge of the world found either that it was impossible to do so or that ignorance was considered undesirable by many young men looking for future brides. Prévost notes that even those who were too young to be "young girls of war" (jeunes filles de guerre), that is, those born after 1905, had taken their older sisters' habits to heart and were freer, more open individuals than their mothers could ever have been twenty years earlier.[4] Prévost's text focuses on young women, born mainly during the first decade of the twentieth century, and contrasts them with the generation of women born in the 1870s or 1880s, which includes the majority of women writers discussed in earlier chapters.

L'Egalité en marche (1989, *Equality on the March*), a history of feminism throughout the Third Republic, confirms Prévost's personal interpretations of the new generation of young women. Remarking on the changes in feminist organizations after the war, Klejman and Rochefort note that "the quest for feminine identity" (la quête d'identité féminine) is less important to the generation following World War I, and that social and political questions take precedent.[5] Women were fighting for practical rights and the "means to defend themselves" rather than for a new identity, which may indicate that they already felt comfortable with their social identities. Further, the new leaders of the feminist groups in the 1920s were mainly active working women: "women lawyers, journalists, doctors or employees; well integrated

---

4. Simone de Beauvoir (born 1908), because of her age and social class, would have been a member of this generational grouping. Her freedom of movement, desire to pursue advanced studies and an independent career, and her parents' realistic view that she would not be able to find a husband among the diminished number of available young men after the war, all indicate her membership in the group Prévost names "la jeune fille d'après-guerre."

5. "Utopia is no longer required. The goal now is less to open up new rapports between the sexes than to give rapidly to women the means to defend themselves and to preserve the peace." (L'utopie n'est plus de mise. L'enjeu désormais est moins d'ébaucher de nouveaux rapports de sexe que donner rapidement aux femmes les moyens de se défendre et de préserver la paix" [Klejman and Rochefort 199]).

professionally" (Klejman and Rochefort 199). The professionalism of this new membership indicates a new generation of women with new perspectives on their roles in the public domain.

We therefore find two opposing portraits of women in the French national conscience during the period immediately following the Belle Epoque. During the war, they were considered active participants in the public domain; in hospitals, factories, and a variety of public sector jobs, their aid was indispensable to the war effort. Although many women did yield their jobs to the returning soldiers following the war's end, they had gained a new attitude and spirit that could never completely conform to nineteenth-century expectations for the submissive housewife. In contrast, the strong effort by government officials attempted to reconfine women to the home and to the traditional duties of motherhood and domestic care. Some of these clashing images of the French woman are evident in the novels about women students and professionals after 1918. Postwar authors' goals for their female characters also tend to fall into the same two distinct categories: those who wanted to promote the new working woman of the war days and those who wanted a return to the submissive nineteenth-century mother and housewife. Because neither protagonist type provided a literary portrait that aroused contemporary debate or curiosity, these works did not have the same critical appeal that the earlier Belle Epoque novels enjoyed.

The Second-Generation Professional Heroine

In the postwar era, we continue to find a number of novels of professional development where the brainy woman character exists, but the author's focus is usually on the second generation of women professionals, no longer on the pioneers in their fields, and these works usually include less open hostility for their protagonists. These novels thus take on a new type of narrative form, and the endings reflect the new status of the protagonist as well as the new time period in which the novels take place.

War and Medical School: **L'Interne**

L'Interne (1920) by Myriam Thelen and Marthe Bertheaume covers the years 1908 to 1919 and follows the development of Jeanne from age seventeen to twenty-eight, as she pursues a career in science and medicine. Jeanne is a high-powered brainy woman in the usual sense, yet she understands herself as belonging to a second generation of women scientists. At age seventeen, when arguing with her father for a chance to study medicine, she quotes Colette Yver's *Princesses de Science* as an example of women scientists who are successful in their careers. This is one of the winning points in her argument, since her father must admit that he was the one who recommended the novel to her. Jeanne also engages in animated debates throughout the text with her old-fashioned sister Hélène (who is twelve years older) on women's role in society. Hélène is obviously a prewar, even pre–Belle Epoque symbol of femininity, and she believes that Jeanne would be happiest as a doctor's wife, rather than as a doctor herself.

Jeanne in contrast can point to a number of established women scientists who have made a life for themselves and thus set an example, and she honors these "pioneers" (Thelen et Bertheaume 1920, 24–25). When speaking of her own situation in medical school, Jeanne appears to consider the battle already won, making such statements as "everything is simplified" (tout s'est simplifié) and "we are used to the presence of women" (on s'est habitué à la présence des femmes). Her remarks confirm not only the idea that women professionals had become a stable feature in the sciences, but also that women working in the public domain in general had become much more common during the war and thus they were no longer objects of scrutiny or criticism. There are several situations in the novel, however, especially when in the company of male students, where Jeanne remarks that she has to be on her guard or they will try to take advantage of her. Thus, the prejudices of men against their future female colleagues has not vanished completely, even though she might hope it were the case.

Jeanne also reflects continually on the difficulties of juggling marriage and career, and on the growing pressures to marry that she is receiving from her sister, uncle, aunt, and an assortment of family friends. Still, she can again turn to her predecessors' examples, including the historical figure Mme Edwards-Pilliet, who was the first woman allowed entrance into the *Internat* in French medical schools in the late 1880s, even though she was a widow with two young children at the time (Thelen et Bertheaume 1920, 83). Jeanne is pleased when her frivolous colleague Madeleine, who had quit medical school to marry and have children, tells her later that she wants to finish her studies and begin practicing medicine alongside her husband because she understands that being a doctor and raising a family are compatible activities (170).

The novel thus includes a wide cast of female characters, including a few older women "pioneers," such as Mlle Poppée, who have been studying five to ten years longer than Jeanne and who act as rather ascetic but inspiring role models for the younger students.[6] In Jeanne's class of first-year students, there exist a number of differing attitudes about the medical profession, from Madeleine's insouciance to Mlle Herpin's practical perseverance to Phoebe's ambitious creativity. Jeanne inserts herself in this particular niche of young women students, the second generation of future women scientists and doctors.

In tandem with these notions of a second, more modern generation of women professionals, the romance plot in this novel is based on modern ideals of equality and collegiality. Jeanne and her colleague André Pascal fall in love, becoming interns and fiancés in the same year. They decide responsibly to finish their studies before marrying, but after a year passes each one begins to wish for an earlier marriage, and they are planning for a September wedding when the war breaks out. André leaves for the front immediately, along with many of his male peers at school. Although Jeanne is worried for these men fighting in the trenches, she also comments at length on the positive effects of the "feminization" of the medical school and on the new authority and respect that her female colleagues at school now enjoy (Thelen et Bertheaume 1920, 189).

The wartime ending of this text means that the renunciation plot is no longer a valid option for the narrative. When Jeanne learns that André has died in combat, she quietly finishes her thesis and then retires to the countryside to become a humble general practitioner. Although she abandons the glories of research and an urban clientele that she and André had dreamed of earlier in their medical studies, there is no question of giving up her career as a doctor. She also adopts her friend Madeleine's daughter, since both Madeleine and her husband died during the war, and she decides to raise the child with the help of her conservative older sister and her grandfather. The fact that she would like these family members with their traditional values to help raise her adopted daughter might indicate that Jeanne desires a return to more conservative roles in childrearing. Yet her decision to continue to work shows a distinct contrast from the final denouement of

---

6. Jeanne is thoroughly impressed, for example, when Mlle Poppée risks her life and poisons herself with a cobra's bite in order to see if her newly developed serum will work as an antidote. Poppée's long hours and dedication to her theories are examples to Jeanne of the intensity with which women scientists must work to succeed (Thelen et Bertheaume 1920, 54–59).

most Belle Epoque novels about scientific heroines. In their conclusion, Thelen et Bertheaume reflect the actual situation of many French women: while government officials were extolling the importance of women as mothers, many women were left widowed or unmarried after the war and knew they would not become mothers at all. For these women, finding work outside the home was more important than raising children.

War and the Sorbonne: La Science et l'amour

In the humanities field, Léontine Zanta's *La Science et l'amour* (1920) presents the diary of a young student of philosophy, Madeleine Hastier, at the Sorbonne during the war years. True to the form and structure of the Belle Epoque novel of educational development, the work includes detailed descriptions of her entrance exams, her first impressions of the halls of the Sorbonne, and her mixed reviews of her first-year courses and professors. A major difference, of course, is that Madeleine is attending the once male-dominated Sorbonne, whereas most Belle Epoque novels for future schoolteachers were set in the single-sex teacher training colleges for women. In the first few chapters of the book, Zanta introduces a wide range of characters who are defined mainly by their participation in a number of informal debates held after class or in the library on philosophical topics, often mixed with arguments over men's and women's future roles in society. The war has influenced their discussions of classic philosophers, and some of the fiercest debates are between the pragmatists and skeptics. The strongest positions, not surprisingly, are usually argued by those speaking up for an early form of "engagement" and theories that can be applied to their situation in the war.

Because the book is set in 1916, the tone is quite different from Belle Epoque novels, as the students also discuss the feminized Sorbonne and the "emptiness" they feel. Madeleine's comments on the triumph of feminism in the Sorbonne reveal her beliefs that it is a phony victory (Zanta 9). Despite this negative sentiment, she and her female peers sense a new duty that they will be called upon to perform: teaching in boys' high schools as well as in girls' schools. Madeleine notes that some of her colleagues have already graduated and been assigned to boys schools, with initially good results. For her, this wartime "experiment" will be a major determinant for the future of feminism in her professional field: "This was an experiment that they had tried, an experiment that could be decisive for the future of feminism, good feminism as we hoped for. Would woman prove herself capable of forming men, in the larger sense of the word?"[7] In contrast with Belle Epoque heroines, Madeleine's concern is not with women's intelligence (sometimes a point of doubt in Belle Epoque novels) nor with their morality (women are occasionally confused or seduced in many Belle Epoque novels), but with their *énergie,* or their ability to discipline a classroom of boys. Her friend Marie Lesage, who has been working in a boys' school for a semester, claims that she has not had problems with her class but cannot vouch for all women teachers in France. This new view of women teachers ready to "form men" (former des hommes) is a major shift from the portraits of women professionals during the Belle Epoque, who worked mainly with a female clientele, whether in the sciences, education, or law. Madeleine's ideal vision of women teaching both boys and girls at the high school level would not become commonplace in France for many years. But the idea that women's moral and intellectual capacities equaled those of men was supported and promoted by another female philosophy student at the Sorbonne who attended eight years after this fictional student: Simone de Beauvoir.

In spite of her strong convictions about the future roles of women in education, Madeleine begins to slip in her own studies due to a number of distractions. She spends a long time away from school to care for her brother when he is seriously injured in the war. During his convalescence, she has heated debates with him on women's purpose in the future. He strongly believes that women should stay at home and reproduce, and his arguments are powerful enough to make Madeleine falter in her convictions. During the same time, she falls in love with a fellow student in philosophy who cannot join the army because of health problems. Jacques is a devout atheist, and when Madeleine begins to return to the church and the teachings of her Catholic upbringing for comfort, he objects to her new love of religion, calling it dogmatic and unthinking. But Madeleine persists, and eventually she converts Jacques, too, bringing him to Mass and Communion. They continue to fight over Berkeley and Locke, skepticism versus pragmatism, and other course-related topics, but their bond grows stronger during the year until Jacques' mother discovers their secret engagement and categorically refuses to allow her son, from a wealthy family of Parisian lawyers, to marry Madeleine, a poor student from a struggling working-class family.

---

7. "C'était une expérience que l'on avait tentée, une expérience qui pouvait être décisive pour l'avenir du féminisme, du bon féminisme que nous voulions. La femme se montrerait-elle capable de former des hommes, au sens large du mot?" (Zanta 81–82).

Despite this blow to her dreams, Madeleine firmly believes that love is good for women intellectuals (les intellectuelles) and that it increases women's abilities to understand and to succeed at their work. The theory of Zanta's character thus contrasts strongly with many pure brainy women protagonists from the Belle Epoque who usually decide that work and love are incompatible. Unfortunately, Madeleine's new belief is tested and fails when she flunks the exams at the end of her first year at the Sorbonne. Zanta surprises the reader with this unusual ending for a women's education novel, since we read throughout the text of advanced discussions and complex arguments in which Madeleine is a leading student and debater among her peers. The fact that she flounders at the end, while most of the others pass with honors, indicates the extent to which her thoughts and study habits have been dispersed during the last months of the school year. Her mentor, Mlle Claire, has confidence that she will pass the exams when she takes them again in October, yet the book concludes with uncertainty and defeat.

Thus the renunciation plot in Zanta's text is also modified from the typical Belle Epoque novel of educational development since Madeleine's potential career, as a philosophy professor, is not threatened by demands from a husband or children or society. Rather, she has failed the exams and limited her career potential through poor study habits and incoherent thought. Furthermore, at the conclusion of the novel, the heroine has not given up her career or her aspirations to become a teacher in order to pursue a love interest. The final lines of the text indicate that Madeleine will persevere and, it is hoped, be able to continue in her chosen field of philosophy.

War and the Country Doctor: Dr. Odile

Similar to *L'Interne*, Bertheaume's and Thelen's other postwar novel, the 1923 *Dr. Odile*, discusses the differences between women of the pre- and postwar era and the opportunities that have opened up for women during World War I. When Odile Winter returns home on vacation from her new position in the distant town of Vic, the narrator comments on the generation gap that now separates Odile from her mother and that keeps them from confiding in each other as they used to (Bertheaume et Thelen 1923, 161). Odile still appreciates her mother's care, but she is sad that they are separated by such different life experiences.

The war has drastically changed women's roles in the small town of Vic, and these changes directly affect Odile's budding career as a doctor. Because women have become an important part of the war effort, Odile's first employer is a local factory, and her first patients are the women employed there, mainly to replace the men who have left for the war front. When the war ends, of course, the women are rapidly laid off and Odile loses her position as the company physician for women employees since there are few women left at the factory. She takes this news with a certain amount of resignation, but she is also sorry to leave her patients whose families and private lives she has begun to know well.

These comments on the changing roles of women in French society notwithstanding, Odile is a classic Belle Epoque brainy woman. She has a strong interest in women's health and women's rights, and she believes firmly that women doctors are better able to communicate with women patients. As such, she conforms to the theories espoused by many Belle Epoque authors that women professionals could best serve women clients, whether in legal matters, medical treatments, or educating girls. Odile is also a reminder of the pure brainy woman from the Belle Epoque because she believes that her duty to the medical profession comes before her own personal happiness. She decides that women like herself who were too busy during school to think about romance are often tempted by the *idea* of being in love when they first begin their careers, even though they are usually not in love at all. The advances of a married man tempt Odile, but eventually she smothers those desires and tells him to do the same. Her attitudes about love are thus strictly objective and commonsensical. She does admit that she might some day fall in love with a true passion, but that she is too young and inexperienced at the moment to do so. She is thus quite different from other postwar women characters who believe either that love and career are compatible or that love is more important than career.

From this brief survey of postwar novels about women students and professionals, a pattern surfaces, one that would explain the lessened popularity of this particular subgenre of the bildungsroman after the war. One of the reasons that these novels may not have enjoyed the same enthusiastic reception as the earlier Belle Epoque texts was the fact that women professionals were no longer considered such unique characters. The women characters themselves constantly remind the reader that they are part of a second generation, not pioneers in their field, and that the challenges and hurdles that existed only ten to twenty years earlier have been cleared for them. The confrontational choice between career, on one hand, and marriage or family, on the other, is also eliminated in two of these novels, either because the fiancé dies on the battlefield or because there are no available men to distract the heroine from her career. These protagonists and their women's communities may have appealed to a specific audience of postwar readers (women who were members of that generation), but they did not pique the general public's curiosity as the earlier portraits of pioneer Belle Epoque heroines and women's communities had. Since the difficulties of the preceding generation had apparently been eliminated, the storylines that these later characters would follow did not contain the same dramatic elements or surprising plot twists found in the prewar novels. None of these later novels won literary prizes, nor did they generate as many reviews and letters in women's magazines.

After the war, there was also a strong antifeminist current in literary circles. A comparison of the misogynist portrayals in Henry Fèvre's *L'Intellectuelle mariée* (*The Intellectual Wife*) to the depictions of women professionals in Yver's *Princesses de science* or *Dames du Palais,* for example, reveals the vast gulf that separates these two views of women. While Yver presented intelligent and productive women who were dragged down by prejudice and chauvinism, Fèvre's text offers us portraits of women who liked to pose as intellectuals but who were actually flighty, acquiescent, or even incompetent professionals. Although these negative portraits might be due in part to the fact that they were written by a man, the fact remains that Fèvre's women intellectuals are ultimately shown to be immature or fraudulent, incapable of sustained intellectual activity.[8] It is for acerbic portraits such as these that I prefer to retain the title "antifeminist," in contrast to the majority of literary critics who feel the need to condemn such writers as Yver or Tinayre or Reval because they included female characters who abandoned their careers for their husbands and children.

Simone de Beauvoir rather infamously dismissed several of these Belle Epoque women writers in her *Mémoires d'une jeune fille range* (*Memoirs of a Dutiful Daughter*). Of Colette Yver, she writes: "My father was no feminist; he admired the wisdom of the novels of Colette Yver in which the woman lawyer or the woman doctor in the end sacrifice their careers in order to provide their children and husband with a happy home. But after all, necessity knows no law: 'You girls will never marry,' he often declared,

---

8. Henry Fèvre was a noted naturalist/anarchist writer in the 1890s and early 1900s, with a number of hit plays in Parisian theaters during the fin-de-siècle period, such as *L'Honneur,* which he also published in novel form (1891). His later work about women, *L'Intellectuelle mariée* (1925), is disappointingly conservative and decidedly antifeminist.

'you have no dowries; you'll have to work for a living'" (de Beauvoir, Kirkup trans. 104).[9] She explains her disappointment as well with Marcelle Tinayre's heroine Hellé: "I had felt some affinity for Hellé, Marcelle Tinayre's heroine. 'Girls like you, Hellé,' her father had told her, 'are fit to be the companions of heroes.' This prophecy had aroused my interest; but I found the bearded, ginger-haired missionary she finally married rather revolting" (Kirkup trans. 144).[10] One might conclude from these statements that Simone de Beauvoir criticized these particular women writers because she felt they were antifeminists. But her attitude about them extends to the entire generation of novelists, both male and female, that had "enchanted my father's youth" (enchanté la jeunesse de papa) (de Beauvoir, Kirkup trans. 109; de Beauvoir 152). When speaking of these writers (Maupassant, Bourget, Daudet, the Goncourt brothers, and others), she claims that they all seemed irrelevant to her own life. Except for the heroines in Colette's *Claudine* and *Mademoiselle Dax* by Claude Farrère, the society described in these writers' works seemed out-of-date and the heroines "inane" or "frivolous" (de Beauvoir 152). After our close analysis of the pioneering professionals and hard-working students of these Belle Epoque works, Simone de Beauvoir's dismissal of them as "inane" or "frivolous" seems incomprehensible. Yet it is apparent that de Beauvoir was in fact part of the *second* generation of women professionals in France. In contrast to the fictional characters in the postwar novels, who respect and give thanks to their pioneering elders, de Beauvoir felt the need to distance herself from those who came before by critiquing them. Not only did she feel that these writers appealed to more conservative readers of an earlier generation, she also dismissed them because she felt that she had moved beyond their writing practices and into the newer realms of surrealist and existentialist fiction. She finds much more in common with her "contemporaries": Barrès, Gide, Valéry, Claudel, for examples (de Beauvoir 269).

France, in general, followed de Beauvoir's lead: it dismissed, forgot, or ignored. As is evident now, those dismissals were rash. The movement for women's equality in the workplace and at home is obviously

9. "Mon père n'était pas féministe; il admirait la sagesse des romans de Colette Yver où l'avocate, la doctoresse, finissent par sacrifier leur carrière à l'harmonie du foyer; mais nécessité fait loi: 'Vous, mes petites, vous ne vous marierez pas.' répétait-il souvent. 'Vous n'avez pas de dot, il faudra travailler'" (de Beauvoir 1958, 154).

10. "Je m'étais sentie assez proche d'Hellé, l'héroïne de Marcelle Tinayre. 'Les filles comme toi, Hellé, sont faites pour être les compagnes des héros,' lui disait son père. Cette prophétie m'avait frappée; mais je trouvai plutôt rebutant l'apôtre roux et barbu qu'Hellé finissait par épouser" (de Beauvoir 1958, 201).

not over, even today; in literature of the early twenty-first century, we find many women protagonists who are still struggling to find their place in corporate and professional culture, and who continue to juggle many tasks in the public and private domains, just as their ancestors did one hundred years ago.[11] Although the discussion of women and work may have waned temporarily during the interwar period, a number of works written after World War II bring up education and profession development for women.[12]

Melanie Hawthorne, in a collection of essays on the politics of literary history in France, makes an important statement about recovering and revising women's history and literature: she claims that it is not only "how previously obscured objects may suddenly come into view, but it is also about how one *reading* may obscure another, and the need for vigilance in not assuming that the first thing that hoves into view is the only thing" (Hawthorne 92). I believe that her statement is especially important when considering these long-forgotten Belle Epoque novels of professional development: while their recent "rediscovery" was a major step in rewriting French literary history, we must be careful in the ways that we re-read and remember them, avoiding the stereotyping and generalizations that caused them to disappear in the first place. If we make a careful analysis of the variations that flourished in the Belle Epoque berufsroman, our new views both of the Belle Epoque and of the generations that dismissed them may not vanish as quickly as did the original works.

Thus, these Belle Epoque novels of professional development remain important texts—and not only because they helped to reshape and redefine the modern heroine at the beginning of the twentieth century. They also introduced a new form of bildungsroman with innovative narrative twists that combined both romance and quest to offer new paths

---

11. I am thinking, for example, of recent novels by Amélie Nothomb, Marie Redonnet, Malika Mokkedem, Claire Martin, Monique Proulx, Nadine Bismuth, and others from Quebec and France whose protagonists are doctors, librarians, computer programmers, writers, translators, hotel managers, among other professions.

12. Simone de Beauvoir herself wrote novels in which the female protagonist's private life is structured by her career in the public sphere. See her *L'Invitée* (1943) for images of women working in the theater and *Les Belles images* (1966) for a discussion of women who design advertising campaigns for domestic products (wood paneling, canned tomatoes, etc.). In the domain of working class women we find Claire Etcherelli's 1967 novel *Elise ou la vraie vie* about a factory worker in Paris during the Algerian War.

for female protagonists in French literature. Although the great dividing line of World War I would temporarily put aside the narratives that these women writers had created, their works act as a crucial link in the development of the French novel in the nineteenth and the twentieth centuries, and they enable us to understand the situations of twenty-first century working heroines in a long-term historical perspective.

APPENDIXES

Appendix 1—Biographical Sketches

All of the authors for whom we have dates (Colette, Harry, Reval, Roger, Tinayre, and Yver) were born in the eight-year period between 1869 and 1877, making them part of the same generation of women writers. All nine writers began their literary careers in approximately the same time period (1890s and or early 1900s). Many were born outside Paris or outside France (Harry was born in Jerusalem, Roger was born in Switzerland) and moved to the capital as children or young adults. Whether or not they lived in Paris, most published their works in Parisian-based journals and used Parisian publishers for their novels.

Babin, Marcelle. Little can be found on this author, who apparently published only the novel *Pharamacienne,* followed by the story *Vie Brisée* in the same volume, in 1907. From the preface of *Pharmacienne,* we know that the author was a pharmacist herself in the provinces and a pharmacy student at the University of Paris. She co-wrote the libretto for a comic opera titled *Idylle en Bretagne,* published and performed in Paris in 1912. The publisher for *Pharmacienne,* J. Siraudeau in Angers, is one of the few non-Parisian publishers in this study.

Colette (1873–1954); née Sidonie-Gabrielle Colette. She married three times, moving to Paris and beginning her writing career with her first husband, Willy. She had a daughter in 1913 with her second husband, Henry de Jouvenel. Beginning with *Claudine à l'école* in 1900, Colette wrote many novels, short stories, and "autobiographical fiction." She was also a prolific journalist and a mime. She was awarded the Légion d'honneur (*chevalier*) in 1920 and promoted to *grand officier* in 1953. She was also the president and first woman member of the Académie Goncourt, among other honors. Colette's life and career has been well documented over the years, both in biographies and critical analyses of her texts. I include her name here for the sake of consistency.

Compain, Louise-Marie. No dates available. Compain was a member of the founding committee of the society that organized the mass movement for women's suffrage in France, the *Union française pour le suffrage des femmes* (French Union for Women's Suffrage, or UFSF). As an officer of the UFSF, Compain participated in the 1911 convention of the International Women's Suffrage Alliance (IWSA) in Stockholm and numerous meetings in France. Compain also devoted herself to women's work and labor law, lecturing and writing on the conditions of working-class women. Her novels include *L'Un vers l'autre* (1903) and *L'Oppobre* (1905).

Harry, Myriam (1869–1958); née Maria Rosette Shapira, married Emile Perrault in 1904. Myriam Harry was born in Jerusalem to a Protestant family (her mother was German, her father a converted Jew from the Ukraine). After the father's suicide, the family returned to Germany, and at seventeen, Harry moved to Paris to become a teacher and also began her literary career. First as columnist for *La Fronde* (with a short story published in 1898), Harry wrote for several journals and published her first novel, *Petites Epouses,* in 1902. Many of her works are "orientalist" in nature, and she is famous as the first recipient of the Femina Prize for *La Conquête de Jérusalem.* The Femina book prize was created after she was denied the Prix Goncourt because she was a woman.

Reval, Gabrielle (1870–1938); née Gabrielle Logerot, married to the poet Fernand Fleuret. Logerot was one of the first graduates (class of 1890) of the Ecole Normale Supérieure de Sèvres founded in 1882, and she taught at the high school for girls at Niort until 1899. In addition to her novels, she also wrote for several newspapers, including *L'Oeuvre* and *Le Journal.* She was awarded the Légion d'honneur, the Prix du Président de la République (1934), and the Portuguese Order of Santiago de l'Epée (1935). She also shaped women's writing as a member of the jury for the Femina Prize.

Roger, Noelle (1874–1953); pseudonym for Hélène Dufour Pittard. Roger was a Swiss novelist, best known for her nine science fiction novels that appeared mainly between the wars, including *Le Déluge* (1922), *Le Nouvel Adam* (1924), *Celui qui voit* (1926), *Le Soleil enseveli* (1928), and *La Vallée perdue* (1939). In these later works, she is a Jean-Jacques Rousseau disciple and holds society responsible for perverting man, distancing him from nature, and bringing him to live in deceit; the impure are punished and the heroes are tragic figures.

Esther de Suze. No dates available; née Esther Bénisti. There is little information on this writer. Before *Institutrice,* she published the novels *Coeur brisé* (1898) and *Journal d'une juive au couvent* (1899), although these do not contain portraits of working women.

Tinayre, Marcelle (1877–1948); née Marguerite-Suzanne-Marcelle Chasteau. She married the painter and engraver Julien Tinayre after receiving the baccalauréat. She began her writing career at an early age, publishing *Vive les vacances* in 1895 and *L'Enfant gaulois* in 1897 under the pseudonym of Charles Marcel. Tinayre contributed regularly to a wide variety of newspapers and periodicals, such as *La Mode Pratique, La Vie Heureuse,* and *Le Temps.* She wrote the first serial story published in Marguerite Durand's *La Fronde* and through that connection made her first contacts in the world of French feminism. In 1908 Tinayre was named to receive the Légion d'honneur (*chevalier*), but she wrote a satirical piece on the award before she received it and her name was removed from the honors list. In 1939 she received the Barthou Prize from the French Academy.

Yver, Colette (1874–1953); née Antoinette de Bergevin. She married Auguste Huzard in 1904. Although she published children's stories when she was only seventeen, Yver's first major novel, *Les Cervelines (The Brainy Women),* did not appear until 1903. Auguste Huzard, an editor for the publishing house of Juven, read the manuscript, and he later claimed to have married her because of it. In 1907, Colette Yver was awarded the "Vie Heureuse" (Femina) Prize for her novel *Princesses de science (Princesses of Science),* and she subsequently became a member of the Femina jury. In later years she worked for the Catholic Church and for the sick, devoting her writing to saints lives and other religious subjects. Her early novels, however, were quite subversive.

Appendix 2—Plot Summaries

La Bachelière (The Female Graduate) 1910, by **Gabrielle Reval**
The novel has two distinct sections; the first depicts the heroine, Gaude Malvos, working alongside her father the famous archeologist Pierre Malvos. Knowing that his funding is running out, she decides in a public ceremony to choose one of her father's wealthy students as a husband so that they may continue their work without interruptions. This decision fails in two ways: the young man requires that Gaude give up her work with her father in order to be a devoted wife and mother, and her father is upset because he believes that his daughter (and most valuable assistant) is giving up the life of the mind for a "banal" existence as wife and mother. The father dies from a heart attack, and Gaude breaks the engagement with the young student so that she can move to Paris to seek her fortune there.

The second part of the novel focuses on Gaude's growing independence and her budding career as a writer. At first, she is rebuffed by her father's publishers, but after taking a series of jobs (research assistant, private school teacher) and moving away from the "protective" cover of her father's reputation and colleagues, she begins to blossom as an independent writer and researcher. She does not see the fruit of her labor, however, as a slightly deranged colleague at the school burns her manuscript (convinced it is heretical writing), and the ending of the novel is ambiguous, as Gaude has decided to leave for Poland (her father's country of origin). Although she anticipates a new start, she leaves with an uncertain future.

Les Cervelines (The Brainy Women) 1903, by **Colette Yver**
The main protagonist in this text is Marceline Rhonans, a high school history teacher and "orientalist" researcher in Brie. There are two other important women professionals as well, Jeanne Boerk, a pathology student at the Briois hospital, and Eugénie Lebrun, a successful novelist and playwright in Paris. All three women are "cervelines" (brainy women) according to Dr. Jean Cécile, the male character who invented this term.

Both Jeanne and Marceline are curiosities in the small city where they work and study, and two young doctors fall in love with them. Jeanne is so devoted to her career (and future advancement in Paris) that she rejects the offer of love and marriage by her supervisor Paul Tisserel. Marceline is tempted by a possible romance with Jean Cécile, but decides that she is not made for a domestic life in the provinces and ends up rejecting his marriage proposal as well. There is also a fairly long flashback by Jean Cécile to his earlier infatuation with another cerveline, Eugénie Lebrun, while he was a medical student in Paris.

The novel ends with Marceline's decision to request support from her former professors so that she can make a trip to Beirut to study the Phoenician culture that is the core of her research and writing.

Claudine à l'école (*Claudine at School*) 1900, by Colette

Colette's first novel, published under her first husband's name, chronicles the final year in public school of fifteen-year-old Claudine in the fictional village of Montigny. Based in part on Colette's memories of her school years, the narrative gives a day-by-day account of girls in a state-run school under the changing laws of the Third Republic. The narrative opens with the students moving in to newly constructed buildings in September and ends with the closing awards ceremony in July.

Influenced by her husband Willy, Colette also included several risqué segments, including references to a lesbian relationship between two of the girls' schoolteachers and a philandering regional inspector who comes to "inspect" the older girls in the school as well as the youngest woman schoolteacher. Claudine describes her coursework, friends and teachers, and end-of-the-year exams, but she also explains her emotional state and her difficulties imagining a future for herself, in the school system or in Montigny "society."

Dames du Palais (*Ladies of the Court*) 1909, by Colette Yver

This text focuses on the budding career of Henriette, a young lawyer in Paris. When the novel begins, she is just starting her legal practice, following in her father's footsteps. But after she marries a fellow lawyer and has a baby girl, her life becomes more complicated. Although she seems to juggle the multiple tasks easily, things become difficult when she begins to compete with her husband for clients. As her talents begin to outshine his, the husband becomes bitter and withdrawn. In the end Henriette decides to give up her practice in order to make her husband happy.

The novel is unusual because it includes many different women lawyers; some are experienced lawyers with a well-known clientele, some are struggling to provide a living for themselves and their children, and others are still students whose futures remains undefined. Yver demonstrates that these women form a community, but there are many different legal styles and professional goals among them.

Institutrice (*Woman Schoolteacher*) 1902, by Esther de Suze
After having been raised as a well-to-do bourgeoise in Marseille, the main character in this novel, Marie-Thérèse Romane, loses both her father and her mother within the space of several weeks and learns after their deaths that her father was ruined, leaving her nothing but debt. At eighteen, suddenly an orphan and a pauper, Marie-Thérèse decides that solitude and hard work are the two things she needs most in life. She therefore pursues the necessary education to receive the brevet supérieur and obtains a teaching post in a village primary school. At the beginning of her stay, Marie-Thérèse spends all her time working out new teaching methods, trying new ways to arrange her house, and taking walks in the mountainous and wintry landscape around her. Although the parents and townspeople think that she is doing a good job overall, she begins to feel lonely. Rumors spread that she is having an affair with the mayor and she must leave the town immediately. The conclusion of the novel explains that she has moved to Marseille and is starting her life over, marrying a young man whom she has met there.

Pharmacienne (*Woman Pharmacist*) 1907, by Marcelle Babin
The main character in this novel, Danielle Dormeuil, age eighteen, suddenly finds herself an orphan with little financial support and a younger brother to care for. Her father's friend Michel Bakitcheff and his son Wilfrid suggest to Danielle that she might pursue a career in medicine, as her father had, in order to support her brother and herself. She immediately begins her studies for the baccalauréat exams and continues with medical school. She becomes the unwitting object of study of the handsome yet Machiavellian Dr. Adrien Clavelan, one of her professors at medical school, because he wishes to know the link between physical and psychological distress. When Danielle becomes seriously ill from an infected scalpel during one of her first autopsies, Clavelan constantly tends to her and reinforces his attentions. At the moment when she is finally beginning to recover, the doctor suddenly reveals to Danielle that he is married. The psychological shock of this news to Danielle triggers a physical relapse, exactly according to Clavelan's predictions.

Her renewed physical suffering, however, does not diminish the "moral suffering" (la souffrance d'amour) that she felt, and therefore Clavelan decides he must end the experiment and never see her again, requiring her to transfer to pharmacy school.

Babin's novel devotes almost one-third of its plot to a description of the heroine's education, from her initial decision to become a doctor, through the different courses taken, exams passed, and diplomas received. But it is more closely related to the scientific novel than the education novel because a major portion of the narrative examines Danielle's negotiations with the town where she has decided to establish her pharmacy. She experiences some of the typical issues involved with clients suspicious of a female professional and must deal with emotional as well as professional disappointments.

In the end, she does meet and marry a local man who is willing to allow her to continue her research and even her public work as a pharmacist. Babin's heroine thus continues her research, although the day-to-day operation of the pharmacy is handed over to her younger brother, who has followed in her career footsteps.

Princesses de science (The Doctor Wife or Princesses of Science) 1907, by Colette Yver

The main protagonist in this novel, Thérèse Herlinge, is a bright young medical student when the novel begins. She marries a fellow student, Fernand Guéméné, and continues with her thesis research until she becomes pregnant. As soon as she has given birth, she returns to her research, but the nine-month interruption leads her to choose a more limited thesis topic. Her work is again interrupted when her husband becomes seriously ill and she stays home to take care of him. When she finally returns to her work, she decides she must give up the thesis and instead establishes a general practice alongside her husband's. Their child, who was being cared for by a wet nurse, dies at an early age, and the couple becomes more and more unhappy. Fernand wishes that Thérèse would give up her career to be a devoted wife and mother; Thérèse cannot imagine a life without science. In the end, after she learns that Fernand has become attracted to the widow of one of his clients, Thérèse renounces her medical practice and her research in order to save her crumbling marriage.

Yver includes a number of other women working in the medical field who serves as antimodels for the main character. These include her peer Dina, who gives up her medical career to marry a fellow doctor, and two older women. One is Dr. Lancelevée, who pursues her high-profile medical career in Paris but maintains a secretive affair with a colleague on the side. The other is Dr. Adeline, who has tried to do everything: have a family and maintain a medical practice. As a result she is exhausted, has not achieved any great professional success, her husband is alienated, and her children are not taken care of properly. These three characters are all examples to Thérèse of the difficulties that women face when trying to juggle professional and personal lives.

La Rebelle (*The Woman Rebel*) 1905, by Marcelle Tinayre

In this novel, the main character is a journalist for the women's magazine *Le Monde féminin*. At the beginning of the text, Josanne Valentin is married to a sick husband and carrying on a fading affair with a wealthy bachelor. These relationships both end (the husband dies and the bachelor marries another woman), and she meets the feminist writer Noël Delysle, whose work *La Travailleuse* (*The Woman Worker*) she reviewed for *Le Monde féminin*. The novel discusses Josanne's career at the magazine, including her rise from a fashion columnist and book reviewer to a full-fledged journalist, doing investigative reporting on topics of her choosing. The narrator also chronicles the ups and downs of her relationship with the jealous and surprisingly conservative Noël. Josanne tries to remain a "rebel" in her public life, that is, in the types of articles that she writes, but in her private life she eventually decides not to insist on feminist principles and renounces her previous life as an adulterer, even though she believes that she had the right to seek pleasure as much as any man. After this renunciation, Noël announces to Josanne's editor that he won't have her for much longer because they are going to be married, and the novel ends with this declaration about Josanne's future.

Sévriennes (*Women of Sèvres*) 1900, by Gabrielle Reval

The first of Reval's trilogy on women students and schoolteachers, this novel focuses on the three years that Marguerite Triel spends at the Ecole Normale Supérieure de Sèvres, the most prestigious state-run teacher training school for women at the time. She is surrounded by an intriguing cast of characters: students with varying personalities and professional aspirations, professors with diverse goals for their students, and a director who provides a model of strength and intelligence for her students, despite her chilly demeanor.

As the novel progresses, Marguerite recounts the day-to-day activities of her classmates, along with major events, such as the departure of certain students for teaching positions or preparations for the final exams. These diary sections are interspersed with sections where the omniscient narrator describes the school's philosophy and other perspectives on its activities. Given her top ranking at the school, the heroine appears poised for a promising career as a high school professor or even as headmistress of a school. In the closing pages of the novel the reader discovers that Marguerite has decided not to take a teaching position but rather to live with and take care of a sculptor named Henri Dolfière.

L'Un vers l'autre (*One Toward the Other*) 1903, by Louise-Marie Compain

Compain outlines the decision by a young wife, Laure Déborda, to leave her conservative husband and become a teacher. The novel briefly describes the year of courses Laure takes to gain her credentials, but it focuses mainly on the trials and tribulations she undergoes as a first-year teacher in a regional école normale for women (teacher training school) in a city with distrusting citizens.

The narrator offers remarkable insights into the developing feminist perspective of the main character, Laure, and the positive influence of her school's director, a single woman who has decided to spend her life directing public schools for girls, opting not to marry or have a family. Although she and the other teachers at the school are all encouraging role models for Laure, the suspicious townspeople and the regional inspectors create tensions in her life that she is unable to tolerate.

In an unusual move in this type of novel, Compain devotes one chapter toward the end of the text to the parallel developments of Laure's husband during the year. Thus the reader receives some justification for the renunciation plot at the end of this narrative: the husband has reformed and forsaken his authoritarian ways that originally drove Laure away. When he comes to the school to tell her he has changed and to ask her to come home, their mountaintop reunion is somewhat rose-colored. Compain, however, depicts them as a happy couple in the follow-up novel that she wrote in 1905.

La Vagabonde (*The Vagabond*) 1910, by Colette

This novel is still well known and currently in print, and I include a brief plot summary here only for the sake of consistency. Recently divorced, Renée Néré has given up a writing career to become a mime performer at a Parisian music hall with her partner Brague. Although her life has become more difficult financially since her divorce from the painter Adolphe Taillandy, she is glad to be on her own after suffering for years from his infidelities.

As the narrative opens, she cautiously begins a new relationship with Maxime Dufferein-Chautel, a wealthy man her age (thirty-four), who originally saw her on the music hall stage. They spend many pleasant moments together, but she leaves him behind when she departs to perform with her partner Brague in a tour of the French provinces. While she is away, Renée and Max begin a correspondence in which she explains that she is worried about future infidelities by Max, in part because of the similarity in their ages but also because she has already been through a failed marriage, while he has never been married. When he writes and asks her to marry him and begins to indicate a more authoritarian (proprietary) style as a future husband, Renée realizes that she cannot continue with him, preferring solitude to domination. The novel ends with her decision to break off the relationship, even though she admits that she cares for him deeply.

REFERENCES

PRIMARY SOURCES

Babin, Marcelle. 1907. *Pharmacienne*. Augers: J. Siraudeau.
Barrès, Maurice. 1988. *Les Déracinés*. Paris: Gallimard; orig. pub. 1897.
Bourget, Paul. 1887. *André Cornélis*. Paris: Fayard.
———. 1902. *L'Etape*. Paris: Plon-Nourrit.
———. 1930. *Le Disciple*. Paris: Société française d'éditions littéraires et techniques; orig. pub. 1889.
Colette. 1984a. *Claudine à l'école*. In *Oeuvres*, vol. 1. Paris: Gallimard; orig. pub. 1900.
———. 1984b. *La Vagabonde*. In *Oeuvres*, vol. 1. Paris: Gallimard; orig. pub. 1910.
———. 2001a. *Claudine at School*. In *The Complete Claudine*. Translated by Antonia White. New York: Farrar, Straus and Giroux.
———. 2001b. *The Vagabond*. Translated by Enid McLeod. New York: Farrar, Straus and Giroux.
Compain, Louise-Marie. 1903. *L'Un vers l'autre*. Paris: Stock.
———. 1905. *L'Opprobre*. Paris: Stock.
———. 1910. *La Femme dans les organisations ouvrières*. Paris: Giard and Brière.
Deries, Léon. 1902, *Journal d'une institutrice*. Paris: A. Colin.
Doche, Gabriel. 1924. *Suzanne Dupré: institutrice*. Foix: Edition du Domaine.
Fèvre, Henry. 1925. *L'Intellectuelle mariée*. Paris: Albin Michel.
Frapié, Léon. 1904. *La Maternelle*. Paris.
———. 1906. *L'Institutrice de province*. Paris: A. Fayard.
Gide, André. 1951. *L'Immoraliste*. Paris: Mercure de France; orig. pub. 1902.
———. 1966. *The Immoralist*. Translated by Richard Howard. New York: Vintage.
Harry, Myriam. 1902. *Petites épouses*. Paris: Calmann-Lévy.
———. 1904. *La Conquête de Jérusalem*. Paris: Calmann-Lévy.
Hue, Gustave. 1903. *L'Avocate*. Paris: Fontemoing.
Margueritte, Paul, and Victor Margueritte. 1899. *Femmes nouvelles*. Paris: E. Plon, Nourrit et Cie.
Mirbeau, Octave. 1900. *Le Journal d'une femme de chambre*. Paris: E. Fasquelle.
Prévost, Marcel. 1900. *Vierges fortes: Léa*. Paris: A. Lemerre.
———. 1900. *Vierges fortes: Frédérique*. Paris: A. Lemerre.
———. 1924. *Nouvelles lettres à Françoise ou la jeune fille d'après-guerre*. Paris: Flammarion.
Reval, Gabrielle. 1900. *Les Sévriennes*. Paris: Ollendorff.
———. 1901. *Un Lycée de jeunes filles*. Paris: Ollendorff.
———. 1902. *Lycéennes*. Paris: Ollendorff.
———. 1904. *L'Avenir de nos filles*. Paris: A. Hatier.
———. 1906. *Le Ruban de Vénus*. Paris: Calmann-Lévy.
———. 1910. *La Bachelière*. Paris: Flammarion.
———. 1924. *La Chaîne des dames*. Paris: G. Crès.
———. 1935. *La Grande parade des Sévriennes*. Paris: Fayard.

Roger, Noëlle. 1912. *Le Docteur Germaine*. Paris: Perrin and Cie.
———. 1915. *Carnets d'une infirmière*. Paris: Attinger Frères.
Suze, Esther de. 1898. *Coeur brisé*. Paris: A. Lemerre.
———. 1899. *Journal d'une juive au couvent*. Paris: A. Lemerre.
———. 1902. *Institutrice*. Paris: Calmann-Lévy.
Thelen, Myriam, and Dr. Marthe Bertheaume. 1920. *L'Interne*. Paris: Plon.
———. 1923. *Le Docteur Odile*. Paris: Plon.
Tinayre, Marcelle. 1896. *Hellé*. Paris: Mercure de France.
———. 1905. *La Rebelle*. Paris: Calmann-Lévy.
UNE institutrice de province. 1905. *L'Evadée*. Paris.
Yver, Colette. 1903. *Les Cervelines*. Paris: Juven.
———. 1903. "Le Cas de conscience d'une avocate." *Un Coin du voile*. Paris: Calmann-Lévy. Pp. 45–91.
———. 1907. *Princesses de science*. Paris: Calmann-Lévy.
———. 1909. *Les Dames du palais*. Paris: Calmann-Lévy.
———. 1920. *Dans le jardin du féminisme*. Paris: Calmann-Lévy.
———. 1929. *Femmes d'aujourd'hui: Enquête sur les nouvelles carrières féminines*. Paris: Calmann-Lévy.
Zanta, Léontine. 1920. *La Science et l'amour: Journal d'une étudiante*. Paris: Plon-Nourrit.

SECONDARY SOURCES

Albertini, Pierre. 1994. *L'Ecole en France, XIXe et XXe siècle*. Paris: Hachette.
Ancelet-Hustache, Jeanne. 1981. *Lycéenne en 1905*. Paris: Aubier Montaigne.
Angenot, Marc. 1983. "On est toujours le disciple de quelqu'un, ou le mystère du pousse-au-crime." *Littérature* 49 (February): 42–55.
Apter, Emily. 1991. *Feminizing the Fetish: Psychoanalysis and Narrative Obsession in Turn-of-the-Century France*. Ithaca: Cornell University Press.
Ardis, Ann. 1990. *New Women, New Novels: Feminism and Early Modernism*. New Brunswick: Rutgers University Press.
———. 1993. "Toward a Redefinition of 'Experimental Writing': Netta Syrett's Realism, 1908–1912." In *Famous Last Words: Changes in Gender and Narrative Closure*, ed. Alison Booth. Charlottesville: University of Virginia Press. Pp. 259–79.
Auerbach, Nina. 1978. *Communities of Women: An Idea in Fiction*. Cambridge: Harvard University Press.
Bakhtin, M. M. 1986. *Speech Genres and Other Late Essays*. Translated by Vern W. McGee. Austin: University of Texas Press.
Barbizet, Claude, and Françoise Leguay. 1988. *Blanche Edwards-Pilliet: Femme et médecin, 1858–1941*. Le Mans: Cénomane.
Barjeau, Mme A. Philip de. 1901. "A Travers les livres: *Sévriennes* de Gabrielle Reval." *La Femme* 23, no. 3 (1 February): 22–23.
———. 1901. "A Travers les livres: *Un Lycée de jeunes filles* and *Lycéennes* de Gabrielle Reval." *La Femme* 23, no. 14 (15 August): 127–28; and 23, no. 15 (1 September): 134–36.
Bartkowski, Frances. 1989. *Feminist Utopias*. Lincoln: University of Nebraska Press.
Beauvoir, Simone de. 1943. *L'Invitée*. Paris: Gallimard.
———. 1966. *Les Belles images*. Paris: Gallimard.
———. 1958. *Mémoires d'une jeune fille rangée*. Paris: Gallimard.

———. 1974. *Memoirs of a Dutiful Daughter.* Translated by James Kirkup. New York: Harper Perennial.
Berenson, Edward. 1992. *The Trial of Madame Caillaux.* Berkeley and Los Angeles: University of California Press.
Bertaut, Jules. 1910. *La Jeune fille dans la littérature française.* Paris: Michaud.
Bompaire-Evesque, Claire. 1992. "Paul Bourget Collaborateur de Maurice Barrès." *Revue d'histoire littéraire de la France* 92, no. 2 (March–April): 218–35.
Bonvoisin, S.-M., and M. Maignien. 1986. *La Presse féminine.* Paris: PUF.
Bourdieu, Pierre. 1984. *Distinction: A Social Critique of the Judgment of Taste.* Translated by Richard Nice. Cambridge: Harvard University Press.
———. 1993. "The Field of Cultural Production, or: The Economic World Reversed." In *The Field of Cultural Production: Essays on Art and Literature.* New York: Columbia University Press. Pp. 29–73.
Branzac, Paule. 1905. "Livres Nouveaux." *L'Evadée,* by "une institutrice de province" and *Sévriennes* by Gabrielle Reval. *La Femme Nouvelle* 2, no. 3 (1 February).
Brombert, Victor. 1961. *The Intellectual Hero: Studies in the French Novel, 1880–1955.* New York: J. B. Lippincott.
Carles, Emilie. 1977. *Une Soupe aux herbes sauvages.* Paris: Robert Laffont.
———. 1991. *A Life of Her Own.* Translated by Avriel H. Goldberger. London: Penguin.
"Ce qu'il nous faut lire d'utile ou d'amusant." 1903. *L'Avocate* de Gustave Hue. *La Vie Heureuse: Guide du lecteur* 2, no. 1 (January): vii–ix.
Charle, Christophe. 1987. *Les Elites de la République, 1880–1900.* Paris: Fayard.
Christian-Smith, Linda. 1990. *Becoming a Woman Through Romance.* New York: Routledge.
Clarétie, Léo. 1907. *L'Ecole des dames.* Paris: Sansot.
Clark, Linda. 1984. *Schooling the Daughters of Marianne: Textbooks and the Socialization of Girls in Modern French Primary Schools.* Albany: SUNY.
———. 1989. "A Battle of the Sexes in a Professional Setting: The Introduction of *Inspectrices Primaires,* 1889–1914." *French Historical Studies* 16, no. 1 (spring): 96–125.
Collado, Mélanie E. 2003. *Colette, Lucie Delarue-Mardrus, Marcelle Tinayre: Emancipation et resignation.* Paris: L'Harmattan.
Couturiau, Paul. 2001. *Séverine l'insurgée: Biographie.* Paris: Editions du Rocher.
Crespelle, Jean Paul. 1976. *La Vie quotidienne à Montparnasse à la grande époque, 1905–1930.* Paris: Hachette.
Curie, Eve. 1937. *Madame Curie.* Translated by Vincent Sheean. New York: Doubleday, Doran.
Damon, Pierre. 1988. *La Vie quotidienne du médecin parisien en 1900.* Paris: Hachette.
"Débuts des Femmes Avocats," 1905. *La Vie Heureuse* 27, no. 9 (September).
Douyère-Demeulenaere, Christine. 2003. *Séverine et Vallès: Le Cri du Peuple.* Paris: Payot.
Duplessis, Rachel Blau. 1985. *Writing Beyond the Ending.* Bloomington: Indiana University Press.
Duquesne, Jacques. 1990. *Catherine Courage.* Paris: Grasset.
Elder, Nancy C., and Andrew Schwarzer. 1996. "Fictional Women Physicians in the Nineteenth Century: The Struggle for Self-Identity." *Journal of Medical Humanities* 17, no. 3 (September): 165–77.

Elliott, Philip. 1972. *Sociology of the Professions*. New York: Herder and Herder.
Etcherelli, Claire. 1967. *Elise ou la vraie vie*. Paris: Denoël.
"Evènements et Menus Faits." On Women in Journalism. 1905. *La Vie Heureuse* 27, no. 11 (November): 4.
Fallières, M. le Président. 1909. "Discours de l'Inauguration de l'Hôtel de la Ligue de l'Enseignement." Repr. in *L'Action Féministe* 2, no. 2 (November): 24–25.
Farrington, Frederic Ernest. 1906. *The Public Primary School System of France with Special Reference to the Training of Teachers*. New York: Columbia University Press.
Felski, Rita. 1989. *Beyond Feminist Aesthetics: Feminist Literature and Social Change*. Cambridge: Harvard University Press.
Finch, Alison. 2000. *Women's Writing in Nineteenth-Century France*. Cambridge: Cambridge University Press.
Flaubert, Gustave. 1984. *L'Education sentimentale*. Paris: Garner; orig. pub. 1869.
Foucault, Michel. 1962. *La Naissance de la clinique*. Paris: Presses Universitaires de France.
France, Anatole. 1893. *Les Opinions de Jérôme Coignard*. Paris: Calmann-Lévy.
———. 1897. *L'Histoire Contemporaine*. Paris: Calmann-Lévy.
Frandon, Ida-Marie. 1989. "Maurice Barrès et le genèse du *Roman de l'énergie nationale*. Autour d'un dénouement abandonné pour *Leurs Figures*." *Revue d'histoire littéraire de la France* 89, no. 2 (March–April): 230–40.
Furst, Lillian. 1997. "Halfway Up the Hill: Doctresses in Late Nineteenth-Century American Fiction." In *Women Healers and Physicians: Climbing a Long Hill*. Edited by Lillian Furst. Lexington: University Press of Kentucky. Pp. 221–38.
Gaillard, Jean-Paul. 1999. *Séverine: Mémoires Inventés d'une femme en colère*. Paris: Plon.
Gatti de Gamand, Isabelle. 1907. *Education—Féminisme*. Paris: V. Girard and E. Brière.
Gelfand, Toby. 1980. *Professionalizing Modern Medicine*. Westport, Conn.: Greenwood Press.
Gennep, Arnold van. 1909. *Les Rites de passage*. Paris: E. Nourry.
Goldberg, Nancy Sloan. 1999. *Woman, Your Hour Is Sounding: Continuity and Change in French Women's Great War Fiction, 1914–1919*. New York: St. Martin's Press.
Gosling, Nigel. 1978. *The Adventurous World of Paris, 1900–1914*. New York: William Morrow.
Grenaudier-Klijn, France. 2004. *Une Littérature de circonstances: Texte, hors-texte et ambiguïté à travers quatre romans de Marcelle Tinayre*. Berne: Peter Lang.
Hardin, James. 1991. "Introduction." In *Reflection and Action: Essays on the Bildungsroman*. Edited by James Hardin. Columbia: University of South Carolina Press. Pp. ix–xxvii.
Hartman, Mary S. 1977. *Victorian Murderesses*. New York: Schocken Books.
Hause, Stephen. 1987. *Hubertine Auclert: The French Suffragette*. New Haven: Yale University Press.
Hause, Stephen C., with Anne R. Kenney. 1984. *Women's Suffrage and Social Politics in the French Third Republic*. Princeton: Princeton University Press.
Hawthorne, Melanie. 2003. "'Une voiture peut en cacher une autre': Twentieth-Century Women Writers Read George Sand." *SubStance*, Special Issue: The Politics of French Literary History, vol. 32, no. 3: 92–108.
Heilbrun, Carolyn. 1988. *Writing a Woman's Life*. New York: W.W. Norton.
Heister, Marion. 1989. *Winzige Katastrophen. Ene Untersuchung zur Schreibweise von Angestelltenromanen*. New York: Peter Lang.

Hirsch, Charles Henri. 1902. "De Mademoiselle de Maupin à Claudine." *Mercure de France* (June): 577–88.
Holmes, Diana. 1996. *French Women's Writing, 1848–1994*. London: Athlone Press.
———. 2006. "Daniel Lesueur and the Feminist Romance." In *A Belle Epoque? Women in French Society and Culture, 1890–1914*. Edited by Diana Holmes and Carrie Tarr. New York: Berghahn Books. Pp. 197–210.
Howells, William Dean. 1881. *Doctor Breen's Practice*. Boston: Osgood.
Jewett, Sarah, Orne. 1999. *A Country Doctor*. New York: Bantam; orig. pub. 1884.
Jullian, Philippe. 1978. "Can-cans and Flappers." Translated by Jennifer Shipton. In *La Belle Epoque: Fifteen Euphoric Years of European History*. New York: William Morrow. Pp. 81–112.
Kern, Stephen. 1992. *The Culture of Love: Victorians to Moderns*. Cambridge: Harvard University Press.
Klejman, Laurence, and Florence Rochefort. 1989. *L'Egalité en marche*. Paris: Presses de la Foundation nationale des sciences politiques des femmes.
Labovitz, Esther Klein. 1986. *The Myth of the Heroine: The Female Bildungsroman in the Twentieth Century*. New York: Peter Lang.
Larnac, Jean. 1929. *Histoire de la littérature féminine en France*. Paris: Editions Kra.
Larson, Magali. 1977. *The Rise of Professionalism*. Berkeley and Los Angeles: University of California Press.
LeGarrec, Evelyne. 1982. *Séverine: Une Rebelle, 1855–1929*. Paris: Seuil.
Leps, Marie-Christine. 1992. *Apprehending the Criminal: The Production of Deviance in Nineteenth-Century Discourse*. Durham: Duke University Press.
Lesueur, Daniel (pseud. of Jeanne Lapauze). 1905. *L'Evolution féminine: Ses résultats économiques*. Paris: A. Lemerre.
Marbo, Camille. 1907. "La Femme intellectuelle au foyer." *La Vie Heureuse* 6, no. 8 (August).
Margadant, Jo Burr. 1990. *Madame le Professeur: Women Educators in the Third Republic*. Princeton: Princeton University Press.
Martin, Benjamin F. 1984. *The Hypocrisy of Justice in the Belle Epoque*. Baton Rouge: Louisiana State University Press.
Martin du Gard, Roger. 1909. *Devenir!* Paris: Société d'éditions littéraires et artistiques.
———. 1913. *Jean Barois*. Paris: Ed. De la Nouvelle revue française.
Martin-Fugier, Anne. 1979. *La Place des bonnes*. Paris: Grasset.
Mayeur, Françoise. 1977. *L'Enseignement secondaire des jeunes filles sous la troisième république*. Paris: Presses de la Fondation Nationale des Sciences Politiques.
Mayeur, Jean-Marie, and Madeleine Rebérioux. 1973. *Les Débuts de la Troisième République, 1871–1898*. Paris: Seuil.
———. 1975. *La République radicale? 1898–1914*. Paris: Seuil.
Meyer, Paulette A. 1997. "They Met in Zurich: Nineteenth-Century German and Russian Women Physicians." In *Women Healers and Physicians: Climbing a Long Hill*. Edited by Lillian Furst. Lexington: University Press of Kentucky. Pp. 151–77.
———. 1999. "From "Uncertifiable" Medical Practice to Berlin Clinic of Women Doctors: The Medical Career of Franziska Tiburtius (M.D. Zurich, 1876)." *Dynamis* 19: 279–303.
———. 2006. "Physiatrie and German Maternal Feminism: Dr. Anna Fischer-Dückelmann Critiques Academic Medicine." *Canadian Bulletin of Medical History* 23, no. 1: 145–82.

Millan, Gordon, Brian Rigby, and Jill Forbes. 1995. "Industrialization and Its Discontents, 1870–1944." In *French Cultural Studies: An Introduction*. Edited by Michael Kelly. New York: Oxford University Press. Pp. 11–53.

Milland, Edmond. 1900. "Les Femmes Avocats." *Le Figaro*. 6 décembre 1900. Repr. in Rossel, André. Edited by *L'Histoire de France à travers les journaux du temps passé: La Belle Epoque, 1898–1914*. Paris: L'Arbre Verdoyant, 1984.

Miller, Michael B. 1981. *The Bon Marché: Bourgeois Culture and the Department Store, 1869–1920*. Princeton: Princeton University Press.

Milligan, Jennifer. 1996. *The Forgotten Generation: French Women Writers in the Interwar Period*. London: Berg Publishers.

Modleski, Tania. 1982. *Loving with a Vengeance: Mass-Produced Fantasies for Women*. New York: Routledge Press.

Monelli, Paolo, 1978. "Introduction." Translated by Olive Ordish. In *La Belle Epoque: Fifteen Euphoric Years of European History*. New York: William Morrow. Pp. 6–15.

Moses, Claire Goldberg. 1984. *French Feminism in the Nineteenth Century*. Albany: SUNY Press.

Nic (pseud. de Jacques Valdour). 1909. *Le Lycée Corrupteur*. Paris: Renaissance Française.

"Nouvel hôpital de Mme Alphen." 1901. *La Femme* 23 no. 1 (1 January): 10.

Offen, Karen. 1984. "Depopulation, Nationalism and Feminism in Fin-de-Siecle France." *American Historical Review* 89, no. 3 (June): 648–76.

O'Monroy, R. and R. Vallier. 1900. *L'Institutrice*. Paris: Librairie théâtrale.

Ozouf, Jacques, and Mona Ozouf. 1992. *La République des instituteurs*. Paris: Seuil.

Ozouf, Mona. 1982. *L'Ecole, L'Eglise, et la République, 1871–1914*. Paris: Cana/Jean Offredo.

———. 1995. *Les Mots des femmes*. Paris: Fayard.

Pernot, Denis. 1992. "Du 'Bildungsroman' au roman d'éducation: un malentendu créateur?" *Romantisme* 76: 105–20.

———. 1998. *Le Roman de socialisation, 1889–1914*. Paris: PUF.

Pert, Camille. 1910. "Le Travail de la femme." In *La Femme*, vol. 4. Paris: Bong.

Phelps, Elizabeth Stewart. 1882. *Doctor Zay*. Boston: Houghton-Mifflin.

Philippe, Charles-Louis. 1900. *Bubu de Montparnasse*. Paris.

Pierrot, Jean. 1981. *The Decadent Imagination, 1880 to 1900*. Translated by Derek Coltman. Chicago: University of Chicago Press.

Pratt, Annis, with Barbara White, Andrea Lowenstein, and Mary Wyer. 1981. *Archetypal Patterns in Women's Fiction*. Bloomington: Indiana University Press.

Proal, Louis. 1890. *La Criminalité féminine*. Extrait du *Correspondant*. Paris: E. de la Soye.

———. 1900. *Suicide et crime passionnels*. Paris: Alcan.

Puibaraud, Louis. 1899. "La Femme criminelle." *La Grande Revue* 9 (May): 393–427.

Rabaut, Jean. 1985. *Féministes à la Belle Epoque*. Paris: France-Empire.

Radway, Janice. 1984. *Reading the Romance: Women, Patriarchy, and Popular Literature*. Chapel Hill: University of North Carolina Press.

Raimond, Michel. 1985. *La Crise du roman*. Paris: José-Corti.

Rambosson, Jules. 1873. *L'Education maternelle d'après les indications de la nature*. Paris: Firmin Didot Frères.

Roberts, Mary Louise. 1994. *Civilization without Sexes: Reconstructing Gender in Post-War France, 1917–1927*. Chicago: University of Chicago Press.
———. 2002. *Disruptive Acts: The New Woman in Fin-de-Siècle France*. Chicago: University of Chicago Press.
Rogers, Juliette M. 1996. "Addressing Success: Fame and Narrative Strategies in Colette's *La Naissance du jour*." *Studies in Twentieth Century Literature* 20, no. 2 (summer): 505–20.
———. 1996. "The Counter-Public Sphere: Colette's Gendered Collective." *MLN* 111, no. 4 (September): 734–46.
———. 1997. "Women at Work: The Femme Nouvelle in Belle Epoque Fiction." *Esprit Créateur* 37, no. 4 (December): 17–28.
———. 2002. "Monstres médicaux: femmes médecins dans la littérature de la Belle Epoque." In *Ecriture et maladie: Du bon usage de la maladie*. Edited by Arlette Bouloumié. Paris: Editions Imago. Pp. 209–18.
———. 2006. "Feminist Discourse in Women's Novels of Professional Development." In *A Belle Epoque? Women in French Society and Culture, 1890–1914*, ed. Diana Holmes and Carrie Tarr. New York: Berghahn Books. Pp. 183–95.
Roussel, Nelly. 1979. *L'Eternelle sacrifiée*. Paris: Syros.
Rousselot, Paul. 1883. *Histoire de l'éducation des femmes en France*, vol. 1. Repr. New York: Burt Franklin, 1971.
Saïd, Edward. 1979. *Orientalism*. New York: Vintage Books.
Sammons, Jeffrey. 1991. "The Bildungsroman for Nonspecialists: An Attempt at a Clarification." In *Reflection and Action: Essays on the Bildungsroman*. Edited by James Hardin. Columbia: University of South Carolina Press. Pp. 26–46.
Sauvy, Anne. 1986. "La Littérature et les femmes." *Histoire de l'édition française*. Vol. 4: *Le Livre concurrencé, 1900–1950*. Dir. Henri-Jean Martin and Roger Chartier. Paris: Promodis.
Seigel, Jerrold. 1986. *Bohemian Paris: Culture, Politics, and the Boundaries of Bourgeois Life, 1830–1930*. London: Penguin.
Shattuck, Roger. 1968. *The Banquet Years*. New York: Vintage.
Showalter, Elaine. 1990. *Sexual Anarchy: Gender and Culture at the Fin de Siècle*. New York: Viking.
Silverman, Willa Z. 1995. *The Notorious Life of Gyp: Right-Wing Anarchist in Fin-de-Siècle France*. New York: Oxford University Press.
Sokel, Walter H. 1991. "The Blackening of the Breast: The Narrative of Existential Education and R. M. Rilke's *The Notebooks of Malte Laurids Brigge*." In *Reflection and Action: Essays on the Bildungsroman*, ed. James Hardin. Columbia: University of South Carolina Press. Pp. 329–61.
Stendhal. 2000. *Le Rouge et le noir*. Paris: Gallimard; orig. pub. 1830.
Stewart, Mary Lynn. 1989. *Women, Work, and the French State: Labour Protection and Social Patriarchy, 1879–1919*. Kingston: McGill–Queen's University Press.
Strumingher, Laura. 1983. *What Were Little Girls and Boys Made Of? Primary Education in Rural France, 1830–1880*. Albany: SUNY Press.
Thiesse, Anne-Marie. 1984. *Le Roman du quotidien: Lecteurs et lectures populaires à la Belle Epoque*. Paris: Chemin Vert.
———. 1997. *Ils apprenaient la France: L'exaltation des régions dans le discours patriotique*. Paris: Editions de la Maison des sciences de l'homme.

Uzanne, Octave. 1910. *Etudes de sociologie féminine: Parisiennes de ce temps, en leurs divers milieux, états et conditions.* Paris: Mercure de France.

Vagogne, Joseph. 1984. *Les Professions libérales.* Paris: PUF.

Valran, Gaston, 1908. *Préjugés d'autrefois et carrières d'aujourd'hui.* Paris.

Van Gennep, Arnold. 1909. *Les Rites de passage.* Paris: E. Nourry.

Waelti-Walters, Jennifer. 1990. *Feminist Novelists of the Belle Epoque: Love as a Lifestyle.* Bloomington: Indiana University Press.

Waelti-Walters, Jennifer, and Steven C. Hause, eds. 1994. *Feminisms of the Belle Epoque: A Historical and Literary Anthology.* Lincoln: University of Nebraska Press.

Weber, Eugen. 1976. *Peasants into Frenchmen: The Modernization of Rural France, 1870–1914.* Stanford: Stanford University Press.

———. 1986. *France: Fin-de-Siècle.* Cambridge: Harvard University Press.

Weiss, John. 1984. "The French Engineering Profession, 1800–1850." In *Professions and the French State, 1700–1900,* ed. J. Geison. Philadelphia: University of Pennsylvania Press.

Yver, Colette. 1907. "Réponse de Colette Yver à Mme Camille Marbo." *La Vie Heureuse* 6, no. 10 (October).

Zola, Emile. 1961 (1877). *L'Assommoir. Les Rougon-Macquart,* vol. 2. Paris: Gallimard.

———. 1964 (1883). *Au bonheur des dames. Les Rougon-Macquart,* vol. 3. Paris: Gallimard.

———. 1964 (1885). *Germinal. Les Rougon-Macquart,* vol. 3. Paris: Gallimard.

———. 1967 (1874). *Le Docteur Pascal. Les Rougon-Macquart,* vol. 5. Paris: Gallimard.

———. 2000 (1874). "Madame Sourdis." Paris: Livre de Poche; orig. publ. 1874.

INDEX

L'Abeille (The Bee), 20
L'Action Féministe (Feminist Action), 20, 30
Affaire Caillaux, 175
Affaire Humbert, 175–76
Affaire Steinheil, 175
agrégation exam, 26, 82
Albertini, Pierre, 16–17, 63
André Cornélis, 55
Angenot, Marc, 55
Angestellteroman, 1n.1
antifeminism, post–World War I emergence of, 214–17
apprenticeship: Barrès's with Bourget, 61; in Chambige affair, 55; in *Dames du Palais* 180, 195; in educational development novels, 47, 49–50; in women writers novels, 152; in Zola, 10
archaeologist: in *La Bachelière*, 72n.29, 128, 130, 133; in *Les Cervelines*, 72n.29; in *La Conquête de Jérusalem*, 28, 71–74; in *L'Immoraliste*, 28, 68; art, in Belle Epoque era, 3–4. *See also* Orientalist
artist: as self-sufficient women, 12; definition of elite vs. popular, 153–54n.4; freedom of, 163; in Zola, 10; lawyer seen as, 184, 195–97; popular, 154, 156; success of, 151, 153–55, 157; suffering of, 156. *See also* Künstlerroman
L'Assommoir, 10
Au Bonheur des dames, 10
Auclert, Hubertine, 4
audience: impact on writer's career, 152–53, 163; impact on writer's personal decisions, 172–73; in *Cervelines*, 153; in *La Rebelle*, 159, 162; in *La Vagabonde*, 156–59; lawyer's effect on, 176, 184, 188, 197; role in *berufsoman* of, 152–53
Auerbach, Nina, 86–87, 183
auscultation, 124, 136

L'Avenir de nos filles (The Future of Our Daughters), 26
L'Avocate (The Woman Lawyer), 36–37

Babin, Marcelle, 8, 38, 114, 141–47, 219
baccalauréat diploma: exams for, 82; Napoléon's creation of, 32; for women, 25–26, 31
La Bachelière (The Female Graduate), 8, 72n.29; "brainy woman" image in, 114; class politics in, 46; plot summary of, 223; as quest narrative, 128–34
Bakhtin, M. M., 46, 79–80
Balzac, Honoré de, 151
Barjeau, Madame A. Philip de, 24
Barney, Natalie, 2
Barrès, Maurice, 44, 46–48, 50, 61–67, 215
Bartkowski, Frances, 87n.9
Béatrix, 15
Beauvoir, Simone de, 150, 206n.4, 214–15, 216n.12
Becquerel, Henri, 113
Bel Ami, 151–52
Belle Epoque literature: Beauvoir's dismissal of, 215; definitions of, 1–2; legacy of, 40–41; male-centered novels in, 48–49, 70–77; professionalization of women in, 33–41; stereotypes in, 5
Les Belles Images, 216n.12
Bentzon, Thérèse, 45
Bertaut, Jules, 22–23
Bertheaume, Marthe, 207–10, 212–13
berufsoman (professional development novel): examples of, 48; legacy of, 40–41; literary, social, and political history and, 7; male authors of, 41, 70–77; sources for, 47–48; style and characteristics of, 11; terminology of, 1; women writer protagonists in, 151–53. *See also* careers for educated women; professional development narratives

bildungsroman: evolution of, 1; historical origins of, 45–47; intellectual figure in, 43; *Les Déracinés* as example of, 62–67; post–World War I period and decline of, 213–17; professional development as theme of, 54, 67–77, 216–17; women lawyers and, 179–85; women scientists and, 114–15

Blackwell, Elizabeth, 11n.15

Bompaire-Evesque, Claire, 61

Bonvoisin, S. M., 19

Bourdieu, Pierre, 153n.4, 156, 160

bourgeois values: in Colette's novels, 90–111; in *Les Dames du Palais*, 188–202; in post–World War I fiction, 205–7; professionalization of women and, 33–41, 54, 153–63; self-sufficient protagonists and, 163–73; women criminals and, 175–76; women scientists as threat to, 115–17

Bourget, Paul, 44, 47–50, 54–61; Barrès and, 61–67; Beauvoir's dismissal of, 215

brainy women (*cervelines*) motif: in Belle Epoque fiction, 8, 21, 38, 72n.29; class politics and, 153–63; historical influences on, 113–14, 116; medical profession and, 121–34; in post–World War I fiction, 208–10, 212–17; "pure," 120, 121, 125–26, 128, 130, 132, 133, 144–45, 186–89, 207, 212–13; romance narratives and, 118–21; scientific careers and, 125–26; "seduced" 120–21, 134–35, 140–41, 186–87, 191, 199–200; self-sufficient protagonist in, 170–73; woman writer protagonists and, 151–56; women lawyers and, 186–95

Branzac, Paule, 24

Brès, Gibelin, 37n.34

brevet, exams for, 82

Brombert, Victor, 43

Caillaux, Henriette, 175–76

Calmette, Gaston, 175–76

Camille Sée Decree, 16

capès diploma, exams for, 82

careers for educated women: in Belle Epoque novels, 151–53; *Les Cervelines* and images of, 125–34; evolution in nineteenth century of, 26–31; legal careers, 175–202; in *Pharmacienne*, 143–47; in *Princesses des sciences*, 134–37; in World War I fiction, 204–5

Carles, Emilie, 30

Carnets d'une infirmière (Notes of a Nurse), 203–4

"Le Cas de conscience d'une avocate," 177n.5

Catherine Courage, 39n.37

Catholic Church: education for women criticized by, 23; in *La Conquête de Jérusalem*, 73–77; Third Republic and, 16, 55

cerveline. *See* brainy woman

Les Cervelines (The Brainy Women), 8, 21, 38, 72n.29; class politics in, 153–63; family life portrayed in, 189–90; historical influences on, 113–14, 116; medical profession in, 121–34; plot summary of, 223–24; as romance narrative, 118–21; scientific careers in, 125–26; self-sufficient protagonist in, 170–73, 195–98; woman writer as protagonist in, 151–56

La Chaîne des dames (The Chain of Women), 205

Chambige, Henri, 55–57, 61

Chauvin, Jeanne, 35

Chéri, 205

Clarétie, Léo, 23

Clark, Linda, 29, 89

class politics: in berufsroman, 60n.14; in bildungsroman, 46; cultural production and, 153–66; in educational novels, 26–28, 49–54, 89–111; in *La Vagabonde*, 156–63; in *Les Cervelines*, 153–56; professionalization of women and, 33–41; teacher training schools and, 28–31; in Tinayre's fiction, 159–63; women criminals and, 175–76

Claudine à l'école (Claudine at School), 8, 13, 25, 30, 219; Beauvoir's comments on, 215; plot summary of, 224; popular success of, 79–80

Coco de Génie, 22
coeducational systems, proposals for, 25
Colette (Sidonie-Gabrielle Colette),
 7–8, 13; Beauvoir's comments on,
 215; biographical sketch of, 219;
 class politics in writing of, 156–63;
 educational themes in novels of,
 25, 29–30, 80–111; education of,
 26; literary types used by, 22–23;
 magazine writing by, 20; post–World
 War I writings of, 205; self-sufficient
 protagonists in fiction of, 168–73;
 woman writer protagonists in fiction
 of, 151–53; women writers in work
 of, 21; World War I writings of, 203
Collado, Mélanie, 6n.13, 7
collegiality, in post–World War I women's
 fiction, 209–17
Commune, education policies and, 15–16
communities of women, in Belle Epoque
 literature, 11–12; in educational
 novels, 86–111; women lawyers *Les
 Dames du Palais*, 178–85
Compain, Louise-Marie, 8, 63n.20,
 80; biographical sketch of, 220;
 conformity in fiction of, 149–50;
 educational novels of, 26, 31, 99–111
*La Conquête de Jérusalem (The Conquest of
 Jerusalem)*, 48, 69–70, 75
counter-public position: definition of,
 108; heroines located in, 108–10
Country Doctor, A, 11n.15
*Crime et suicide passionnels (Suicide and
 Crimes of Passion)*, 52
criminal acts: by bourgeois women,
 175–76; in *La Conquête de Jérusalem*, 75;
 in *L'Immoraliste*, 69–77; in professional
 development novels, 51–54
*La Criminalité féminine (Feminine
 Criminality)*, 51–52
Cubists, 4
cultural production: by self-sufficient
 protagonists, 170–73; by women
 writers, 153–63
Curie, Eve, 117n.5, 121n.11
Curie, Marie, 113–14, 117n.5, 130n.26,
 134, 150, 177; biographies of, 121n.11
Curie, Pierre, 113–14, 117n.5, 121n.11

*Les Dames du Palais (Ladies of the
 Court)*, 8, 35, 37; brainy woman
 motif in, 186–95; plot summary of,
 224–25; post–World War I misogyny
 contrasted with, 214; as professional
 development narrative, 114, 177–202;
 self-sufficient protagonists in,
 195–202; women lawyers in, 177–202
Dans le jardin du féminisme (In the Garden
 of Feminism), 205
Daudet, Alphonse, 215
Debussy, Claude, 4
"Débuts des femmes avocats" ("The
 Beginnings of Women Lawyers"), 36
Decadent movement, 2, 7
Delarue-Mardrus, Lucie, 7
department stores, women's careers in, 29
Les Déracinés (The Uprooted), 47–50,
 61–67, 76–77, 99
diagnosis, 122, 124, 131, 136, 188
Dilthey, Wilhelm, 45
director: in *Sévriennes*, 94, 96, 98–99;
 of L'Ecole Normale de Sèvre, 24,
 93; of home for unwed mothers in
 La Rebelle, 162; of hospital in *Les
 Cervelines*, 122, 124; of magazine in
 La Rebelle, 161; of private schools, 25,
 39; of teacher training school in *L'Un
 vers l'autre* 31. *See also* teaching careers,
 educational development novels
Le Disciple (The Disciple), 47, 49–50,
 54–61, 76–77
*Disruptive Acts: The New Woman in Fin-de-
 Siècle France*, 5
Distinction, 153n.4
divorce: in *Les Cervelines*, 155, in *Dames
 du Palais*, 185, 188, 191–93, 195,
 198; in *La Vagabonde*, 156, 158, 169;
 practice of divorce law, 35; women's
 right to, 4
Le Docteur Germaine, 203–4
Le Docteur Pascal, 10
Docteur Pascal, 43
doctor. *See also* medical profession,
 professional development novels
Dr. Odile, 212–13
Dr. Breen's Practice, 11n.15
Dr. Zay, 11n.15

domestic duties: balanced with work responsibilities in *Dames du Palais*, 189–90

domestic service: professionalization of women and, 39–41; women's employment in, 26–28

domesticated workspaces: in *La Bachelière*; *Les Cervelines*; *Dames du Palais*, 190; *Princesses de sciences*

Dumur, Louis, 22

Duplessis, Rachel Blau, 122n.16

Duquesne, Jacques 39n.37

Durand, Marguerite, 5, 19

Duruy, Victor, 15–16, 91, 93

Ecole de Médecine de Paris, women's admittance into, 37

L'Ecole, L'Eglise, et la République, 1871–1914 (School, Church, and Republic), 16

L'Ecole des dames (The School for Ladies), 24

École Normal Supérieure de Sèvres, 16, 26, 60n.14, 80, 113, 205

economics, in educational novels, 49–54

educational development novel: of Belle Epoque era, 8, 12, 15–41, 59–61; coeducational system proposals, 25; in Colette's novels, 89–111; critics of, 23; defined, 1; dreams and disappointments in, 79–111; examples of, 47–48; inspector system in, 102n.28; literary trends in, 22–23; narrative structure of, 49–54, 81–111; *Pharmacienne* as example of, 142n.37; political and historical hypotheses for, 26; in post–World War I period, 205, 210–12; renunciation plot in, 199–202; scientific novels compared with, 115–21; teaching careers and, 28–31. *See also* secondary schools for girls; teaching careers

Education sentimentale, 43

Edwards-Pilliet, Blanche (Doctor), 114, 177, 208

L'Egalité en marche (Equality on the March), 206–7

Elise ou la vraie vie, 216n.12

Elliott, Philip, 32–33, 39, 179

emergence, in bildungsroman, 46

Emilie ou la jeune fille auteur, 45

employment for women, in post–World War I period, 205–6

equality, in post–World War I women's fiction, 209–17

erziehungsroman. See educational development novel

L'Etape, 49

Etcherelli, Claire, 216n.12

"L'Eternelle Sacrifée" ("The Eternal Sacrificed Woman"), 25n.20

Etudes de sociologie féminine: Parisiennes de ce temps (Studies in Feminine Sociology: Parisian Women of Today), 20, 28

Eugénie, Empress, 37

Europe, influence of Belle Epoque in, 2–3

L'Evolution féminine; ses résultants économiques (Femine Evolution: Economic Results), 26

examination system in France, in women's educational novels, 81–82, 103–11

Exposition Universelle, 3

Fallières (President), 30

Falloux law of 1850, 15

family relations: in post–World War I women's fiction, 208–17; in *Princesses de sciences*, 134–47; self-sufficient women protagonists and, 168–73; women lawyers and role of, 181–85, 188–95; in women's scientific novels, 118–21, 125–26. *See also* marriage; motherhood

Farrère, Claude, 215

Fauvists, 4

Favres, Jules, 177

Felski, Rita 108, 108n.34, 110

Fémina magazine, 19–20, 160

feminism: Belle Epoque literature and, 2–5, 7, 150–51; Catholic Church on threat of, 24; in post–World War I women's writing, 204–7, 210–17; women lawyers in fiction and, 186–95

féministe (the feminist) as literary type, 22

Feminist Novelists of the Belle Epoque: Love as a Lifestyle, 2, 7–8

"Femme intellectuelle au foyer, La" ("Intellectual Woman at Home"), 149
La Femme dan les organisations ouvrières (Woman in Workers Organizations), 26
La Femme (journal), 39
La Femme Nouvelle (The New Woman) (journal), 20, 24
Femmes d'aujourd'hui: enquête sur les nouvelles carrières féminines (Women of Today: A Study of the New Feminine Careers), 175n.1, 205
femmes nouvelles: in Belle Epoque literature, 11; in professional development novels, 53–54; in scientific novels, 120–21; Third Republic educational reforms and, 17–18. See also self-sufficient women
Femmes nouvelles (novel), 151n.3
Ferry, Jules, 16–17
Fèvre, Henry, 217
Le Figaro, 35, 176
fille du peuple (daughter of the people) as literary type, 22
Finch, Alison, 44–45
fin-de-siècle studies, Belle Epoque era and, 1–2, 5
Flaubert, Gustave, 43
Forbes, Jill, 1
Forgotten, Generation, The, 118n.7, 150n.2
Foucault, Michel, 38, 115
France: bildungsroman in, 1–2, 46; dismissal of Belle Epoque literature in, 215–16; educational reforms of, 15–16, 19–20, 28–31, 55, 63–67, 93–111; employment hierarchy in, 31–32; exam system in, 81–82, 103–11; gendered social positions in, 48–49; influence of Belle Epoque in, 2–5; twenty-first-century literature in, 216; women scientists in, 115–16. See also Third Republic (France)
France, Anatole, 44n.2
"free" professions (France), women's absence from, 31–32
French Women's Writing, 7
La Fronde (The Revolt), 19–20, 151n.3

Gatti de Gamand, Isabelle, 25
Gelfand, Toby, 115–16
Germinal, 10
Gide, André, 4, 44, 48–50, 67–77, 215
Goldberg, Nancy Sloan, 6, 9, 150n.2, 203
Goncourt brothers, 215
La Grande parade des Sévriennes (The Great Parade of Sévres Women), 205
Gueydan, Berthe, 176
gynecology: in *Princesses de sciences*, 35; women's specialization 39

Harlequin Romances, 118n.8
harassment: in *Les Cervelines*, 38; in *Pharmacienne*, 38, 142, 144; in professional development novels 120; in *L'Un vers l'autre*, 104; of women students, 38
Harry, Myriam, 19n.19, 48, 67–77, 220
Hartman, Mary S., 175–76
Hause, Stephen, 4, 87n.11
headmistress: first contact with, 85–86; in *Claudine à l'école*, 82, 88–39; in *L'Un vers l'autre* 100–101, 103; in *Sévriennes*, 94. See also director
Heilbrun, Carolyn, 6n.13
Heister, Marion, 1n.1
Hirsch, Charles-Henri, 22–23
Histoire de la littérature féminine en France, 6
Holmes, Diana, 7–9, 118, 150–51
Hôtel de la Ligue de l'Enseignement (Hotel for the League of Education), 30
Howells, William Dean, 11n.15
Hue, Gustave, 36–37
Humbert, Thérèse, 175–76
Huzard, Auguste, 133n.30

Idylle en Bretagne, 219
Ils apprenaient la France (They Taught France), 64
L'Immoraliste (The Immoralist), 48–49, 67–77
Impressionists, 3–4
independent woman. See self-sufficient women
inspector: in *Claudine à l'école*, 88; in *L'Un vers l'autre*, 102; in *Sévriennes*, 98–99.

See also teaching careers, educational development novels
Institutrice (Woman Schoolteacher), 8, 31, 80–111, 225
intellectuals, in French literature, 43–44
intellectuelle (the intellectual girl) as literary type, 22
L'Intellectuelle mariée (The Intellectual Wife), 214
Internat (medical school entrance), 208
L'Interne, 207–10

jeune filles (young girls) as literary type, 22
Jewett, Sarah Orne, 111n.15
Journal d'une femme de chambre (Diary of a Chambermaid), 27–28
journalism: in Tinayre's fiction, 159–63; women in, 19–22, 157
Jullian, Philippe, 5

Klejman, Laurence, 206–7
Klumpke, Augusta, 114n.3
Künstlerroman: defined, 1; principles of, 47; women protagonists in, 151n.3

Laïcité, 16
Lapauze, Jeanne, 26, 30
Larnac, Jean, 6
Larson, Magali, 33–35, 131n.38
lawyer: in Dames du Palais 35, 175–200. See also legal profession, professional development novels
Lectures de la femme (Women's Reading), 20
legal profession, women in: barriers to practice by, 36–41; in Belle Epoque fiction, 8, 12–13, 34–41, 177–202. See also Les Dames du Palais (Ladies of the Court)
LeGarrec, Evelyne, 21
Le Rouge et le noir, 43
Lesueur, Daniel (pseud.). See Lapauze, Jeanne
licence diploma, exams for, 82
L'Invitée, 216n.12
Lippmann, Gabriel, 113
literacy rates for French women: class politics and, 26–28; Third Republic educational reforms and, 17–19, 22–23

L'Un vers l'autre (One Toward the Other), 8
Le Lycée corrupteur (The Corrupting High School), 23
Lycéennes, 83–86

Madame Bovary, 38n.35
"Madame Sourdis," 10
Mademoiselle Dax, 215
magazines and periodicals, for women, nineteenth-century popularity of, 18–23
Maignien, M., 19
La Maison de Claudine (Claudine's House), 205
male protagonists, in educational development novels, 49–54, 67–77
Marbo, Camille, 149
Margadant, Jo Burr, 25–26, 94
marriage: post–World War I misogyny and, 214–17; in post–World War I women's fiction, 207–17; in Princesses de sciences, 137–47; in professional development novels, 76–77; self-sufficient women and, 163–73; women lawyers and role of, 181–95; in women's scientific novels, 118–21, 125–26; women writers' discussion of, 149–50, 156–63
Martin, Benjamin F., 176
Martin du Gard, Roger, 44n.2
Martin-Fugier, Anne, 27
masculine elements, of women lawyer protagonists, 187–95
Maupassant, Guy de, 151–52, 215
medical profession: barriers to women in, 10n.15, 34–41; in Les Cervelines (The Brainy Women), 121–34; history in France of, 115–16; in post–World War I fiction, 207–10, 212–17; women's entrance into, 114–15; in women's science novels, 117–21; in World War I fiction, 203
Mémoires d'une jeune fille range (Memoirs of a Dutiful Daughter), 214–15
mentor-disciple: comparison of in Le Disciple and Les Déracinés, 61–62, 62n.17; in La Bachelière, 129, 130; in Les Cervelines 122, 127; in Claudine

à l'école, 88–89; in *La Conquête de Jérusalem*, 72–74; in *Dames du Palais*, 179–80; *Les Déracinés*, 62–67; in *Le Disciple*, 55–60; in *L'Immoraliste* 68–69; in male novels, 50; male and female relationships compared, 60n.14, 99 Orientalism in Belle Epoque literature and, 68–77; in *Pharmacienne* 142; in post–World War I fiction, 208–17; in professional development narratives, 50–54, 65–67; for in *La Rebelle* 152; in *Sévriennes* 94; in *L'Un vers l'autre* 103; in *La Vagabonde* 152; women lawyers, 179–85; in women's educational novels, 79–80, 103–11; in women's scientific novels 115, 117; for women writer protagonists, 152–53. *See also* apprenticeship
Meyer, Paulette, 11n.15
Millan, Gordon, 1
Milland, Edmond, 35–36
Millerand, Alexandre, 3n.5
Milligan, Jennifer, 9, 119n.7, 150n.2, 205n.3
Mirbeau, Octave, 27–28
misogyny, post–World War I emergence of, 214–17
Modleski, Tania, 118n.8
moral and behavioral guidelines: negative effects of novels and, 52–54; Third Republic educational reforms and, 28–31
Moses, Claire, 4
motherhood: cultural norms of, 28–29; in *Les Dames du Palais*, 180–85, 188–95, 198–202; in post–World War I fiction, 205; in *Princesses des sciences*, 138–44
murder, by women, 175–76

La Naissance de la clinique, 38n.35
La Naissance du jour (Break of Day), 205
Napoléon Bonaparte, educational reforms of, 32–33
Napoleonic Code, 181
nationalism: in Belle Epoque literature, 48; French educational reform and, 16–17, 64–67
Naturalist school, 55

newspapers: serial novels in, 18–20; women journalists and, 19–22. *See also* magazines and periodicals
Nobel Prize, for Marie Curie, 113–14
Nouvelles lettres à Françoise ou la jeune fille d'après-guerre (New Letters to Françoise, or the Postwar Young Girl), 206

obstetrics, 39
Orientalism: in Belle Epoque novels, 48, 68–77; in *La Conquête de Jérusalem*, 71–77; women writers, 72n.29
Orientalism, 68n.24
Orientalist: in La Conquête de Jérusalem, 71; female orientalists in *La Bachelière* and *Les Cervelines* 72n.29. *See also* archaeologist
Ozouf, Mona, 6n.13, 16, 63, 106n.33

Palais de l'Electricité, 3
"Paris-by-Night" motif, in Belle Epoque era, 5
Paris-province opposition, in nineteenth-century novels, 43
paternalism, towards women lawyers, 183–85
pathology: student of, in *Les Cervelines*, 121; pathologist in *Les Cervelines*, 122, 125. *See also* medical profession, scientific novels
patriotism, Third Republic educational reforms and, 16–17
Peasants into Frenchmen: The Modernization of Rural France, 1870–1914, 17
pediatrics, 39
Pelletier, Madeleine (Dr.), 114n.3
Pernot, Denis, 47
Pert, Camille, 20–21, 36, 157
Le Petit Journal, 36
Pharmacienne (Woman Pharmacist), 8, 83; autobiographical elements in, 219; "brainy woman" image in, 114, 116; plot summary of, 225; as professional development narrative, 38, 141–47
Phelps, Elizabeth Stewart, 11n.15
pioneer: as character type, 11–13, 29; in *La Bachelière*, 129, 132; in *Les Cervelines*, 126; in *Dames du Palais*,

183; in *L'Interne*, 208–9; in male novels of professional and educational development, in *Pharmacienne*, 142. *See also* brainy woman (cerveline)
politics: in educational novels, 102–11; women criminals and, 176
Post-Impressionists, 3–4
post office, women's careers in, 29
power relations, in scientific novels, 115–21
prestation de serment (oath taking), 36
Prévost, Marcel, 130n.26, 206
Princesses de sciences (The Doctor Wife or *Princesses of Science)*, 8, 35, 134–47, 208; family life protrayed in, 189–90; historical influences on, 113–14; plot summary of, 226–27; post–World War I misogyny contrasted with, 214; romance narrative in, 118–19; self-sufficient protagonist in, 196; women scientists in, 116; women writers' critique of, 149
Prix Femina (Prix Vie Heureuse), 19, 48, 134
Prix Goncourt, 48; exclusion of women from, 19
Proal, Louis, 51–52
professional development narratives: in Belle Epoque literature, 7–12; criminal acts in, 51–54; *Les Dames du Palais* as example of, 175–202; male protagonists in, 49–54, 70–77; *Pharmacienne* as, 141–47; post–World War I misogyny and, 214–17; second-generation professional heroines, 207–17; sociological and historical theories of, 31–41; women writer protagonists in, 151–53; in World War I fiction, 204–5
Professionalizing Modern Medicine, 115–16
les professions libres, 31–32
professor: of English language in *L'Un vers l'autre*, 103; of history in *Les Cervelines*, 126; of history in *L'Immoraliste*, 69; of law in *Dames du Palais* 179–80; of literature in *L'Un vers l'autre*, 100; of literature in *Sévriennes*, 97; of medicine in *Pharmacienne* 116;

143; of music in *Claudine à l'école*, 89; of pathology in *Les Cervelines*, of philosophy in *Les Déracinés*, 62, 65; of philosophy in *Le Disciple*, 57–58; of philosophy in *Le Science et l'amour*, 212; of philosophy in *Sévriennes*, 97. *See also* education development novels; teaching careers
Proust, Marcel, 4
provincial and regional culture, educational reforms and, 64–67
public sphere, women in: in Belle Epoque literature, 9; in *Pharmacienne*, 144–47; in post–World War I fiction, 208–17; self-sufficient protagonists of women writers and, 170–73; women criminals and, 175–76; women lawyers and, 184–85, 188–95

quest narrative: in *La Bachelière (The Female Graduate)*, 128–34; in Belle Epoque novels, 76–77; in *Les Cervelines (The Brainy Women)*, 125–34; in *Les Dames du Palais*, 180–85; in women's science novels, 119–21

Rabaut, Jean, 19n.9
Rachilde, 2, 7, 177
Radway, Janice, 118n.6
Rambosson, Jules, 28–29
Ravel, Maurice, 4
Reading the Romance, 118n.6
La Rebelle (The Woman Rebel), 8, 21; mentor relationships in, 152; plot summary of, 227; self-sufficient protagonist of, 163–73, 198; woman writer as protagonist in, 151–53
renunciation plot: in *Les Dames du Palais*, 199–202; in post–World War I women's fiction, 208–17; in professional development novels, 54
Republic Mother image, in World War I fiction, 20
Reval, Gabrielle, 8–9, 60n.14; *La Bachelière* written by, 128–34; biographical sketch of, 220; brainy woman image in novels of, 38; careerism in novels of, 29; educational

novels of, 24, 26, 80–111, 114;
Orientalism in work of, 72n.29;
post–World War I novels of, 205
revoltée (the revolted girl) as literary
type, 22
Rigby, Brian, 1
Rise of Professionalism, The, 33–34
Les Rites de passage, 81–82
Roberts, Mary Louise, 5, 130n.26
Rochefort, Florence, 206–7
Roger, Noëlle, 203–4, 220
role model: in *Claudine à l'école,* 92–93;
in *Dames du Palais,* 180; in *Institutrice,*
105; in *Princesses de sciences,* 133, 140;
in scientific novels, 115; in *Le Science
et l'amour,* 209; in *L'Un vers l'autre,*
99–100, 101, 103; maternal in
Sévriennes, 97. See also mentor-disciple
romance narrative: in *La Bachelière
(The Female Graduate),* 128–34; in
Belle Epoque novels, 52–54; in *Les
Cervelines (The Brainy Women),* 125–34;
in post–World War I fiction, 209–17;
in *Princesses de sciences,* 136–47; in
science novels, 117–21; self-sufficient
protagonists and, 152, 159, 163–73;
women writers of, 12
roman d'apprentissage, defined, 1
*Le Roman de l'énergie nationale (The Novel
of National Energy),* 61
Roussel, Nelly, 25n.20
Rousselot, Paul, 15–16

Saïd, Edward, 68
sales clerk: in department stores and post
offices, 29n.26; in Zola, 10
Sand, George, 45
Satie, Eric, 4
Sauvy, Anne, 18 19n.9
schoolteacher: compared to other
professions, 34; in *La Bachelière*
131–33; married couples, 105–7;
Third Republic patriotism of, 63–64.
See also teaching careers, educational
development novels
science, women professionals in, 117n.5,
130n.26, 134, 150, 177
La Science et l'Amour, 210–12

scientific novels: in Belle Epoque era, 8,
12, 34–41, 113–47; in post–World
War I period, 210–17; "supermom"
phenomenon in, 121n.11; women
protagonists in, 34–41, 113–47,
150, 177
secondary schools for girls: access
to university educations and, 31;
coeducational proposals and, 25–26;
criticism of, 23; establishment in
France of, 15–16, 19–20; impact on
literary trends of, 21–22; lycée system,
32; magazines for, 20
secretary: in *La Bachelière,* 129, 131; in
Dames du Palais 191, 193–94, 197–99;
in Zola, 10
self-sufficient women: in Belle Epoque
literature, 12; as lawyers, 195–220; as
writers, 163–73
serial novels *(roman-feuilleton),*
nineteenth-century popularity of,
18–19
Séverine, 5, 21, 177
Sévriennes (Women of Sèvres), 8, 29,
60n.14, 65n.21; community of women
in, 180–82; educational themes of,
80–111; plot summary of, 227–28
sexual harassment: in *Pharmacienne,*
143–47; of professional women, 38–41
sexuality: in Colette's novels, 88–111; of
self-sufficient women protagonists,
165–73
Sido, 205
social aspirations of women: in Belle
Epoque novels, 8; in educational
novels, 49–54; professional
development and, 32–41; women
lawyers and, 181–85
sociological theory, in professional
development novels, 57–61
Sociology of the Professions, 32–33
Sokel, Walter, 46–47, 57
Staël, Germaine de, 45
status socialization, professionalization of
women, 32–41
Steinheil, Meg, 175–76
stereotypes, Belle Epoque images as, 5
students, women as, 8

Suffrage des Femmes organization, 4
suffrage movement, women criminals and, 176
superintendent: in *Claudine à l'école*, 88; in *L'Un vers l'autre*, 101–2, 104. See also inspector, teaching careers, educational development novels
supervisor: of medicine in *Pharmacienne*, 116, 143; of pathology in *Les Cervelines*, 122–24, 125. See also director, professor
Suze, Esther de, 8, 31, 80, 84, 104–8, 220

Taine, Hippolyte, 55
teaching careers: training schools for, 15–16; for women, 28–31, 177; women lawyers compared with, 179–85. See also educational development novel; secondary schools for girls
technical training, access for women to, 34–41
telephone operators, 28
Thelen, Myriam, 207–10, 212–13
La Théorie des passions (Theory of the Passions), 56
thesis novel (roman à thèse), 62n.16
Thiesse, Anne-Marie, 18–19, 64
Third Republic (France): educational reforms of, 16–17, 28–31, 55, 63–67, 93–111; mothering guidelines of, 28–29; Orientalist writings in, 74n.31; women's lives in, 15
Tinayre, Marcelle, 7–9; Beauvoir's dismissal of, 215; biographical sketch of, 221; conformity in fiction of, 149–50; fiction of, 21; magazine writing by, 20; self-sufficient women in fiction of, 163–73; women writer protagonists in fiction of, 151–53, 159–63; World War I writings of, 203
transformisme period, impact on women of, 3
Le Travail de la femme (Women's Work), 20
typists, 28

Ulliac-Trémadeure, Sophie, 45
Une Soupe aux herbes sauvages (A Life of Her Own), 30–31
university educations, access for women to, 31
L'Un vers l'autre (One Toward the Other), 31, 63n.20, 80–111, 181; plot summary of, 228
utopianism, in educational novels, 90–111
Uzanne, Octave, 3, 20, 28

La Vagabonde (The Vagabond), 8, 21; class politics in, 156–63; mentor relationships in, 152; plot summary of, 228–29; self-sufficient protagonist of, 168–73, 195–97, 205; woman writer portrayed in, 151–53
Valdour, Jacques, 23
Valéry, Paul, 4, 215
Valran, Gaston, 33
van Gennep, Arnold, 81–84
Victorian Murderesses, 175
La Vie Heureuse (The Happy Life), 19–20, 36–37, 149–50, 160; women lawyers discussed in, 175n.1
vitrioleuses, 175
Vivien, Renée, 2
Von Morgenstern, Karl, 45

Waelti-Walters, Jennifer, 2, 7–8, 87n.11, 150
Weber, Eugen, 2.n3, 17, 35–38
Weiss, John H., 32
Wilde, Oscar, 70n.27
Winzige Katastrophen, 1n.1
"Woman, Your Hour Is Sounding": Continuity and Change in French Women's Great War Fiction, 1914–1919, 150n.2, 203
women: in Belle Epoque literature, 8–14; communities of, in Belle Epoque literature, 11–12, 86–111, 178–85; as criminals, 51–54, 175–76; education reforms in France for, 15–41; in legal profession, 34–41, 175–202; as murderers, 175–76; Orientalism and, 74–77; in science, 113–47; as self-sufficient protagonists, 163–73, 195–202
women's unions: history of, 26; newsletters for, 20

Women's Writing in Nineteenth-Century France, 44–45
women writers: acceptability as career choice, 21; as Belle Epoque literature protagonists, 2.n2, 4, 6, 8, 12–13, 21, 151–53; class politics and, 153–63; educational and class backgrounds of, 26n.22; history in French literature of, 151–52; in interwar period, 118n.7; in journalism, 19–22, 157; literary criticism by, 149; in nineteenth century, 10; post–World War I obscurity of, 13
workplace activity, in women's professional development novels, 53–54
World War I, women writers' fiction during, 203–17
World War II, French literature following, 216
Writing Beyond the Ending, 122n.16

Yette, 45
Yver, Colette, 8–9; Beauvoir's dismissal of, 214–15; biographical sketch of, 221; class politics and work of, 153–63; conformity in fiction of, 149–50; documentary-style postwar fiction of, 204–5; magazine writing by, 20; Orientalism in works of, 72n.29; post–World War I misogyny and fiction of, 214; professional development in novels of, 35, 37–38; response to Marbo by, 149–50; scientific novels of, 113–14, 126–47; self-sufficient women in fiction of, 170–73, 195–202; woman writers in fiction of, 151–53; women lawyers in fiction of, 175n.1, 177–202; women writers in work of, 21; World War I writings of, 203

Zanta, Léontine, 210–12
Zola, Emile, 10, 43, 46, 49, 164–65n.20

www.ingramcontent.com/pod-product-compliance
Lightning Source LLC
Chambersburg PA
CBHW031548300426
44111CB00006BA/216